# Human Resources
# in Latin America and the Caribbean

Jere R. Behrman

**Published by the Inter-American Development Bank**
**Distributed by The Johns Hopkins University Press**

Washington, D.C.
1996

The views and opinions expressed in this publication are those of the authors and do not necessarily reflect the official position of the Inter-American Development Bank.

**Human Resources in Latin America and the Caribbean**

© Copyright 1996 by the Inter-American Development Bank

Inter-American Development Bank
1300 New York Avenue, N.W.
Washington, D.C. 20577

Distributed by
The Johns Hopkins University Press
2715 North Charles Street
Baltimore, MD 21218-4319

Library of Congress Catalog Card Number: 96-77716
ISBN: 1-886938-08-3

# PREFACE

Human resource investments in education, training, health, and nutrition are increasingly recognized as vital to economic development and social reform in Latin America and the Caribbean. Helping the poor to become more productive draws them into the development process and at the same time makes development more equitable and sustainable.

This book looks at the current condition of the region's human resources and how it relates to economic growth. A survey of programs in the region finds that, although Latin America's human resources fare relatively well by international comparison, important gaps and inadequacies in investment in recent years are cause for concern.

A country's investments in education, health, and nutrition are critical links in development, and, if successfully targeted, can lead to a more equitable pattern of growth. Evidence indicates, for example, that the education of women can have a positive impact on the education, health, and nutrition of children, due in part to lower fertility rates and in part to the fact that women direct an important part of their resources to their children.

The value of broad educational coverage is confirmed by the book's findings; however, the Inter-American Development Bank also supports improving the quality of education in all countries in the region. Recent evidence shows that the quality of education is actually more important than the number of years a child stays in school. In fact, for middle- and higher-income countries in the region, the quality of education may well be the most important factor in productivity gains. This is also true in the lower-income countries, but in these countries productivity is enhanced even more by investments in health and nutrition.

Another important component of development in the region is training, to prepare workers to work in more efficient and modern industries. The author demonstrates empirically that training is most effective if it is directed to people with good basic schooling.

For policymakers and government officials, this book offers important suggestions about how changes in human resource policies could substantially improve returns in several key components of development. With a more skilled labor force, countries will be able to adapt more quickly to changes in the world economy and enjoy greater productivity growth over the long term.

Nohra Rey de Marulanda, Manager
Integration and Regional Programs Department
Inter-American Development Bank

# ACKNOWLEDGMENTS

This study was prepared by Jere R. Behrman, William R. Kenan Jr. Professor of Economics at the University of Pennsylvania, Philadelphia, Pennsylvania, while he served as a consultant to the IDB.

The study builds on papers by eleven individual research teams from the eight Latin American and Caribbean research institutes that participated in the IDB's Second Round of Meetings of Regional Research Networks on "Human Resources in the Adjustment Process," "Social Service Delivery Systems: An Agenda for Reform," and "Social Security Systems in the Region: Alternatives for Reform." The coordinators of the meetings were Ricardo Paredes, Mario Cristián Aedo, and Francisco Eduardo Barreto de Oliveira. The research teams were headed by Ricardo Paes de Barros, Marisa Bucheli, Alvaro Zerda Sarmiento, Juan Diego Trejos, Isidoro Santana López, Juan Luis Bour, Gustavo Márquez, and Patricio R. Mujica.

Boxes and sidebars on special topics were prepared for this study by Roberto Cavalcanti de Albuquerque, Ricardo Paes de Barros, Santiago Levy, Jacqueline Mazza, Rosane Silva Pinto de Mendonça, Ricardo Paredes, Alberto Petrecolla, Luis Riveros, and James Alan Shope. Research assistance was provided by Juan Antonio Rivas, Ryan Schneider, and Russell Lamb. Juan Carlos Ginarte prepared the figures.

The project was conducted under the guidance of Nohra Rey de Marulanda, Manager of the IDB's Integration and Regional Programs Department; Willy Van Ryckeghem, Senior Regional Economic Advisor of the IDB's Regional Operations Department 1; and Frederick Jaspersen, former Chief of the IDB's Development Policy Research Division. In addition, Gabriela Baer, Frederick Jaspersen, Nohra Rey de Marulanda, Jacqueline Mazza, Ricardo Morán, and Willy Van Ryckeghem provided useful comments on the first draft of this study and José Núñez del Arco provided useful editorial guidance.

# CONTENTS

# LIST OF BOXES

# LIST OF FIGURES

# CHAPTER

# OVERVIEW

## Motivation

Human resource investments in schooling, health and nutrition, and training are increasingly considered major components of successful economic development strategies. Recent analyses of economic development experiences and the academic literature both stress the critical role of human resources.

Studies that synthesize the last four decades of applied economic development experience emphasize that appropriate human resource policies are as critical to successful development as are macroeconomic stability, exposure to the competitive pressures of selling on world markets, and physical infrastructure investments. It has, in fact, become accepted that human resource development should be the basic objective of economic development, because it lifts people out of poverty and enables them to expand their capabilities.

In addition, recent academic literature on new neoclassical growth models highlights the critical role of increasing returns to scale and of externalities to human resource stocks in explaining divergences in different countries' economic growth paths and multiple growth equilibria (Box 2.1). This literature places considerable emphasis on the importance, for a country's growth and development, of the initial conditions of its human resources—that is, on how rich or poor a country is in terms of human resources, given that country's development level. The greater the human resources with respect to other selected dimensions of initial development, such as real per capita income, the better a country's development prospects. Economies with greater human resources for a given level of initial per capita real income level are more likely to be able to adapt to changing markets and technologies and to grow and prosper.

The recent emphasis on human resource investments as an integral part of development policy reflects the following perception: human resources are critical because human resource enrichment is a central aspect of poverty alleviation and of development in itself, and also because human resource investments have important positive productivity effects. Such effects are particularly helpful in facilitating adjustment to changes under uncertainty, which are of increasing significance as the world becomes more integrated, as markets and technology change ever more quickly, and as larger numbers of developing countries adopt export-oriented strategies. In addition, considerable human resource investments are seen as having facilitated the rapid growth of East Asia and Southeast Asia by ensuring widespread distribution of the benefits of that growth. This growth with equity creates greater incentives to sacrifice current consumption of goods, services, and leisure in order to contribute to the growth process.

Despite this growing emphasis on human resources as central to the development process, however, human resources in Latin America and the Caribbean have only recently received much attention. Analysis of the role of human resources was conspicuously absent from earlier Latin American and Caribbean thought on development strategies, as noted in surveys of such thinking by Corbo (1992) and Iglesias (1992). Earlier debates on Latin American development, rather, were concerned with macro imbalances, prospects in international markets, inward versus outward orientation, debt issues, and macro dimensions of structural adjustment.

The poor economic performance of the 1980s in most of the region, moreover, led to "a severe deterioration in productive conditions and in the labor situation" (PREALC, 1991). Even at the beginning of the 1980s, nearly every economy in the region had a labor demand that was not expanding as fast as labor supply. With the slowdown of economic growth from an average of 5.5 percent per year for 1950–1980 to 1.2 percent per year in the 1980s, labor market imbalances worsened. Open employment increased to levels higher than 10 percent in many cases, despite an annual growth in public sector employment of 3.7 percent in the 1980s, with a growing structural component stemming from mismatches and from an effective deterioration of unemployed human resources (Mazza, 1992; Riveros, 1990a).[1] Real wages generally declined during this period. Moreover, the composition of employment shifted toward

---

[1] Comparisons of unemployment rates among countries in the region are difficult because of different definitions. For instance, in Argentina and Mexico the usual definition includes those who were employed less than a minimum number of hours per week. Chile, Colombia, and Costa Rica include all of those who declare that they have been actively looking for work during the reference week. Jamaica and some other Caribbean states include discouraged workers, which leads to considerably higher rates. The sensitivity to the definition used is reflected in alternative estimates for open unemployment in the first quarter of 1991 by the

small-scale firms and toward the lower-wage informal sector, i.e., from 25 percent of nonagricultural informal sector employment in 1980 to 35 percent in 1989 (Riveros, 1992a).[2] The structural reform process during that period—toward fiscal balance, trade liberalization, and privatization—led to further imbalances in human resources, as the demand for labor shifted toward tradables and toward the private sector. It also led to reduced government support for human resources.[3]

Looking forward, Iglesias (1992) emphasizes the current movement toward a new Latin American consensus on development, in which human resource investments will have a major role. In this emerging consensus, macro and international balances are established, incentives to increase productivity (including deregulation) are created, and equitable and sustained growth is attained through new investments.[4] These include important investments in human resources so that work forces can adapt to rapidly changing markets and so that the benefits of future economic growth can be widely shared by the population. Iglesias observes that:

> Among the policies aimed at improving the situation of the poorer sectors and at making economic growth compatible with social concerns, none perhaps is more important than upgrading human resources and incorporating them into the productive system. The past decade has been characterized by a growing insertion of the Latin American economies into the world markets, together with new demands with regard to the quality of these economies' macroeco-

Statistical Office of Mexico (and reported by Riveros, 1992a): 2.3 percent with the official definition, 5.5 percent if those who worked less than 15 hours a week are included, and 11.1 percent if those with income lower than the minimum wage are included. Even though different definitions across countries make cross-country comparisons difficult, in all of these countries the average unemployment rate increased by the mid 1980s and declined very slowly thereafter.

[2] In part, the shift to smaller firms stemmed from the breakup of larger firms into smaller ones and from increased use of subcontracting to small firms by medium-sized and large firms (PREALC, 1991).

[3] Cline (1991) does argue that the labor displacement from trade liberalization in the region has been less severe than feared, probably because real exchange rate depreciations have buffered the shock of import liberalization.

[4] Although there is movement toward such a consensus, clearly not all countries in the region have adopted policies consistent with this consensus. As of this writing, Brazil, for instance, has not established effective internal balance in terms of governmental deficits, even though the external balance in terms of the international balance of payments has improved substantially in the past decade, and employment creation has been impressive. The numbers employed increased from about 40 million in 1981 to roughly 56 million in 1991 (Barros, 1992).

nomic policies, the modernization of their productive structures, and the competitiveness of their exports—all of which require new knowledge, technological innovation, new organizational forms, and better-qualified human resources. At the same time, the relatively higher levels of welfare and complexity in Latin American countries following the postwar period of growth have accentuated the internal stratification within their societies, favored the emergence of various interest groups, and furthered distributional struggles. . . . Consequently, the identity and interests of the different groups depend increasingly on their technical know-how, their skill at developing proposals, and their ability to negotiate agreements with the government or other social groups. Finally, the trend toward increasing the professionalism and technical knowledge of authorities in the executive branch and in the parliaments and other representative bodies, as necessitated by the growing complexity of modern life, makes it possible that the groups represented will have less to say about the handling of their own problems unless they assume greater responsibility and become more technically competent. This combination of economic, social, and political factors underscores the importance of human resources in Latin America's current economic and political development (Iglesias, 1992, 112–13).

Iglesias also observes that:

. . . education and the development of human resources, once considered strictly from the social perspective, become key factors in economic development. The gap that Latin America must bridge in this area is determined on the one hand by the persistence of poverty and social inequality and on the other by the demands created by the speed of productivity and technological change (Iglesias, 1992, 152).

Within the emerging Latin American and Caribbean consensus on development, human resource investments are thus being viewed ever more widely as a central element in programs of integrated economic development, social reform, and poverty reduction, in which the poor are to become more productive and increasingly empowered and thereby able to contribute to the creation of more equitable sustained development processes.

Such programs clearly require macroeconomic stability, effective use of international and domestic markets, and governmental reforms to promote progressive increases in productivity. But to ensure opportunities for widespread participation of the poor so they can emerge out of poverty within the dynamic economies of the future, the programs also require substantial human resource investments in the poor.

Human resource investments are required to (i) facilitate the shorter-term adjustment process through which production and employment adapt to changing incentives arising from greater integration into the international economy, and (ii) increase the prospects for longer-run sustained productivity growth (Mazza, 1992). Greater human resource investment will contribute to the pursuit of social reform through which all members of society can be given the opportunity to enjoy the benefits of development.

Given the emerging consensus on the critical role of human resources for both shorter-run adjustment and longer-run equitable productivity growth in Latin America and the Caribbean, a review of human resources in the region is in order.

## Approach

This study is a review of basic aspects of human resources in the Latin American and Caribbean region. The second chapter examines why human resources are important to the region, discussing their impact on poverty alleviation and on economic growth and development. The third chapter is an overview of the current condition of human resources in the region. The fourth chapter analyzes the determinants of human resource investments, with attention to both the role of private decisions and the role of official policy. It also surveys the strengths and limitations of the region's human resource programs in education, health and nutrition, and training. The fifth and final chapter outlines general and specific aspects of the region's human resource policy options for the 1990s.

These chapters draw on several types of knowledge. Whenever possible, they are based on recent aggregate quantitative analysis or on empirical analysis at the micro level. But such analysis is difficult: it may depend on the market and policy context, which may shift as a result of changes in macro and market policies. In addition, data limitations often make it difficult to control for unobserved factors, such as ability and motivation, that may obscure the causal effects of human resource investments and the true determinants of those investments.

Therefore, to obtain as good a basis as possible for policies, hard evidence from careful, systematic empirical analysis must be supplemented by insights of simple models, by expert judgments, and by general evidence showing that individuals and economic entities respond substantially to incentives. This study pulls together evidence based on these various types of knowledge, to characterize the impact, condition, and determinants of human resource investments in the region, as well as the most promising human resource policies.

The region is clearly no more homogeneous with regard to human resources than with regard to most of its other features. Concerning human resources in the region, Miguel Urrutia (1991) has said, "Generalizations are treacherous, and generalizations about Latin America...are often based on the analysis of only one or two countries." Some countries in the region, such as Chile and Costa Rica, apparently have relatively rich human resources in a number of dimensions, while others, such as Brazil and Haiti, have much poorer human resources. This study attempts to describe the common human resource experience in the region, as well as the ways in which the experiences of particular countries differ from the common experience.

## Major Messages

Because human resources are determined by and have effects within complex interlinked socioeconomic systems, and because substantial limitations exist with regard to the information available about human resources, generalized messages about human resources in the region can be misleading or oversimplified. The basic results of this study can be summarized in four major messages, but the nuances of these messages are also important and should not be overlooked.

*Point 1. Human resources have an important impact on productivity and distribution in Latin America and the Caribbean.*

High levels of schooling and good health and nutrition relative to a country's initial level of development are associated with relatively good subsequent macroeconomic performance. These human resources operate through myriad channels—creating direct productivity effects, altering expenditure patterns, inducing further human resource investments, and/or reducing population pressures.

Increases in post-primary schooling facilitate adjustment to market changes by reducing the cost of acquiring new specific human capital (although for lower school levels the possible loss of specific human capital investments induced by the previous economic regime may outweigh the gains from switching to new productive activities). In addition, schooling variations are consistent with a substantial portion of the income variance in the region, with more schooling associated with lower probabilities of being in poverty.

The returns to human resource investments do tend to vary with a country's level of development and its initial human resource stock. For very low income populations, rates of return to health and nutrition in terms of productivity may be greater than those to education. For middle and higher-income populations, rates of return to education in terms of productivity are considerable. In economies in which schooling is relatively limited, the highest rate of return may result from improving the quality and quantity of basic primary schooling; for countries with more extensive schooling experience, the return may be higher for investments in more advanced levels of schooling. Likewise, in countries with poorer health and nutrition conditions, the returns may be highest to interventions to control infectious disease and increase infant and maternal care. In other cases, where demographic and epidemiological transitions are already well underway, health problems may be increasingly dominated by the so-called adult diseases of development.

In most economies in the region, the rates of return to additional human resource investments tend to be higher for females than for males, in part because of the greater role of female schooling in determining health, nutrition, and fertility. And although there may be high medium and long-term returns to such investments, these are not likely to produce many quick fixes in the form of human capital investments that have large immediate effects on productivity, simply because most human resource investments have long gestation periods. One possible exception is training; evidence in this area is still relatively limited, but given the substantial role that training has played in Latin America and the Caribbean, there would likely be high returns to additional systematic analysis of and investment in training. The rates of return to human resource investments also depend on the overall national context and development strategy and are likely to increase with greater macro balance, increased market orientation, and greater integration into world markets.

*Point 2. The condition of human resources in Latin America and the Caribbean is relatively good in some dimensions in comparison with international experience, but there are some important gaps and some evidence of inadequacies in recent investments relative to what would be desirable.*

In comparison with international experience and controlling for per capita income, the available crude indicators suggest that aggregate human resource schooling and health/nutrition conditions in the region are relatively good, with relatively small gender gaps favoring males. But human resource conditions in some countries in the region, such as Brazil and Venezuela, fare poorly in aggregate comparisons. In addition, there are a number of reasons to suspect that recent human resource investments in the entire region have been less than what would be desirable.

The relatively good condition of the aggregate human resource indicators in the region vis-à-vis international experience reflects in part merely the relative persistence of human resource stocks in a period in which national real per capita incomes have declined rather than grown. Had these income growth figures been better in the past decade, the relative condition of human resources might well have appeared less satisfactory, even by the crude indices for which data are available.

At some more disaggregate levels for which reasonably comparable data are available, such as the stock of secondary schooling, the region lags behind international experience. The limited secondary schooling stock among adults in economies that are more integrated into rapidly changing world markets is likely to limit possibilities for growth.

In terms of public investment in human resources, the region has, on average, fared less well recently in comparison with international experience. This decline stems in part from the disruptions of the lost decade of the 1980s, which may have a negative effect on the future condition of human resources.

This problem is compounded by the fact that the region is currently undergoing certain major changes, such as demographic and epidemiological transitions and the spread of AIDS. Although the effects of these changes are not yet prominent in the aggregate statistics, it is clear that they are altering the composition of health service needs. The delivery of needed services related to health and other human resources has not yet adjusted sufficiently.

If the region is to succeed in its aspirations for rapid economic growth, greater investment in human resources will be needed. Investment in the poorer members of society is an effective means of improving the welfare and increasing the productivity and income of many such individuals. These gains are important, given the relatively great income inequalities and the associated high incidence of poverty in the region, particularly in rural areas and among certain ethnic groups.

*Point 3. Although many of the returns to human resource investments are private, there are important productivity-related and distributional reasons for public policy support for selected human resource investments in the region.*

The fact that a given human resource investment has a high rate of return is not, in itself, a reason for public support of that investment in terms of productivity (although a public subsidy might be justified in terms of equity for the poorer members of society). From the point of view of productivity and efficiency, what is really important is whether the social rates of return to given human resource investments are greater than the private rates of return. If that is the case, then there is an efficiency reason for public subsidies for given human resource investments, or for changes in investments to lessen or remove the difference between the social and private returns.

Much of the advocacy for greater public support for human resource investment ignores the question of whether there are discrepancies between social and private rates of return. Such advocacy, therefore, could lead to the wrong composition of public support for these investments and obscure the socially more attractive policy options by suggesting overly broad policy needs. For instance, most of the evidence on the high rates of return to schooling in terms of wages or outcomes such as health and fertility does not address the question of whether there are differences in private versus social effects that can be lessened through human resource investments.

Nevertheless, for some aspects of human resource investment, the efficiency rationale for public policy support seems strong, both because of externalities that are not transferred through markets and could not best be remedied by changing markets, and because of public good aspects such that more for one individual does not mean less for others. An important example of both is the control of contagious diseases.

Greater adjustment capacity as a result of more schooling and training, so that workers can adapt more rapidly to changing economic conditions, also has important positive external social benefits beyond the private benefits, by lessening aggregate employment problems. Information and knowledge generated by better-schooled and better-trained individuals are likely to involve important externalities and public good characteristics. For instance, such individuals are more likely to explore marketing and technological innovations, thus providing information to others about the usefulness of such innovations.

Public support for human resource investments may also be warranted to compensate for the fact that capital markets do not function well for such investments. To improve policies from a productivity and efficiency perspective, public support should be directed not toward human resources indiscriminately, but toward those human resource investments for which the social rates of return exceed private returns.

*Point 4. Some relatively small modifications to public provision of services related to human resources can have high returns, but there can be potentially larger gains from more substantial policy changes.*

Within the present general framework of human resource service delivery, certain changes are likely to bring high returns in a number of countries. These include wide provision of textbooks and writing materials in schools; more closely linking training programs to the needs of employers; ensuring that publicly subsidized training programs provide general (not firm-specific) training and build upon sufficient general education; extending to all children expanded basic immunizations; mounting more extensive information campaigns on addictive substances and sexually transmitted diseases (STDs); subsidizing means of restricting the spread of STDs; improving safe motherhood and infant monitoring and care; making short-course chemotherapy against tuberculosis more widely available; disseminating manuals on therapeutic drugs (including use, dosage, and adverse reactions) to more pharmaceutical providers; ensuring adequate supplies of pharmaceuticals to clinics; promoting wider use of generic pharmaceuticals; streamlining pharmaceutical selection and procurement; promoting development of preventive and chronic care facilities so that acute care facilities are not used for chronic care; and expanding the collection of information about the impact and determinants of human resources.

There are probably even larger potential gains from substantial policy reforms that would make service delivery more responsive to incentives and more directed toward market failures—including, most importantly, information problems. These changes might include symmetrical policy treatment for private and public suppliers, incentive schemes through markets or voucher systems, and better monitoring and publicizing data on value added in various services related to human resources.

# CHAPTER

2

## IMPACT OF HUMAN RESOURCES

What are the patterns of human resource investment in Latin America and the Caribbean and how do they affect economic growth, poverty, economic distribution, and other important outcomes? This chapter assesses recent studies and provides new aggregate evidence on the impact of human resources on poverty and on economic growth in the region. To the extent possible, it also documents the importance of quality in human resource investment, as well as the relative importance of investing in females versus males, in different ethnic groups, in rural versus urban residents, and in different types of services (for instance, basic versus advanced schooling, curative versus preventive health care). The chapter also discusses the effect of overall economic strategy and of human resource investment on productivity and equity. The difficulties in obtaining hard evidence on some supposed effects of human resource investment (such as externalities) are also considered.

Recent surveys of the relation between aggregate indicators of human resources and economic performance in the region suggest that there is no systematic association. The survey by Aerate (1991), for instance, concluded that:

> Apparently no clear systematic relationship exists between performance in economic indicators and social indicators. Brazil grew very rapidly in economic terms but did not do well in social development. On the other hand, Costa Rica and Panama combined rapid growth with a significant improvement in social indicators, while Haiti stagnated in both economic and social development. The Central American statistics, with the exception of those for Costa Rica, show below-average economic and social development.

Until now, however, there has been no systematic examination of how the ratio between a country's level of human resources and its initial level of development can affect its subsequent economic trajectory. This is

## Box 2.1. The New Neoclassical Growth Models

Neoclassical growth models have long shaped the intuition of academic economists about long-run growth, in part because of their simplicity and elegance. In these models, the rate of return on investment and the rate of growth of per capita product are decreasing functions of the level of per capita capital stock, and over time, wage rates and capital-labor ratios eventually converge across countries. That is, initial conditions and subsequent shocks have no long-run effects on output or consumption. For instance, an exogenous reduction in the capital stock causes an increase in the price of capital assets, which induces an offsetting increase in investments. In the absence of technological change, per capita product converges to a steady-state value with no per capita growth, because of diminishing returns to per capita capital.

The new neoclassical growth models focus on human resource investments with externalities and returns to scale. Romer (1986) presents an equilibrium growth model of endogenous technological changes in which long-run growth is driven primarily by the accumulation of knowledge. New knowledge is produced with diminishing returns, but with positive externalities in the form of productivity benefits for others than the developer or owner of the knowledge, since knowledge is not perfectly patented or kept secret. The stock of knowledge, however, has increasing returns in the production of consumption goods. Therefore, knowledge and per capita output can grow without limits, the rate of investment and the rate of return on capital stock may increase with increased capital stock, and the levels of per capita product need not converge across countries. Human resources are central to the growth process, and active policies favoring human resources have a growth payoff because of the externalities and increasing returns associated with such investments.

Lucas (1988) first adapts the neoclassical growth model by adding externalities such as how the average level of human capital affects a worker's productivity in addition to the worker's own human capital stock. This modification permits permanent differences in per capita incomes across countries to be main-

the focus of the new classical growth economics (Box 2.1). To explore the aggregate effects of human resources on subsequent economic outcomes, this chapter considers how aggregate human resources, controlling for per capita real income in 1965, have been associated with the growth in various economic indicators since 1965, as well as with recent levels of such indicators. The evidence on this association provides a basis for assessing the different trajectories that countries in the region might be expected to follow, given their current patterns of human resource development relative to per capita income.

tained. Lucas also considers a model in which human capital has only external effects on many commodities, each with different learning-by-doing, and on international trade. He shows that such a model is consistent with very different levels and rates of growth across countries, as well as with sudden jumps in production patterns and growth rates in response to small changes in world prices. Once again, externalities suggest a possible major role for policies favoring human resource investments.

Azariadis and Drazen (1990) add technological externalities with a threshold property to Diamon's (1965) overlapping generations neoclassical growth model; within this model, returns to scale can change very rapidly, and there can be multiple, locally stable, balanced growth equilibrium paths. Among the externalities they consider are labor augmenting spillovers from human capital investments. For instance, more knowledge may make it easier to acquire still more knowledge, so that countries with high human resource investments relative to their per capita income can experience subsequent periods of high sustained growth. Such a framework, once again, implies that policies to support human resource investments may increase growth because of positive externalities.

Thus, this new neoclassical growth literature provides systematic aggregate theoretical models in which human resources are central, positive externalities of human resources may justify policy support of human resource investments to increase growth, per capita income may grow without bounds rather than approach a steady state, initial conditions relating to the stock of human resources relative to per capita income may be critical, responses to shocks may be considerable rather than marginal, and growth experiences may diverge among countries. These models have been prominent in the recent academic literature and have been cited frequently in the more applied human resource literature as part of the rationale for policies favoring human resource investments. However, there are questions about how much of the "new" neoclassical growth literature really is new and about the nature of the empirical support for these models (for instance, Behrman, 1990a).

*Source:* Prepared by the author.

Both aggregate and disaggregate analysis are employed in this chapter to assess the relation between investment in human resources and important outcomes such as wages or health. Such estimates are usually based on cross-sectional data. Estimating the associations between human resources and such outcomes is straightforward, but estimating the extent to which the human resources cause the outcomes is much more difficult. This is so because there are unobserved individual characteristics (ability, motivation), family characteristics (parental role models, genetic endowments, connections regarding school admissions and jobs), and community characteristics (role models, labor market opportunities, health conditions) that may affect both the human resource investment and the outcomes studied. Such factors at the household and community level also make it very difficult to estimate possible externalities of human resources from micro data, which is a serious limitation in that such externalities may be an important part of the rationale for policy interventions (as will be discussed later in greater detail). The better studies control for such factors.

## Determinants of Human Resource Investments and Their Impact—Preliminary Points

Many empirical studies of human resources ignore simple analytical considerations, with the result that the interpretations and policy justifications given may be quite misleading. Therefore, before turning to empirical evidence about the impact of human resource investment in the region, we briefly summarize some of these considerations. Because the determinants of human resource investments affect the interpretation of the relations between the investments and outcomes of interest to policymakers (such as wages), let us begin with individual or household demand for investment in human resources. Analysis of this demand establishes the foundation for interpreting empirical evidence of human resources in the region, and for considering policies that further human resource investment.

Households and the individuals in those households are the proximate sources of demand for most human resource investment, given their predetermined assets, their productive functions, and the current and expected prices of inputs used in human resource investments and of the outcomes of the production process. All of this can be summarized in the present discounted value of expected marginal benefits for different human resource investments for a given individual (hereafter, "marginal benefits"), as in Becker's (1967) Woytinsky lecture (see the downward-sloping line in Figure 2.1A). The marginal benefit curve slopes downward if plotted against human resource investments because (i) human resource investments have diminishing returns, (ii) individuals possess given endowments (genetic and environmental), and (iii) to the extent that human resource investments take time (such as schooling and training), greater investments imply greater lags in obtaining returns and a shorter post-investment period in which to reap those returns. In this case, equilibrium human resource investment in the individual is at a level at which the marginal benefit equals the marginal cost of the investments, since for any lesser investment the marginal benefit is greater than the marginal cost, so gains can be made by increasing the investment (and vice versa).

**Figure 2.1. Marginal Benefits and Marginal Costs Determining Human Resource Investments (H)**

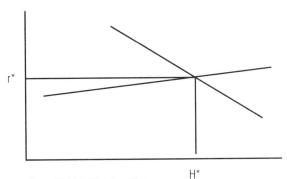

Figure 2.1A Initial Equilibrium

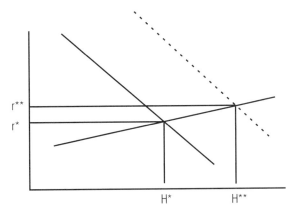

Figure 2.1B Equilibrium with Higher Marginal Benefits (Dashed Line)

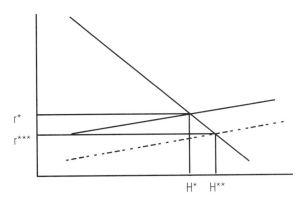

Figure 2.1C Equilibrium with Lower Marginal Costs (Dashed Line)

The marginal cost is also in present discounted value terms, since some of these costs may be experienced in the future. These marginal costs may increase with human resource investments because of the increasing opportunity costs of devoting more time to such investments (especially for schooling and training), and because of the increasing marginal costs of borrowing on financial markets. The marginal cost curve slopes upward in the figure. The equilibrium human resource investment for this individual is H* where the two curves intersect, with both the marginal benefit and the marginal cost equal to r*.

If the marginal benefit curve is higher for every level of human resource investment, as shown by the dashed line in Figure 2.1B, then all else equal, the equilibrium human resource investment (H**) and the equilibrium marginal benefit (r**) both are greater. The marginal benefit curve may be higher for a number of possible reasons that can be illuminated by comparing two individuals who are identical except for one of the following differences:[1]

• One individual may have greater endowments (such as more ability and drive) that are rewarded in schooling and in post-schooling labor markets and that stem from some combination of genetic and home environmental factors. Such an individual invests more in human resources in equilibrium, which means that to estimate the impact of human resource investments on some outcome, one cannot simply consider the association between the human resource investment and the outcome (for example, between years of schooling and wage rates) without also controlling for the endowments underlying the different human resource investments.

• One individual may have better health and a longer expected life because of complementary investments, so that the post-investment period in which that individual reaps the returns to the investment is greater, and therefore the expected returns are also greater.

• One individual may have human resource investment options of higher quality (for instance, access to higher-quality public schools or public health services), so that the marginal benefits for a given level of investment are higher, and the equilibrium investments are greater.[2]

---

[1] For some of these comparisons (for instance, the last three), the otherwise identical individuals would have to live in different societies and economies.

[2] If the investor (or the investor's family) must pay at the margin for greater quality, the amount of the investment does not necessarily increase with a higher-quality option. What happens to the equilibrium investment in this case depends on where the marginal cost curve for the higher-quality option is, in addition to the location of the marginal benefit curve.

• One individual may have greater marginal benefits to a given level of such investments because of labor market discrimination that favors that individual because of gender, race, language, family, village, or ethnic group. For instance, estimated rates of return to schooling are lower in Bolivia and Guatemala for indigenous workers than for those of European descent (Psacharopoulos, 1993), which would seem to induce smaller schooling investments by indigenous people, as indeed has been observed (Box 3.2).

• The returns to investing in one individual may be greater than the returns to investing in another (for instance, if traditional gender roles dictate that children of only one sex support their parents in old age, then parents may have greater incentives to invest in children who are likely to provide such support).

• One individual may have greater marginal benefits to a given level of such investments because of greater externalities from the human resource investments of others in the same labor market (for instance, because of greater knowledge).

• One individual may have greater marginal benefits to a given level of investment because of being in a more dynamic economy in which the returns to such investments are greater.

• One individual may live in a more stable economy so that the discount rate for future returns is lower and thus the marginal benefit of future returns is greater.

If the marginal cost is lower for every level of human resource investment, as shown by the dashed line in Figure 2.1C, ceteris paribus, the equilibrium human resource investment (H***) is greater, and the marginal benefit (r***) at the higher investment level is lower. The marginal cost might be lower for a number of reasons that can be illuminated by comparing two individuals who are identical except for one of the following differences:

• One individual may have lower-cost access to educational and health services related to such investments because of greater proximity to such services or lower user charges.

• One individual may have lower opportunity costs for time used for such investments (for instance, because of gender specialization in household and farm tasks performed by children).

• One individual may come from a household with greater access to credit because of greater wealth or status.

• One individual may face lower utility costs of such investments because of cultural norms (for instance, if girls past puberty are not allowed to intermingle with males outside the family in transit to school or in school, the preference costs of schooling will be lower for boys than for girls).

This simple framework systematizes three critical common sense points for identifying the impact of human resource investments on important outcomes such as labor productivity, and for understanding when there may be efficiency reasons for governments or private firms to subsidize human resource investments.

First, human resource investments are associated with a number of individual, family, community, and labor market characteristics: individual abilities, motivations, and inherent robustness; family support, role models, household gender roles, connections, and genetic endowments; community role models, quality of community health and educational services, and stock of community production inputs complementary to individual human resource investments; and labor market segmentation by gender, ethnic, and racial groups. To identify the impact of human resource investments on a particular outcome, therefore, it is important to control for these characteristics. Simple estimates that do not control for them may attribute to human resource investments not only the true effect of those investments but also the effects of all other individual, family, community, and labor market characteristics that are in the background. Given the limitations of the available data, it is difficult to control for such characteristics. But for some studies of the impact of human resources in Latin America and the Caribbean, such controls appear to have made a considerable difference. Without such controls, mere associations between human resource investments and certain outcomes should not be assumed to indicate that the human resource investments by themselves actually cause the outcomes.

Second, empirical returns to human resource investments are observed for a given macroeconomic, market, and regulatory environment. If macro policies reduce the costs of investment in physical capital and reduce the rewards for investment in human resources, these factors need to be taken into account in evaluating the prospective returns from new human resource investments. If labor market discrimination or glass ceilings have limited the advancement and thus the financial returns to human resources of groups identified by gender, ethnicity, or race, then possible labor market changes need to be taken into account in assessing future returns to investing in the human resources of such individuals.

Third, the marginal benefits of human resource investment in a particular individual may differ depending on the point of view from which these benefits are evaluated. Two such possibilities are important for this report: externalities and specific returns. Let us examine both.

## Externalities

Externalities to human resource investments are effects that are not transferred through markets. If an individual who is more educated contributes to marginal productivity beyond what she or he is paid, there is a positive externality, and the social marginal benefit is greater than the private marginal benefit. Or if an individual adjusts rapidly to changing circumstances and by virtue of that adjustment provides information to others about whether or not there are economic rewards to such an adjustment, there is a dynamic externality in the form of information about the changing world. Or if an individual is cured of a contagious disease, not only does that individual benefit from the medical intervention, but others who may have been at risk if that individual had not been cured benefit as well. In all of these cases, the social marginal benefit curve is greater than the private one that does not take externalities into account, as in Figure 2.1B, where the social marginal benefit curve is represented by the dashed line and the private marginal benefit curve by the solid line.

With such positive externalities, the private incentives are to underinvest in human resources, since the private marginal benefits are below the private marginal costs for human resource investments beyond H*, even though the desirable investment from a social point of view is H**.[3] But if the individual benefits from positive externalities because of the human resource investments of others that increase the rate of return to human resource investment in her or him (just as others benefit from her or his human resource investments), then there is less of a gap between the private and social marginal benefits. For instance, if the rate of return to one's own schooling is higher because of the externalities of greater knowledge, then the private marginal benefits curve is higher than if there were no such externalities.

## Specific Returns

Returns to some investments may be specific to a particular economic entity rather than more general. General human resources have broad productivity returns throughout the economy, while specific human resources apply only to a particular entity, such as a firm. Basic literacy and numeracy are general forms of human resources while knowledge of idiosyncratic production or management processes may be specific forms. From an indi-

---

[3] To focus on the benefits of these externalities, this statement assumes that the private marginal costs and the social marginal costs are equal.

**Box 2.2. Schooling, Growth, and Distribution in Brazil**

The links among Brazil's economic performance, social condition, and political participation in the 1970s and 1980s have been examined extensively in studies by the Institute for Applied Economic Research (IPEA) and the National Institute for Advanced Studies (INAE).

In the 1970s, high per capita GDP growth (6.1 percent per year) was followed by rapid improvement of broad social indicators, sharp poverty reduction (from 46 percent to 20 percent of households), and significant narrowing of regional and urban-rural disparities. Moreover, the electorate climbed from 61 percent to 84 percent of the over-18 population, and a gradual process of political openness took place, leading to freedom of expression and rule of law. The decade can be seen as having achieved convergence between economic dynamism and social inclusion, as well as some political-institutional improvements.

In the 1980s, unsuccessful macroeconomic adjustments led to falling per capita income and increased poverty (from 20 percent to 26 percent of households). But social indicators were more resilient and continued to improve, and interzonal and urban-rural gaps continued to diminish, albeit slowly. The electorate grew to more than 90 percent of the over-18 population, and democracy was fully established under a new constitution in 1988. The decade can be viewed as having asymmetrically combined economic stagnation, social inclusion, and political-institutional advancement.

In both decades, personal income inequality remained fairly stable although very high. (The Gini coefficient went down from 0.64 to 0.62 in the 1970s and up to 0.63 in the 1980s.) The poor and nonpoor benefitted from

vidual point of view, there may not be an incentive to invest sufficiently in specific forms of human capital because the individual cannot reap the full marginal gains from such investments in the labor market. That is, the marginal benefits from such investments may be like the solid downward-sloping line in Figure 2.1B. From the point of view of the firm, on the other hand, the benefits may be greater, as shown by the dashed line in Figure 2.1B. Therefore, the firm has an incentive to use resources to induce the individual to invest more in specific human capital than the individual would on his or her own.

Such incentives are greater, of course, the longer the individual is expected to work with the firm, so that the firm can reap the returns to such investments. For this reason, the firm may wish to design a labor contract that creates incentives, such as increasing compensation, to encourage workers with specific human capital to continue with the firm.

Individuals with more general human resources are also usually able to learn better, so the return to investing in their specific human resources growth in the 1970s; the income share of the lowest 40 percent of households in fact increased from 6.7 percent to 7.5 percent during this decade. Both the poor and the nonpoor suffered from stagnation in the 1980s; the poor suffered somewhat more in that the income share of the lowest 40 percent of households declined to 7.2 percent.

Progress in education was impressive in Brazil during the last two decades, particularly given the rapid population expansion in the 1960s (3.0 percent per year) and 1970s (2.5 percent), which substantially increased the numbers of school-age children. Formal literacy climbed from 66 percent of the over-15 population in the early 1970s to 81 percent by the end of the 1980s. Since 1980 there has been enough primary school capacity to enroll virtually all of the relevant age group. Nonetheless, repetition, dropout, and functional illiteracy rates were very high. By the end of the 1980s, only 41 percent of the over-20 population had four or more years of schooling, and scarcely 21 percent had 8 or more years.

Brazilian education and income distribution are strongly correlated. About 40 percent of personal income inequality is related to education. The average income of over-20 workers with more than 5 years of schooling in the 1980s was 55 percent higher than that of the total over-20 work force. And 72 percent of the poor workers were illiterate or had less than 1 year of schooling. Studies suggest that low skills limited the capacity of the poorer members of society to gain from growth in the 1970s or to find alternatives to escape poverty in the 1980s.

*Source:* Roberto Cavalcanti de Albuquerque.

will be greater. Moreover, while the value of much specific human capital in declining production activities may be lost with changes in the economy, those with more general human resources are able to adjust more rapidly to those changes and can be retrained at lower cost. Therefore, particularly in periods of adjustment, there may be greater advantages to having considerable general human capital, even if substantial specific human capital from past training and learning is lost.

## Impact of Schooling

Schooling is the most emphasized form of human resource investment, and is widely perceived to have high social returns in terms of greater productivity, improved health, and reduced fertility (see Box 2.2). This section considers aggregate and micro evidence regarding the impact of schooling in Latin America and the Caribbean.

### Aggregate Estimates of the Impact of Initial Schooling

A question of considerable interest is whether differences in schooling from the levels predicted by real per capita income[4] (hereafter, "initial schooling") affect subsequent outcomes, as suggested by recent economic growth models (Box 2.1). This can be determined for medium-term development only with the passage of a decade or more. Nevertheless, insight can be gained about these prospects by examining the associations between initial schooling in 1965 and (i) subsequent average annual growth rates, (ii) recent socioeconomic outcomes, and (iii) recent socioeconomic outcomes relative to those predicted by recent per capita real income. Schooling can be represented either by total years of schooling implied in enrollment rates (Table 2.1), or by more disaggregated measures that focus on enrollments at different levels (that is, primary, secondary, and tertiary, as in Table 2.2), or as a function of gender (Table 2.3).

These analyses have yielded several main findings:

*Finding 1. Initial total schooling investments are associated with subsequent growth levels and other key outcomes.*

Initial schooling is positively associated with subsequent real per capita GNP growth, with the growth rate about 0.35 percent higher for every grade by which initial schooling exceeds the level predicted by real per capita income. This means, for instance, that the difference between recent schooling (controlling for per capita income) of 3.8 grades for Ecuador and –0.9 grades for Brazil in Figure 3.1 and Table 3.1, all else equal, would translate into a considerable difference (1.6 percent a year) in growth of real per capita GNP.

This relation is somewhat fuzzy, however, as reflected in Figure 2.2, which plots initial schooling versus growth rates for 20 countries in the region. Still, only six of the countries in the region fall into the northwest or southeast quadrants, with negative values of initial schooling and positive growth (Guatemala, Haiti, and Honduras) or vice versa (Bolivia, Jamaica, and Peru). Moreover, the estimates in tables 2.2 and 2.3 (discussed below) indicate more precise relations between more disaggregate representations of initial schooling—in particular, primary schooling and the gender gap in schooling—and subsequent growth.

---

[4] Note that controlling for initial real per capita income means that the schooling indicators are not representing general development, to the extent that such development is associated with real per capita income.

**Figure 2.2.  Average Annual Percentage Growth in Real Per Capita Income versus Actual Minus Predicted Total Schooling, 1965**

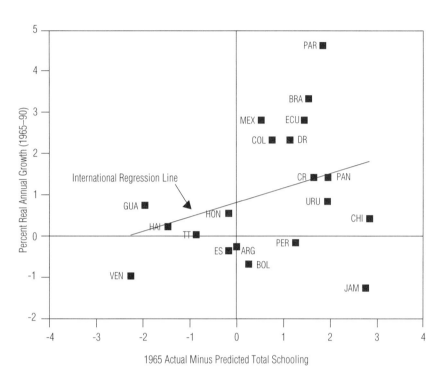

Two important channels through which initial schooling affects real per capita GNP growth and other selected outcomes also are suggested by the other estimates in part 1 of Table 2.1. First, export growth has been higher by 0.7 percent per year for every extra grade of initial schooling. Competition on international markets through exports is widely perceived to be a critical component of strategies to accelerate productivity growth, and thus this channel is an important one. Second, population growth has been lower by about 0.20 percent a year for every extra grade of initial schooling. Lower population growth, of course, reduces pressures on governmental subsidies for schooling and a number of dimensions of health services, or permits better quality schooling and health services. Lower population growth also tends, relatively speaking, to reduce pressures on the poorer members of society, since family sizes tend to be inversely associated with income. The estimated magnitude of the effects of initial schooling through increased export growth and reduced population growth is substantial. To illustrate, these estimates imply that the Brazil-

**Table 2.1. Impact of One More Year of Initial 1965 Total Schooling, Correcting for Real Per Capita Income, on Subsequent Growth and Recent Levels of Various Variables in Latin America and the Caribbean**

| 1. Average annual growth (%) in: | | 3. Recent actual levels - predicted values | |
|---|---|---|---|
| GNP per capita (1965–90) | 0.35** | Total primary enrollment rate, 1987 | 3.7* |
| Manufacturing earnings/employer | | Female primary enrollment rate, 1987 | 4.6* |
| (1970–80) | 0.85* | Total secondary enrollment rate, 1987 | 5.2 |
| Export growth (1980–90) | 0.70 | Female secondary enrollment rate, 1987 | 4.6 |
| Population growth (1965–80) | −0.26 | Schooling for a synthetic cohort, total, 1987 | 0.71 |
| **2. Recent level variables** | | Schooling for a synthetic cohort, female, 1987 | 0.92 |
| Private consumption/GDP (%), 1990 | −4.0 | Adult literacy rate, female, 1985 | 6.8 |
| Medical care/private consumption (%), | | Adult literacy rate, male, 1985 | 5.4 |
| 1990 | −1.1 | Life expectancy at birth, female, 1988 | 1.8 |
| Share of population 15–64 years, 1990 | 1.5 | Life expectancy at birth, male, 1988 | 1.9 |
| Share of population 0–14 years, 1990 | −2.2 | Infant mortality/1,000 births, 1988 | −8.1 |
| Crude birth rate per 1,000, 1990 | −2.4 | Risk of dying by age 5/1,000 births, | |
| Total fertility rate, 1990 | −0.4 | female, 1988 | −9.8 |
| Infant mortality rate (1,000 live births) | | Risk of dying by age 5/1,000 births, | |
| female, 1990 | −8.9 | male, 1988 | −12 |
| Under 5 mortality rate (1,000 live births) | | Risk of dying by age 5/1,000 births, | |
| female, 1990 | −11.8 | male-female, 1988 | 1.8 |
| Under 5 mortality rate (1,000 live births) | | | |
| male, 1990 | −13.4 | Birth attended by health staff, 1985 | 7.3 |
| Life expectancy at birth, female, 1990 | 2.0 | Low birth weight, 1985 | −1.6 |
| Life expectancy at birth, male, 1990 | 2.0 | % central government expenditure on housing, | |
| | | social security, welfare, 1988 | 6.0 |
| | | % GNP government expenditure on housing, | |
| | | social security, welfare, 1988 | 2.2 |
| | | Crude birth rate per 1,000, 1988 | −2.4 |
| | | Total fertility rate, 1988 | −0.4 |

*Note:* Based on initial 1965 total schooling, correcting for real per capita income. All point estimates are significantly nonzero at the 5 percent level, except those indicated by * are significantly nonzero at the 10 percent level and those indicated by ** are significantly nonzero at the 20 percent level.
*Source:* Based on regression estimates by the author.

Ecuador schooling difference noted earlier translates into a 3.2 percent yearly increase in the export growth rate and a 0.9 percent yearly decline in population growth.

The estimated impact of initial schooling on outcomes two decades or more later is also substantial. The effects in Table 2.1 cluster into three groups, each of which we shall discuss in turn.

First, the composition of total GNP and of private and government expenditures is changed. For every additional grade of initial schooling, private consumption declines by 5.0 percent; the share of private consumption devoted to medical care falls by 1.1 percent; and the shares of

# Table 2.2. Impact of Initial 1965 Schooling Enrollments at Different Levels, Correcting for Real Per Capita Income, on Subsequent Growth and Recent Levels of Various Variables in Latin America and the Caribbean

| | Actual-Predicted 1965 Enrollments (%) | | |
|---|---|---|---|
| | Primary | Secondary | Tertiary |
| **1. Average annual growth (%) in:** | | | |
| GNP per capita (1965–90) | 0.072 | -0.081* | — |
| Manufacturing earnings/employer (1970–80) | 0.18 | -0.16 | -0.35** |
| Export growth (1980–90) | 0.22 | -0.17** | — |
| Population growth (1965–80) | 0.017** | -0.071 | -0.10* |
| Population growth (1980–90) | — | -0.054 | -0.090 |
| **2. Recent level variables** | | | |
| Private consumption/GDP (%), 1990 | -0.34 | — | — |
| Medical care/private consumption (%), 1990 | -0.10 | — | 0.48** |
| Share of population 15–64 years, 1990 | 0.089* | — | -0.98 |
| Share of population 0–14 years, 1990 | — | -0.21** | -0.88* |
| Crude birth rate per 1,000, 1990 | -0.11** | — | — |
| Crude death rate per 1,000, 1990 | -0.098 | 0.073** | — |
| Total fertility rate, 1990 | -0.024* | — | — |
| Infant mortality rate (1,000 live births), 1990 | -0.68* | — | — |
| Under 5 mortality rate (1,000 live births), female, 1990 | -0.99 | — | — |
| Under 5 mortality rate (1,000 live births), male, 1990 | -1.1 | — | — |
| Life expectancy at birth, female, 1990 | 0.20* | — | — |
| Life expectancy at birth, male, 1990 | 0.19* | — | — |

| | Actual-Predicted 1965 Enrollments (%) | | |
|---|---|---|---|
| | Primary | Secondary | Tertiary |
| **3. Recent actual levels - predicted values** | | | |
| Male-female primary enrollment rates, 1987 | -0.23 | — | 0.86* |
| Total secondary enrollment rate, 1987 | — | 0.93 | — |
| Female secondary enrollment rate, 1987 | — | 1.0 | — |
| Schooling for a synthetic cohort, total, 1987 | — | — | 0.23* |
| Adult literacy rate, female, 1985 | 0.48 | — | — |
| Adult literacy rate, male, 1985 | 0.33 | — | 1.2** |
| Life expectancy at birth, female, 1988 | 0.10** | 0.14** | — |
| Life expectancy at birth, male, 1988 | 0.11** | 0.15 | — |
| Infant mortality/1,000 births, 1988 | — | -0.98** | — |
| Risk of dying by age 5/1,000 births, male, 1988 | -0.64** | -1.2** | — |
| Risk of dying by age 5/1,000 births, male-female, 1988 | -0.11 | -0.15** | — |
| Low birth weight, 1985 | 0.11 | — | -0.47* |
| % GNP government expenditure on housing, social security, welfare, 1988 | 0.13* | -0.14** | — |
| Crude birth rate per 1,000, 1988 | — | -0.31 | — |
| Total fertility rate, 1988 | -0.018* | -0.042 | — |

*Note:* Based on initial 1965 total schooling, correcting for real per capita income. All point estimates are significantly nonzero at the 10 percent level and those indicated by ** are significantly nonzero at the 20 percent level. (Coefficient estimates not included are not significantly nonzero at the 20 percent level, but the variables are in the underlying regressions).
*Source:* Based on regression estimates by the author.

central government expenditure and of GNP devoted to housing, welfare, and social security increase, respectively, by 6.0 and 2.2 percent.[5] The decline in the private consumption share is offset primarily by increases in government consumption and private investment, which, if used efficiently, increases growth prospects through physical capital accumulation. The reduced share of private consumption devoted to medical care may reflect better health. The increase in central government expenditures on housing, welfare, and social security might be expected to improve the lot of the poor, but these expenditures in most Latin American and Caribbean countries largely benefit the middle and upper classes.

Second, total schooling, enrollments at various levels, and adult literacy (all controlling for recent per capita income levels) are higher. For every additional grade of initial schooling, two decades later the primary enrollment rate is 3.7 percent higher (5.6 percent for females), the total secondary enrollment rate is 5.2 percent higher (5.6 percent for females), schooling increases by 0.7 grades (0.9 for females), and adult literacy is around 6 percent higher (6.8 percent for females). Given the range of recent schooling differentials (controlling for income) in the region, the differences in schooling investments two decades later associated with the differential in initial schooling can be considerable indeed. And these persistent positive schooling effects across the decades, if they impact economic growth and other factors, mean that growth and human development can diverge among countries because of initial schooling differentials.

Third, fertility and mortality rates are lower, population is smaller with a smaller share of young dependents, and life expectancies are higher because of initial schooling investments.[6] For every additional grade of initial schooling, 20 to 25 years later there are 0.4 fewer births per 1,000, 2.4 fewer crude births per 1,000, infant mortality per 1,000 live births falls by about 8, under-five mortality per 1,000 live births falls by between 10 and 13 children (somewhat more for boys), the share of the population in the 0 to 14 age range is 2.2 percent less and in the 15 to 64 age range is 1.5 percent greater (so the dependency rate falls), and life expectancy at birth increases by about two years. Once again, given the range of recent schooling differentials in the region (controlling for income), the differences in demographic outcomes and health 20 to 25 years later, because of

---

[5] The shares related to central government expenditure on housing, welfare, and social security are controlled for real per capita income.

[6] Most of these effects occur whether or not there is control for per capita real income for the recent level variables.

the differential in initial schooling, can be substantial. These induced demographic and health differentials are important in themselves in directly improving welfare, and they tend to be particularly important for those living in poverty. And, like schooling effects, they may have a persistent ongoing positive impact on the development trajectory, as discussed below in greater detail.

*Finding 2. Impact of initial schooling enrollments varies by schooling levels.*

The recent composition of schooling enrollments differs substantially across countries in the region. For primary school, some countries (such as Colombia, the Dominican Republic, Ecuador, Mexico, and Peru) had enrollment rates 20 percent or more above international experience (controlling for real per capita income), while others (such as El Salvador, Guatemala, and Trinidad and Tobago) had rates 8 percent to 10 percent below. For secondary school, some countries (such as Chile and Peru) had enrollment rates more than 20 percent above international experience (controlling for real per capita income). For tertiary enrollments, some countries (such as Argentina, Ecuador, and Uruguay) were at least 20 percent above international experience, and others (such as Trinidad and Tobago) were 10 percent below. Does the composition of such investments make a difference, and if so, how? To provide insight into these questions, Table 2.2 summarizes significant estimates of the association between the composition of schooling enrollments in 1965 (controlling for real per capita income) and subsequent growth and levels of variables two decades or more later.[7] These estimates suggest which schooling levels were most important in attaining desired outcomes.

The estimates imply, for instance, that initial high primary school enrollments were particularly important in attaining higher per capita GNP growth and export growth. They suggest that a 30 percent initial difference between recent primary enrollment rates relative to international experience (such as that between Colombia and Guatemala), all else being equal, is associated with a 2.1 percent difference in subsequent annual per capita GDP growth rates and a 5.4 percent difference in subsequent annual export growth rates. High initial secondary school enrollments, and to a lesser extent, tertiary school enrollments are associ-

---

[7] The underlying estimates do not control for 1965 schooling, given real per capita income, because of high multicollinearity (for instance, the bivariate correlation between schooling and primary enrollment in the region in 1965 was 0.94, and that between schooling and secondary enrollment was 0.80).

ated with lower subsequent population growth. The estimates further suggest that a 30 percent difference relative to international experience in secondary school enrollments (approximately the differential between Chile and Venezuela) implies about a 1.8 percent lower annual population growth rate.[8]

There are also some differences in the apparent importance of initial enrollment rates at the three different schooling levels for some outcomes 20 to 25 years later. High initial primary school enrollments, for instance, are particularly strongly associated with subsequent reductions in the share of private consumption in GDP and in the share of private consumption going to medical care; increases in the share of GNP going to central government expenditures on housing, social security, and welfare; declines in low birth weights, in gender differences favoring males in child and infant death rates, in total fertility, and in infant and child mortality;[9] declines in the gender gaps favoring males in primary schooling enrollments; higher adult literacy rates; and greater life expectancies at birth. High initial secondary school enrollments are particularly strongly associated with subsequent higher secondary school enrollments and a gender gap favoring males in those enrollments; and declines in infant mortality, total fertility, and crude birth rates (all controlling for per capita income).

In turn, high initial tertiary enrollment rates are particularly strongly associated with a shift in the age structure of the population from 0 through 14 year-olds to 15 through 64 year-olds, increased total schooling, and reduced incidence of low birth weight (the mechanism for the last two effects presumably is a relatively high proportion of highly trained individuals in the teaching and medical professions).

Thus, for the 20 to 25 years subsequent to 1965, in most respects having high initial primary school enrollments was most important in the region. For those countries with relatively low current primary school enrollments (such as El Salvador, Guatemala, and Trinidad and Tobago), the future payoffs from increasing those enrollments would seem to be substantial. For other countries with relatively high primary school enrollments, however, greater future payoffs may come from increasing secondary and tertiary enrollments in order to be more competitive with an increasingly educated international work force.

---

[8] The estimates for tertiary school enrollments are somewhat larger but less precise.

[9] Nevertheless, high initial secondary enrollments may be more important for the total fertility rate, infant mortality rate, and the gender gap in infant and child mortality rates.

**Table 2.3. Impact of Initial 1965 Schooling Difference by Gender (Female–Male), Correcting for Real Per Capita Income, on Subsequent Growth and Recent Levels of Various Variables in Latin America and the Caribbean**

| 1. Average annual growth (%) in: | | 3. Recent actual levels - predicted values | |
|---|---|---|---|
| GNP per capita (1965–90) | 1.3 | Male-female primary enrollment rate, 1987 | −3.9* |
| | | Total secondary enrollment rate, 1987 | −6.5** |
| **2. Recent level variables** | | Persistence to grade 4, female, 1984 | −22 |
| Medical care/private consumption (%), 1990 | 1.7 | Persistence to grade 4, male, 1985 | −18 |
| | | Adult literacy rate, male, 1985 | −2.9 |
| Total fertility rate, 1990 | −0.45** | Adult literacy rate, male-female, 1985 | −5.7 |
| Infant mortality rate (1,000 live births), 1990 | −13** | Life expectancy at birth, female, 1988 | 3.0 |
| | | Life expectancy at birth, male, 1988 | 2.9 |
| Under 5 mortality rate (1,000 live births), female, 1990 | −16** | Infant mortality/1,000 births, 1988 | −12** |
| | | Risk of dying by age 5/1,000 births, female, 1988 | −21 |
| Under 5 mortality rate (1,000 live births), male, 1990 | −19** | Risk of dying by age 5/1,000 births, female, 1988 | −21 |
| Life expectancy at birth, female, 1990 | 4.1** | Crude birth rate per 1,000, 1988 | −2.3** |
| Life expectancy at birth, male, 1990 | 4.1** | Total fertility rate, 1988 | −0.35** |

*Note:* Based on initial 1965 total schooling, correcting for real per capita income. All point estimates are significantly nonzero at the 5 percent level, except those indicated by * are significantly nonzero at the 10 percent level and those indicated by ** are significantly nonzero at the 20 percent level.
*Source:* Based on regression estimates by the author.

*Finding 3. There is an impact on human resources from the composition of 1965 schooling investments by gender (controlling for per capita real income).*

Recent gender gaps favoring males in schooling investments are small in most Latin American and Caribbean countries compared with international experience. There is, however, considerable variation in such gender gaps among countries in the region. For total schooling in 1987, the Dominican Republic and Peru favor females by two grades or more relative to international experience, but only by 0.5 grades or less in Bolivia and Mexico. Are such differences in schooling investments by gender associated with differences in subsequent socioeconomic performance? Table 2.3 summarizes how adding the gender difference in schooling to the impact of the schooling differential from the level predicted by international experience (both 1965) changes the subsequent outcomes.[10]

Probably the most striking result in this table is the strong association between a gender gap favoring females in schooling and the subse-

---

[10] The coefficient estimates of the initial gender gap are significantly nonzero, at least at the 20 percent level.

quent annual rate of growth of per capita GNP. The estimates in the table indicate that an initial gender gap favoring females by 1.5 grades (approximately the difference between Peru and Bolivia in 1987) is associated with a subsequent growth rate increase of almost 2 percent a year. The mechanisms for this effect are not clear from the other growth rates, none of which is significantly affected by the inclusion of the initial gender gap in addition to the initial difference between total schooling and the level predicted by international experience.

Estimates of the significant impact of the 1965 gender gap on recent outcomes, however, suggest that the gender gap in schooling has important effects on demographic and health outcomes. One grade higher initial female relative to male schooling is associated with a subsequent drop in total fertility of about 0.4 births per 1,000, declines in infant mortality of 12 to 13 children per 1,000 live births, and drops in under-five mortality of 16 to 21 per 1,000 live births. In part because of drops in infant and child mortality rates, life expectancies at birth are 3 to 4 years greater.[11] Therefore, important mechanisms for the longer-run impact of gender gaps in schooling appear to be reduced population pressure through reduced fertility, decreased use of resources to deal with infant and child morbidity and mortality,[12] and higher returns to human resource investments because of greater life expectancies. There are also other significant associations of such gaps with recent schooling investments relative to international standards that control for real per capita income. One grade more of initial schooling for females relative to males is associated with a 3.9 percent reduction in the recent male-female adult primary school enrollment gap and a 5.7 percent reduction in the recent male-female adult literacy gap. Therefore, there is hysterisis, with the initial gender gaps in schooling tending to be perpetuated over long periods of time.[13]

Thus, the aggregate estimates suggest that the returns to investment in schooling of females are greater than for males. Smaller initial gender

---

[11] These results hold whether or not there is control for real per capita income.

[12] The share of medical care in private consumption expenditure increases with higher initial schooling of females relative to males. But the overall reduction in infant and child morbidity and mortality probably entails reduction in the time devoted to caring for the sick, which may more than offset the increase in the monetary expense.

[13] The estimates also indicate that larger initial gender gaps favoring females may reduce secondary school enrollment and the persistence to grade four for males and females. But these estimated associations may be misleading. The reduction in secondary schooling is associated with an increase in primary schooling, although the coefficient estimate of the latter is quite imprecise. The estimated effect on the persistence to grade 4 appears to be something of an artifact of the correlation between total initial schooling and the gender gap in that schooling: when the gender gap is added to the regression with the total initial schooling, the coefficient estimate on total schooling doubles and becomes significant.

gaps favoring males in schooling in the region lead to higher overall economic growth rates, lower population growth, and improved health and life expectancies.

*Micro Evidence on Schooling Impact*

The available empirical evidence on schooling impact varies considerably in coverage and quality. With respect to coverage, for instance, many studies consider the determinants and impact of schooling, but relatively few consider other forms of education such as adult training programs. With respect to quality, many studies ignore a number of estimation problems (Box 2.3). The empirical evidence therefore has to be interpreted with care and supplemented with the insights gained from simple but powerful economic models, as discussed above. Nevertheless, some systematic patterns do emerge from the studies. Here we examine these systematic patterns in some detail.

*Finding 4. The impact of schooling on wages and economic productivity is considerable, with returns relatively high to lower schooling levels and to general schooling as opposed to technical-vocational schooling, and at least as high on average for females as for males.*

A large number of studies report substantial associations among years of schooling and wages, earnings, and productivity. Table 2.4 summarizes estimates of private and social rates of return to schooling by regions of the world. The private rates of return are the estimated returns on all private costs of schooling, including the opportunity cost of students being in school instead of in the labor market. The social rates of return (as the term is used in this literature) adjust, in addition, for government schooling expenditures (for instance, teachers' salaries in public schools), but do not incorporate externalities. The estimates in Table 2.4 imply that in developing countries the rates of return to schooling are high, that these rates do not decline very rapidly with the level of development, that they are highest in developing countries for lower schooling levels, and that the returns to schooling in Latin America and the Caribbean generally have been at least as high as in other regions, with the exception of the private rates of return in Africa. Other disaggregations of the same underlying country estimates suggest that the rates of return to schooling are higher for women than for men in developing countries,[14] higher for general aca-

---

[14] Note that if the gender wage gap favoring males becomes smaller with higher schooling levels, then the rate of return to increasing schooling may be higher for women than for men even if wages and salaries are currently lower for women than for men.

## Box 2.3. Common Estimation Problems in Assessing the Impact of Human Resources

Undertaking social science research is difficult, in part because of the lack of experimental data. Estimation problems abound in existing studies of the impact of human resources in the Latin American and Caribbean region (as well as elsewhere). This report does not dwell in detail on these problems, but the interpretations presented here are sensitive to such problems, four of which are summarized below.

First, many studies do not control well for the implications of the simple framework presented earlier in this chapter; i.e., that individuals with higher human resource investments in, say, years of schooling are likely to come from families that reinforce such investments and are likely to have had lower marginal costs for such investments and access to higher-quality schools. The estimates in such studies probably suffer, therefore, from omitted-variable biases. The association of years of schooling with outcomes such as wage rates, fertility, and child health does not necessarily represent causality because in most estimates, years of schooling represents not only time in school but also factors that are correlated with years of schooling, such as ability, family background, and schooling quality. To understand the impact of years of schooling on such outcomes, one needs to control for these other factors, as do some—but not many—existing studies.

The second problem is that most studies do not control for sample selectivity. That is, for explicit examples, in estimating the impact of adult schooling on wage rates or on choices of treatment for sick children, the studies do not control for the facts that wages are reported only for individuals who elect to participate in the labor force and that curative treatment choices are made only by those who perceive morbidity. The individuals who receive wages or who perceive morbidity are not likely to be randomly selected (for instance, in many developing country contexts, those with more assets are likely to select themselves out of wage labor markets into family farms and firms; certain types of morbidity, likewise, are more likely to be perceived by individuals who are more integrated into capital city and international information systems). Therefore, the failure to control for the sample selection process may considerably bias the estimated impact of human resource investments. Similarly, if studies do not control for who attends certain types of schools (public versus private, vocational versus general, regular versus experimental), the results may not be informative about the school effects because of the selected nature of the students.

demic secondary schools than for vocational-technical secondary schools, and higher for employment in the private sector than in the public sector.

Such estimates imply that schooling, particularly at the primary level, is a very good investment, both privately and socially, in Latin America and

Third, many of the studies do not control for simultaneity. For instance, healthier and better nourished individuals may perform better in school and have higher wages and greater productivity, but that does not mean that better health and nutrition cause better performance in school and in labor markets. Parents who invest more in their children's schooling plausibly might invest more in their children's health and nutrition; so that children who are healthier perform better in school in part because such parental concern leads to more investment in both health and schooling, not only because better health leads to better school performance. In this case, control for simultaneity probably would result in a smaller estimated impact of child health and nutrition on schooling success. On the other hand, there may be differences in the extent to which parents are interested in child health versus child schooling, because of either preference or rate of return differences, so that parents who invest more in child health tend to invest less in child schooling. In this case, control for simultaneity probably would result in a larger estimated impact of child health and nutrition on child schooling success than if there were not such control. Adults with more income may purchase more health and better nutrition, so the health/nutrition-to-income/productivity association may reflect causality in either direction. In either case, simultaneity needs to be controlled in order to obtain estimates of the impact of improved health and nutrition on performance in school and in labor markets.

Fourth, data measurement problems may obscure the nature of underlying relations. Random measurement errors in right-side variables, such as in schooling in a wage determination relation, cause biases toward zero in the estimated coefficients—and thus underestimates of the effects of human resources. But systematic measurement errors may work in the opposite direction. For instance, schooling is usually represented in socioeconomic analysis by years or grades of schooling, with no control for quality. But the quality of schooling appears to vary greatly and would seem to have an impact on various outcomes of interest, including years of schooling. If school quality does have an impact and higher school quality is correlated with more schooling, then the failure to control for schooling quality in estimates of schooling impact results in upwardly biased estimates of the effect of extending years of schooling, since in the statistical analysis, grades of schooling implicitly represent not only the effect of grades but also the effect of quality.

*Source:* Prepared by the author.

the Caribbean. They also imply that there is not likely to be an equity-productivity trade-off, because the returns are highest for primary schooling (for which further expansion is likely to enroll mostly children from very poor families), and because the returns are higher for females than for males.

**Table 2.4. Average Rates of Return to Schooling**
*(Percent)*

| Region/Country Type | Private | | | Social | | |
|---|---|---|---|---|---|---|
| | Primary | Secondary | Tertiary | Primary | Secondary | Tertiary |
| Africa | 45 | 26 | 32 | 26 | 17 | 13 |
| Asia | 31 | 15 | 18 | 27 | 15 | 13 |
| Latin America | 32 | 23 | 23 | 26 | 18 | 16 |
| Intermediate | 17 | 13 | 13 | 13 | 10 | 8 |
| Advanced | — | 12 | 12 | — | 11 | 9 |

*Source:* Psacharopoulos (1985, Table 1).

Such estimates are not completely credible, however, because they imply that investment in schooling has such phenomenally high returns. Investment with a real annual rate of return of 32 percent (in this table, the private rate of return to primary schooling in the region), together with reinvestment of the proceeds of such investment, implies that investors could double their real assets in a little more than two years; and the real rate of 23 percent on secondary and tertiary schooling implies the possibility of doubling real assets in three years. If investments were available such that almost every family could so greatly increase its real assets in such short periods of time, economic growth would be much higher than ever before observed.

The problem is that the estimates in the standard studies that underlie Table 2.4 do not deal well with the estimation problems summarized in Box 2.3. Possible pitfalls in the standard estimates of the returns to schooling include: failure to control for ability, motivation, and family connections (all of which may affect schooling and earnings), leading to an exaggeratedly positive correlation between schooling and earnings; failure to distinguish between quantity and quality of schooling; failure to control for geographical aggregation biases such as regional price variations, or such as blending poor areas with limited physical capital and low schooling levels into the same samples as areas having extensive physical capital and high levels of schooling (for instance, northeastern and southeastern Brazil); failure to control for school dropouts and class repeaters; and failure to control for unobserved household and community variables.

Most of these pitfalls have long been recognized as possible problems in standard estimates of the returns to schooling. But whether or not they are serious problems is an empirical question, and data and procedures suitable for exploring their importance in developing economies have not been available until recently. When such data and procedures are used, the estimated rates of return to schooling tend to be about half of those in Table 2.4, with a greater reduction in the estimates for primary schooling because that is where grade repetition and dropping out are concentrated (Behrman, 1990a,b). Even at these reduced levels, however, the estimates still suggest that schooling probably has a fairly high rate of return in Latin America and the Caribbean.

One other aspect of the calculation of the social rates of return in Table 2.4 probably means that they are overstated for Latin America and the Caribbean in comparison with the rates of return in parts of Asia or the advanced economies—namely, the social rates as calculated do not adjust for distortions in output prices between domestic and international markets. Therefore, if more schooling enables an individual to receive high earnings in an activity that is not competitive in international markets but that is able to prosper behind protectionist barriers, the standard calculations result in high estimated private and social rates of return to schooling even though there may be a social loss in having that industry.

Finally, as noted earlier, the available social estimates do not incorporate externalities. If the latter are positive, as is often claimed, then total returns to schooling may be higher than the most careful present estimates suggest, perhaps with different effects for different schooling levels. One possibly very important externality of higher levels of schooling, for instance, pertains to additions to knowledge. Indicators of the extent of additions to knowledge are imperfect, but the number of scientific articles produced per million inhabitants is one suggestive measure (Table 2.5). By this indicator, in 1980 there was substantial variance among countries in the region: a ratio of about 65 to one between Chile on one end and the Dominican Republic and Ecuador on the other. The region as a whole lagged far behind the advanced developing countries, but the leading five or six countries in the region had additions to knowledge of the same order of magnitude as countries such as Spain or Portugal. In any case, bearing in mind the limitations of this indicator, the extent to which public subsidies to tertiary schooling could be justified on this basis varies considerably. Much more careful examination is needed to determine the extent to which subsidies would be warranted on the basis of this indicator.

*Finding 5. Schooling is related to adjustment capacity, but possibly in a nonlinear manner.*

In most countries in the region, open unemployment (Table 2.6) increased substantially in the mid 1980s (with the spread of adjustment efforts) and then declined slowly (more rapidly in Chile than in most other countries because of accelerated growth and the relatively flexible labor market). In most countries (but not in Colombia), real wages dropped

**Table 2.5. Scientific Articles per Million Inhabitants in Selected Countries, 1980**

**Developed countries**

| | |
|---|---|
| Israel | 892 |
| U.S.A. | 742 |
| Canada | 692 |
| Switzerland | 513 |
| France | 343 |
| Germany | 331 |
| Japan | 161 |
| Spain | 74 |
| Portugal | 18 |

**Latin America and the Caribbean**

| | |
|---|---|
| Chile | 64 |
| Argentina | 39 |
| Costa Rica | 38 |
| Venezuela | 27 |
| Brazil | 13 |
| Mexico | 11 |
| Cuba | 8 |
| Peru | 5 |
| Guatemala | 3 |
| Colombia | 3 |
| Dominican Republic | 1 |
| Ecuador | 1 |

*Source:* Brunner (1989, Table 85), as reproduced from M. Roche y Y. Freites, "Producción y flujo de información en un país periférico americano" (Venezuela). *Interciencia*, Vol. 7, No. 5, Sept.–Oct. 1982.

significantly in the early and mid 1980s and in many cases in the late 1980s (Table 2.7). Important differences in wage composition, with greater drops in informal sector wages, have reflected in part the shifts in relative prices against nontradeables, and in part the residual employer nature of informal markets (that is, the informal market often is characterized as absorbing all those who cannot obtain employment in the formal sector).

Despite the widespread increases in open unemployment and the decreases in real wages, López and Riveros (1990) report no statistical connection between wage fluctuations and observed disequilibria in the labor market. Regression analyses for Argentina, Brazil, Chile, Colombia, Mexico, Peru, and Uruguay show that the effect of open unemployment on observed nominal wage changes is either insignificant or positive. Riveros (1990a, 1992b) interprets these regressions to mean that labor market distortions are important: "It is highly likely that the lack of wage responsiveness to labor market disequilibrium is due to the presence of rigidities associated with prevailing regulations and institutions. This

**Table 2.6. Unemployment Rates in Selected Latin American Economies, 1980–1991**

| | 1980 | 1981 | 1982 | 1983 | 1984 | 1985 | 1986 | 1987 | 1988 | 1989 | 1990 | 1991* |
|---|---|---|---|---|---|---|---|---|---|---|---|---|
| Bolivia | — | — | — | 8.5 | 6.9 | 5.8 | 7.0 | 7.2 | 11.6 | 10.2 | 9.5 | 8.1 |
| Colombia | 10.0 | 8.7 | 9.3 | 11.0 | 13.2 | 14.0 | 13.8 | 11.7 | 11.5 | 9.6 | 10.2 | 10.3 |
| Costa Rica | — | — | — | 8.5 | 6.6 | 6.7 | 6.7 | 5.9 | 6.3 | 3.7 | 5.4 | 5.0 |
| Peru | 7.0 | 6.8 | 6.6 | 9.0 | 8.9 | 10.1 | 5.4 | 4.8 | 7.9 | 7.9 | 8.1 | — |
| Mexico | 4.5 | 4.2 | 4.2 | 6.7 | 6.0 | 4.8 | 4.3 | 3.9 | 3.5 | 2.9 | 2.8 | 2.6 |
| Brazil | 6.3 | 7.9 | 6.3 | 6.7 | 7.1 | 5.3 | 3.6 | 3.8 | 3.8 | 3.3 | 4.3 | 5.0 |
| Chile | 11.8 | 10.9 | 20.3 | 18.9 | 18.5 | 17.2 | 13.1 | 11.9 | 10.2 | 7.2 | 6.6 | 7.9 |
| Uruguay | 6.8 | 7.5 | 11.9 | 15.5 | 14.0 | 13.1 | 10.7 | 9.3 | 9.1 | 8.6 | 9.2 | 9.2 |
| Argentina | 2.5 | 4.8 | 5.3 | 4.7 | 4.6 | 6.1 | 5.6 | 5.9 | 6.3 | 7.8 | 8.6 | 6.5 |
| Venezuela | — | — | — | 11.2 | 14.3 | 14.3 | 12.1 | 9.9 | 7.9 | 9.7 | 10.5 | 10.9 |

*Source:* Riveros (1992a, Table 6, based on Inter-American Development Bank data). Rates may not be comparable across countries because of different definitions.
* Preliminary.

**Table 2.7. Real Wages in Selected Latin American Economies, 1980–1991**

|  | 1980 | 1981 | 1982 | 1983 | 1984 | 1985 | 1986 | 1987 | 1988 | 1989 | 1990 | 1991* |
|---|---|---|---|---|---|---|---|---|---|---|---|---|
| Colombia | 100 | 101.3 | 104.7 | 110.1 | 118.1 | 114.6 | 120.1 | 119.2 | 117.7 | 119.1 | 120.1 | 116.6 |
| Costa Rica | — | — | — | 70.8 | 78.5 | 84.7 | 92.2 | 97.8 | 98.2 | 85.2 | 85.7 | 87.2 |
| Peru | 100 | 101.8 | 110.2 | 93.4 | 87.2 | 77.6 | 97.5 | 101.3 | 76.1 | 41.5 | 43.9 | 38.7 |
| Mexico | 100 | 103.5 | 102.2 | 80.7 | 75.4 | 76.6 | 72.3 | 72.8 | 72.1 | 75.8 | 77.9 | 77.2 |
| Brazil | 100 | 108.5 | 121.6 | 112.7 | 105.7 | 112.7 | 121.8 | 102.4 | 107.1 | 107.2 | 85.5 | 84.4 |
| Chile | 100 | 108.9 | 108.6 | 97.1 | 97.2 | 93.5 | 95.1 | 94.7 | 101.0 | 102.9 | 104.7 | 109.7 |
| Uruguay | 100 | 107.1 | 106.5 | 84.5 | 71.1 | 68.1 | 71.9 | 75.4 | 76.3 | 76.3 | 72.8 | 72.6 |
| Argentina | 100 | 89.4 | 80.1 | 101.5 | 129.5 | 107.5 | 108.1 | 99.6 | 95.7 | 81.5 | 68.3 | 76.6 |

Source: Riveros (1992a, Table 7, based on Inter-American Development Bank data).
* Preliminary.

would indicate that reducing relatively high unemployment may demand eliminating distortions and policy interventions instead of only pursuing aggregate demand policies" (Riveros, 1992b). Another factor would seem to be that in countries such as Colombia, Mexico, and Venezuela, labor costs did not drop nearly as much as did real wages, because nonwage benefits increased.

Even though there is no evidence of a close inverse relation between aggregate wages and open unemployment, there might be a relation between schooling and adjustment. During periods of adjustment, the relative gainers are, a priori, those who do not have as much specific human capital to lose and those who can acquire new specific human capital most cheaply. Therefore, adjustment capacity is not necessarily associated simply linearly with schooling, but is likely to reflect the interaction between specific and general human capital (as defined earlier in this chapter.) Those with no schooling are likely to have little specific human capital to lose but also are likely to acquire new specific human capital only at great cost. Those with more general human capital are more likely to be able to acquire new specific human capital relatively cheaply but also are more likely to already have greater amounts of specific human capital, the value of which may be reduced or lost because of adjustment. The costs of adjustment are likely to be greatest for those with the greatest gap between specific human capital and general human capital (because the cost of acquiring new specific human capital is likely to be inversely associated with the stock of general human capital). The relation between adjustment capacity and schooling, therefore, is an empirical question.

In Chile the average schooling level in the tradeables sector increased much more rapidly than that in the nontradeables sector between 1970–1973 and 1984–1992, such that the previously fairly large schooling gap between the two sectors was almost eliminated (Table 2.8). With trade liberalization, more-schooled workers were attracted to, and better able to adjust to, the expanding tradeables sector (Paredes, Riveros, Balmaceda, Manzur, and Núñez, 1993). In this case, with relatively highly schooled workers, the dominant tendency was that more-schooled workers could acquire the specific human capital in the expanding tradeables sector more quickly and cheaply than could less-schooled workers.

For Brazil the story is somewhat more complicated, apparently because the labor force is less schooled. Because of inflation, there have been substantial fluctuations in real wages. Barros, Cardoso, and Urani (1992, as reported in Amadeo et al., 1993) show that both unemployment and inflation effects on real income are negatively correlated with schooling and that it is easier to protect income against unemployment than against inflation. Amadeo et al. (1993) present estimates of wage sensitivity in

**Table 2.8. Average Grades of Schooling for Workers in Tradeable and Nontradeable Sectors in Chile, 1970–1992**

|  | Tradeables | Nontradeables |
|---|---|---|
| 1970–73 | 7.4 | 8.3 |
| 1974–79 | 8.0 | 9.0 |
| 1980–83 | 8.7 | 9.3 |
| 1984–92 | 9.5 | 9.7 |

*Source:* Paredes, Riveros, Balmaceda, and Manzur (1992, Table 5), as calculated from the labor force survey.

Brazil to the level of national economic activity, in terms of the wage earners' schooling levels (Figure 2.3). The relationship among wage sensitivity, national economic activity level, and wage earners' schooling is expressed in an inverted $U$ shape. Wage sensitivity increases with initial schooling, reaches a peak with upper primary schooling, and falls with further schooling, such that the wages of those with superior (tertiary) schooling are the least sensitive. Those with upper primary schooling (5 to 8 years) thus apparently have the largest gap between specific and general human capital and therefore tend to suffer most (gain least) in the adjustment process. But for a given level of specific human capital, schooling increments reduce the cost of adjustment because they reduce the gap between specific and general human capital.

*Finding 6. Variability in schooling is associated with the variability in income distribution and whether individuals are below the poverty line.*

Countries in the region historically have had high levels of income inequality in comparison with other developing countries. Figure 2.4 gives the ratio of the income of the highest 20 percent of households to the income of the lowest 20 percent of households for all developing countries for which such data were presented in a recent international compilation. For the seven Latin American and Caribbean countries included, these ratios range from 9.1 in Jamaica to 26.1 in Brazil. Among these seven countries, only in Jamaica does the highest 20 percent of households not have at least 10 times as much income as the lowest 20 percent of households. Among the 13 developing countries from Asia and Africa for which similar data are available, these ratios range from 3.7 for Bangladesh to 23.6 for Botswana (which is far above the second-highest ratio for African and Asian countries in the chart: 11.7 for Sri Lanka). Among these 13 Asian and African countries, only four have ratios as high as ten to one. A ratio of ten to one or higher is the norm in the Latin American and Caribbean region, but is the exception in Africa and Asia.

**Figure 2.3. Degree of Brazilian Wage Sensitivity to Macroeconomic Conditions, by Schooling Level**

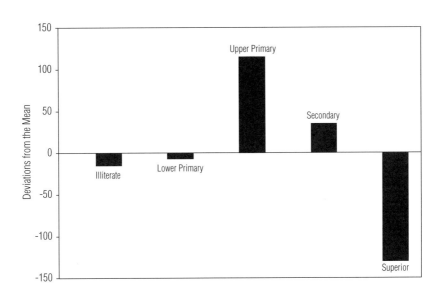

A recent study (Psacharopoulos et al., 1992) examines the changes in income inequality and poverty in the region in the 1980s and the relation among schooling, income inequality, and poverty.[15] In the 1980s income inequality rose in Argentina, Bolivia, Brazil, Guatemala, Honduras, Panama, Peru, and Venezuela and fell in Colombia, Costa Rica, Paraguay, and Uruguay. During the same decade, poverty as indicated by a headcount measure increased in Argentina, Brazil, Guatemala, Honduras, Panama, Peru, and Venezuela and decreased in Bolivia, Colombia, Costa Rica, Paraguay, and Uruguay. Brazil, Guatemala, Honduras, and Panama had the greatest inequality in the region, and Paraguay and Uruguay had the least.

---

[15] This study is based on analysis of data from 30 household surveys for 18 countries in the region (for 12, the availability of two surveys made comparisons over time possible). The data sets are not all comparable across countries because in some cases (Argentina and Paraguay) the data are for metropolitan areas only, and in other cases (Bolivia, Colombia, Ecuador, El Salvador, Peru [Lima], and Uruguay) they refer to urban areas only. A variety of measures of income distribution (deciles, Gini coefficients, Theil index, the Lorenz curve) and of poverty (headcount measures, the poverty gap, the Foster-Greer-Thorbecke $P_2$ measure) are presented. (The summary here refers to the Gini measure of inequality [but the Theil index is used for the decompositions] and the headcount measure of poverty, although the same basic patterns hold for the other measures.) For more details and qualifications, see Psacharopoulos et al., 1992).

**Figure 2.4. Ratio of Income of Highest 20 Percent of Households to Lowest 20 Percent, by Income**

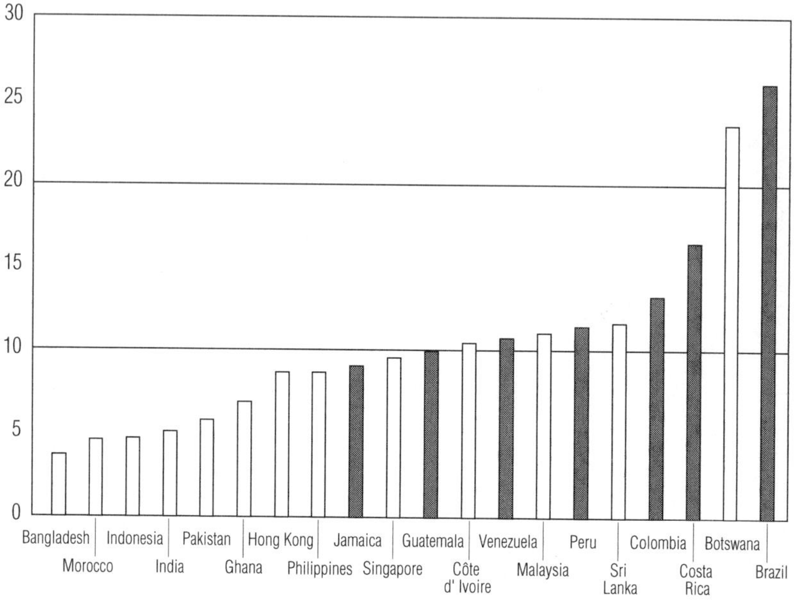

Source: World Development Report 1992, World Bank.

The poverty headcount measure increased from 28 percent in 1980 to 33 percent in 1989. In 1989, approximately 43 percent of those in the region who lived in poverty were in Brazil, 11 percent lived in Mexico, and 11 percent lived in Peru. An additional 19 percent lived in relatively small countries, including Bolivia, El Salvador, Guatemala, Haiti, Honduras, and Nicaragua. Costa Rica and Uruguay had the lowest poverty levels measured, and Guatemala and Honduras had the highest. During the decade, poverty shifted from being a predominantly rural phenomenon to being predominantly urban, even though the incidence of poverty remained higher in rural areas.[16] Measures of income inequality and of poverty incidence rose during recession and fell during recovery.

A decomposition of the inequality in the distribution of workers' income (including only individuals at least 15 years of age in the labor force with

---

[16] In 1980 the incidence of poverty was 46 percent of the population in rural areas and 18 percent in urban areas: 55 million people in the rural areas and 40 million people in urban areas lived in poverty. In 1989 the incidence of poverty was 54 percent in rural areas and 24 percent in urban areas, with 65 million people in rural areas and 73 million in urban areas living in poverty.

positive income) indicates that variations in years of schooling were associated with about a quarter of the income inequality, and variations in age, employment sector, and employment category were associated with smaller proportions of income variance.[17,18] In addition, low schooling (in years) is the characteristic most associated with being in the bottom 20 percent in workers' income; on average, those with no schooling had a 56 percent probability of being in the bottom 20 percent of the workers' income distribution, while those with primary schooling had a 27 percent probability, those at the secondary level a 9 percent probability, and those with university schooling a 4 percent probability. These results indicate "the overwhelming preeminence of education" and that "clearly . . . education is the variable with the strongest impact on income inequality" (Psacharopoulos et al., 1992).

Of course, these studies do not consider the incomes of those not in the work force. They also do not control for a number of individual, family, and community characteristics such as ability, motivation, family connections, school quality, and labor market conditions; therefore, schooling probably is partially proxying for these characteristics in this analysis. But even if only half of the estimated effect reflects the causal effects of schooling (and the other half these other characteristics), the estimates suggest that schooling can have an important effect on equalizing incomes and alleviating poverty.

*Finding 7. The impact of years of schooling on nonmarket outcomes appears as great or greater for females as for males; therefore, the total effect of female schooling tends to be greater than that of male schooling.*

As discussed earlier, the household is the locus of decisions regarding many nonmarket outcomes such as health, nutrition, and fertility. So it is not surprising that considerable associations exist between parental (particularly maternal) schooling and such outcomes. Although these associations tend to be lessened when there is control for omitted variables, the impact still seems to be fairly large in a number of cases.

---

[17] In these decompositions, education is divided into four groups (0–5 years, 6–8 years, 9–12 years, 13 or more years), age is divided into four categories (15–25 years, 26–40 years, 41–55 years, 56 or more years), the employment sector is divided into eight groups (agriculture, mining, manufacturing, transportation-communication-utilities, construction, commerce, financial services, and services), and employment is divided into three or four categories depending on the country (employees [sometimes divided between public and private sector], self-employed, and employers).

[18] Altimir and Pinera (1979), using information from around 1970, report that schooling (together with occupation) is the most important characteristic in similar decompositions.

Several recent studies, for instance, examine the family and community determinants of child height (an indicator of long-run health and nutrition) and child survival in different regions of Brazil (Thomas, Strauss, and Henriques, 1990, 1991; Thomas and Strauss, 1992). These studies find strong positive effects of parents' schooling on both child height and child survival, with that for the father weaker than for the mother in the survival relation. For the urban Northeast, relative to having illiterate parents, a child with a literate mother (father) is about 1.6 per cent (1.2 percent) taller, with a mother (father) who has completed elementary school about 2.5 percent (2.6 percent) taller, and with a mother (father) who has completed secondary schooling or more about 5.2 percent (5.8 percent) taller.[19]

Parental schooling apparently is proxying in part, however, for other parental endowments not controlled in the base estimates. If the calculations include parental height to control partially for such endowments, the coefficient estimates on parents' schooling drop by 20 to 50 percent in the height regressions, although not in the survival relation. The effects of paternal education on height are not significantly different from those of maternal education, but maternal education does have a significantly larger effect on child survival. Finally, there are stronger parental education effects in the urban areas. This fact suggests that parental education is complementary with the broader range of health-related services available in urban areas.

Another set of studies considers the determination of child and maternal health, child schooling and survival, household nutrition, and fertility in Nicaragua (Behrman and Wolfe, 1987a, 1987b, 1989; and Wolfe and Behrman, 1987). Using standard approaches, these studies estimate strong effects of women's schooling in improving health, nutrition, and child schooling and in reducing mortality and fertility. The data set used has the special feature of including in the sample adult sisters of many of the respondents. Having the adult sibling data permits control for common childhood family background characteristics of the women, such as their common genetic endowments, role models in their childhood family and community, habits learned as a child, the quality of neighborhood schools, and the environment in which they were raised.[20] Control for the common childhood family background of the adult sisters changes the estimated impact of maternal schooling. For the child outcomes and for fertility, such control leads

---

[19] For the urban South the effects are slightly smaller. For the rural Northeast and South, they are significantly smaller.

[20] The intuition behind the control for shared family background is simple. If some outcome (Y) depends linearly on parental schooling (S) and shared family background characteristics

to a smaller estimated impact of mother's schooling. But there remain strong and basically unchanged estimated effects of mother's schooling on household nutrition and on women's health, even with such controls.

Thus, women's schooling seems to have effects on a number of non-economic outcomes that generally are at least as strong as the impact of men's schooling, and that persist (albeit perhaps in modified or reduced form) with control for estimation problems of the sort discussed in Box 2.3. These effects strengthen the case that greater female schooling has an impact on economic outcomes.

*Finding 8. The impact of schooling quality appears to be considerable, although there have been very few studies.*

Although few studies have been done on the exact impact of schooling quality on subsequent outcomes in developing countries, the studies that do exist suggest that the effects of quality enhancement are considerable and that the rate of return to improving schooling quality is at least as great as the rate of return to expanding school systems at present quality levels. The framework described earlier can illuminate the role of school quality. The solid downward-sloping line in Figure 2.1B shows the marginal schooling benefits for a particular individual, given the quality of schools provided by the government. Were better-quality schooling provided, the same individual's marginal schooling benefits would be higher, as indicated by the dashed line. This fact has two important implications. First, for a given level of schooling (say, $H^*$), the rate of return to years of schooling is a positive function of schooling quality (as indicated by the dashed marginal benefit curve rather than $r^*$ for the solid marginal benefit curve); therefore, schooling quality should increase the rate of return to given years of schooling. Second, if the marginal cost of funds is not vertical, individuals (or their parents) in equilibrium invest in more years of schooling if quality is higher ($H^{**}$ instead of $H^*$), so there is a positive association between an individual's years of schooling and schooling quality. Therefore, if schooling quality is important, the failure to include it in

---

that are not observed in the data set (F), the usual estimation of this relation ($Y = aS + bF + \ldots$) results in biased estimates of the effect of parental schooling if parental schooling is correlated with the unobserved family background. In standard estimates, S represents not only the effect of schooling per se but also the effects of correlated dimensions of childhood family background. But if the relation for one sister is subtracted from the relation for the other sister, the resulting expression does not include any of the unobserved common family background characteristics, so it effectively permits estimation of the impact of S with control for the common family background characteristics.

standard estimates results in an upward bias in the estimated return to years of schooling, because this estimated rate of return incorporates in part the return to schooling quality.

Some studies have provided information about the empirical effects of school quality in Brazil (Behrman and Birdsall, 1983; Behrman, Birdsall, and Kaplan, 1993). Let us consider the results of these studies:

• School quality should be included along with school quantity in the analysis of labor market and noneconomic outcomes.

• A substantial upward bias exists in the estimated rate of return to years of schooling if schooling quality is excluded. The estimated private rate of return in the labor market in terms of income to years of schooling is 20.5 percent, about the same order of magnitude as in Table 2.4, given that average schooling in Brazil is fairly low. Once schooling quality is incorporated into the analysis, however, the estimated private return to years of schooling falls to 11.0 percent. Therefore, if schooling quality is important, as suggested by these empirical estimates, the standard procedure (which ignores schooling quality) overstates the private rate of return to increasing years of schooling of a given quality by more than 80 percent.

• The social rate of return to schooling quality is as high as, or even higher than, the social rate of return to number of years of schooling.

• Schooling quality and years of schooling interact; higher quality increases the return to years spent in school, as in Figure 2.1B. As a result, there is an equity-productivity trade-off in the sense that there are greater productivity gains for society if years of schooling and schooling quality are concentrated among fewer individuals instead of spread broadly. This trade-off implies that there are circumstances in which societies might be better off extending secondary rather than primary schooling, contrary to the usual interpretation of estimates such as those in Table 2.4 (Colclough, 1982; Psacharopoulos, 1985).[21]

These results raise questions about the efficiency of the current allocation of resources between schooling quality and quantity, and about a possible equity-productivity trade-off, given that productivity gains may be larger from concentrating schooling resources among fewer individuals than from spreading these resources broadly in low-quality schools. The nature of the equity-productivity trade-off, moreover, may have subtleties: some quality improvements may require more household inputs from poor households, and other quality improvements may actually free such resources for poor households (Box 4.1).

---

[21] These estimates also suggest that the difference between earnings functions for migrants and nonmigrants in standard estimates largely disappears if there is control for schooling quality.

## Impact of Health and Nutrition

Human resource investments are not limited to schooling and training. They include investments in health and nutrition. Considerable variations exist among Latin American and Caribbean countries in life expectancy and mortality outcomes related to health and nutrition investments. In most countries in the region, recent life expectancies at birth are higher than would be predicted by international experience (controlling for real per capita income), but a considerable range does exist, with Jamaica approximately 14 years above and Bolivia 2 to 4 years below the international regression line. Are such differences across countries associated with subsequent experiences regarding growth and levels of key outcomes? As with schooling, such questions can be explored by looking at the association between initial 1965 life expectancies[22] and the experience over the next quarter century, and by considering micro evidence.

### Aggregate Estimates of the Impact of Initial (1965) Life Expectancies

*Finding 9. Life expectancies (controlling for real per capita income) are associated with subsequent growth levels and other key outcomes.*

Table 2.9 summarizes estimates of significant association in Latin America and the Caribbean among initial life expectancies (life expectancies in 1965 relative to the country's real per capita income in 1965), subsequent growth rates, and recent levels of other key variables.[23]

In Table 2.9, initial life expectancy is positively associated with subsequent real per capita GNP growth, as shown in an additional 0.15 percent

---

[22] In addition to life expectancies, infant and child mortality rates have been widely used to characterize aggregate health and nutrition experience. For Latin America and the Caribbean, in the past three decades life expectancies at birth and infant and child mortality rates are almost perfectly correlated (even after controlling for per capita income for both), so not much insight would be gained by considering both of these indicators of health and nutrition.

[23] Initial life expectancies and initial schooling are positively correlated (with a bivariate correlation of 0.67). Each additional year of initial schooling is associated with 2.7 years of additional life expectancy. Because of this correlation and the relatively small number of observations (data are generally available for 20 Latin American and Caribbean countries), the point estimates in the regressions underlying Table 2.8 tend to become very imprecise if initial schooling is added to the specification (and likewise for those underlying Table 2.1 if initial life expectancy is added to that specification). For this reason, the results with both initial schooling and initial life expectancy are not summarized in this report. But the reader should keep in mind that the estimated effect of one initial human resource indicator represents in part the effect of the other. Their relative importance varies with the outcome, with each appearing relatively more important than the other in about half the estimates.

**Table 2.9. Impact of Initial 1965 Life Expectancy, Correcting for Real Per Capita Income, on Subsequent Growth and Recent Levels of Various Variables in Latin America and the Caribbean**

| 1. Average annual growth (%) in: | | 3. Recent actual levels - predicted values | |
|---|---|---|---|
| GNP per capita (1965–90) | 0.15 | Adult literacy rate, female, 1985 | 1.5 |
| Export Growth (1980–90) | 0.44 | Adult literacy rate, male, 1985 | 0.93 |
| Population growth (1965–80) | −0.056* | Adult literacy rate, male-female, 1985 | −0.54 |
| | | Life expectancy at birth, female, 1988 | 0.54 |
| **2. Recent level variables** | | Life expectancy at birth, male, 1988 | 0.57 |
| Private consumption/GDP (%), 1990 | −0.90 | Infant mortality/1,000 births, female, 1988 | −2.9 |
| Share of population 15–64 years, 1990 | 0.35 | Risk of dying by age 5/1,000 births, female, 1988 | −3.5 |
| Share of population 0–14 years, 1990 | −0.55 | Risk of dying by age 5/1,000 births, male, 1988 | −4.0 |
| Crude birth rate per 1,000, 1990 | −0.63 | Risk of dying by age 5/1,000 births, | |
| Crude death rate per 1,000, 1990 | −0.17 | male-female, 1988 | −0.43 |
| Total fertility rate, 1990 | −0.098 | Low birth weight (%), 1985 | −0.32 |
| Infant mortality rate | | Crude birth rate per 1,000, 1988 | −0.52 |
| (1,000 live births), 1990 | −3.2 | Total fertility rate, 1988 | −0.095 |
| Under 5 mortality rate (1,000 live births), | | | |
| female, 1990 | −4.1 | | |
| Under 5 mortality rate (1,000 live births), | | | |
| male, 1990 | −4.6 | | |
| Life expectancy at birth, female, 1990 | 1.0 | | |
| Life expectancy at birth, male, 1990 | 0.99 | | |

*Note:* Based on initial 1965 total schooling, correcting for real per capita income. All point estimates are significantly nonzero at the 5 percent level, except those indicated by * are significantly nonzero at the 10 percent level and those indicated by ** are significantly nonzero at the 20 percent level.
*Source:* Based on regression estimates by the author.

annual growth rate per quarter century for every year of difference in initial life expectancies. This relation is consistent with a large proportion of the Latin American and Caribbean growth experience. Thus, although schooling is the most emphasized human resource, life expectancies are a better indicator of recent Latin American and Caribbean economic growth rates. The point estimate means that, all else being equal, the recent gap between Jamaican and Bolivian life expectancies relative to international experience will be associated with a difference in future real per capita GNP growth rates of 2.4 percent per year—a considerable effect. Figure 2.5 plots GNP growth rates in the 1965–1990 period in the region against initial life expectancies. For only 30 percent of the 20 countries are the signs of initial life expectancy and of the subsequent GNP growth rate opposite (Argentina, El Salvador, Haiti, Honduras, Guatemala, and Jamaica).

Initial life expectancy also has a significant positive association with subsequent export growth and a significant negative association with population growth. The estimates indicate that for every additional year of initial life expectancy, the annual growth rate of exports is 0.44 percent higher and the annual population growth rate is 0.056 percent lower. Differences in life

**Figure 2.5.  Average Annual Percentage Growth in Real Per Capita Income versus Actual Minus Predicted Total Life Expectancy in 1965**

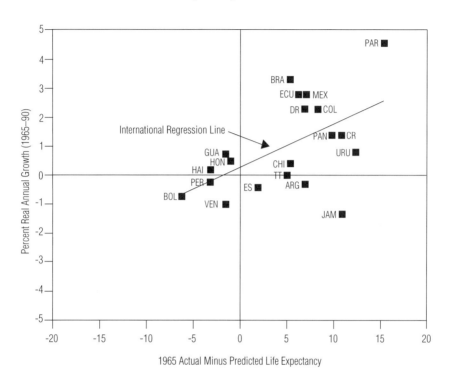

expectancies of the magnitudes observed recently in the Latin American and Caribbean may thus be associated with large increases in export growth and with large decreases in population growth, both of which tend to be associated importantly with successful development experiences.

The estimated impact of initial life expectancy on outcomes two decades or more later is also significant in a number of cases. For every additional year of initial life expectancy, (1) the share of private consumption in GDP is lowered by 0.9 percent (and the share of investment and government expenditure increased); (2) total fertility rates decline by about 0.10 child; (3) the share of the population in the prime adult 15-to-64 age range increases by 0.35 percent; (4) infant and child mortality rates fall by 3.5 to 5.6 children per thousand live births; (5) life expectancy at birth increases from 0.5 to 0.6 years (controlling for real per capita income), which suggests persistency of the underlying effects across generations; and (6) adult literacy is higher by 1.5 percent for females and 0.9 percent for males (so the gender gap in such rates falls by about 0.5 percent). These changes are for

**Table 2.10. Impact of Initial 1965 Gender Gap in Life Expectancy (Female–Male), Correcting for Real Per Capita Income, on Subsequent Growth and Recent Levels of Various Variables in Latin America and the Caribbean**

| 1. Average annual growth (%) in: | | 3. Recent actual levels - predicted value | |
|---|---|---|---|
| Population growth (1965–80) | −0.32 | Life expectancy at birth, male, 1988 | −0.96* |
| | | % central government expenditure on | |
| **2. Recent level variables** | | housing, social security, welfare, 1988 | 8.5 |
| Education/government expenditure (%) 1990 | −2.2 | % GNP government expenditure on | |
| Share of population 15–64 years 1990 | 0.84** | housing, social security, welfare, 1988 | 2.0 |
| Share of population 0–14 years 1990 | −1.7* | Crude birth rate per 1,000, 1988 | −1.3** |
| Crude birth rate per 1,000, 1990 | −1.7* | | |
| Crude death rate per 1,000, 1990 | −0.86 | | |

*Note:* Based on initial 1965 total schooling, correcting for real per capita income. All point estimates are significantly nonzero at the 5 percent level, except those indicated by * are significantly nonzero at the 10 percent level and those indicated by ** are significantly nonzero at the 20 percent level.
*Source:* Based on regression estimates by the author.

the most part desirable in themselves. In addition, they tend to free resources for higher current or future real per capita consumption and to increase the expected returns to investments in human resources through schooling and training by increasing life expectancies. Thus, initial life expectancy has considerable and substantial associations with subsequent development achievements in the Latin American and Caribbean region.

*Finding 10. There is an impact by gender from the composition of 1965 initial life expectancy (controlling for real per capita income).*

Just as gender differences in schooling may affect socioeconomic outcomes, so may gender differences in health and nutrition investments affect such outcomes. Table 2.10 presents estimates for cases in which initial female life expectancy relative to initial male life expectancy is significantly associated with subsequent outcomes, even with control for initial average life expectancy. These gender effects are less widespread than are those noted for schooling (Table 2.3). Nevertheless, there is some evidence of such gender impacts on demographic outcomes and on the composition of government expenditures.

With regard to demographic outcomes, one-year higher female relative to male initial life expectancy is associated with 0.3 percent lower annual population growth rate, a 0.9 persons per thousand lower crude death rate, a 1.7 percent reduction in the share of the population under 15 years of age, and a related 0.8 increase in the population share of 15- to-64 year olds. These changes tend to be desirable in themselves and also to increase economic productivity. With regard to the composition of government expenditures, one-year higher female relative to male initial life expectancy is associated with a 2.2 percent reduction in the share of central government expenditures on education and an 8.5 percent increase in the share of central government expenditures on housing, social security, and welfare. Thus, charges are induced in the composition of central government expenditures on human resources. In important part, these charges reflect the shift in age composition away from children.

### Micro Evidence on Impact of Health and Nutrition

*Finding 11. There appear to be some positive effects of better health and nutrition on schooling performance and labor productivity for low-income populations in developing countries, although these effects may differ substantially from those suggested by associations that do not control for simultaneity and unobserved family characteristics.*

Very few studies in this area have attempted to control for the estimation problems noted in Box 2.3 (see Behrman, 1993a for a survey). Studies that do control for these problems suggest that for low-income rural areas, labor productivity and school productivity respond to longer-run health and nutrition status, and less commonly, to shorter-run health and nutrition status. For very poor areas in which there has not been rapid technological change, in fact, the returns to investing in health and nutrition appear larger than the returns to increasing schooling, if only because the returns to schooling are estimated to be relatively low in such contexts.

*Finding 12. Preventive and basic health care seem to have higher returns than does curative health care during the early stages of economic development, which is characterized by the dominance of communicable childhood diseases and malnutrition. With development, there is an epidemiological transition toward diseases of adults and the elderly, which results in more complex patterns of relative returns.*

The general tendency for fertility rates to decline in the region implies shifts in the age structure of populations toward older individuals, with substantial impact also on the patterns of morbidity. Such shifts are intensified by urbanization, industrialization, adoption of new techniques and technologies, and behavioral changes (leading perhaps to increases in motor vehicle injuries, industrial accidents, exposure to pesticides and other toxic chemicals, smoking, cardiovascular disease, cancer, ischemic heart disease, and sexually transmitted diseases). Looking forward, the most dramatic increases in mortality in the region are likely to be caused by adult chronic, noncommunicable diseases, as these diseases become more common and childhood infectious and parasitic diseases decline. All of these shifts are occurring in conjunction with technological changes in treatment (such as oral rehydration therapy [ORT],[24] short-course multiple-drug chemotherapy for tuberculosis and leprosy, population-wide antihelminth therapy, simplified surgery, and new vaccines against measles, hepatitis B, and polio) and with technological changes in epidemiological monitoring capacities. One overall effect will be changes in the relative returns to the various types of health interventions. Such changes are likely to depend also on the particular details of each country.

## Impact of Training

*Finding 13. Systematic evidence on returns to training is relatively limited, but a priori analysis and expert judgments are that returns to well-designed programs with strong linkages with employers may be considerable.*

According to Riveros (1992b), traditional training programs in the region have had high returns in some cases, although other observers have a less optimistic appraisal (for instance, Middleton, Ziderman, and Van Adams, 1991). The most studied national experience probably has been that of Colombia, with emphasis on the *Servicio Nacional de Aprendizaje* (SENA), the national learning service. One prominent study of Bogota data (Jiménez, Kugler, and Horn, 1989) concludes that the social rates of return to long courses exceed 20 percent, and those for short courses exceed 10 percent (the estimated rate of return to secondary schooling in Colombia). The tendency is toward higher rates of return for more experienced workers with more formal schooling. The study emphasizes that the higher rates of return to the long courses contrast with the widely held view that short courses are more cost effective than longer ones, the basis of the trend toward more short courses in Colombia and many other countries in the region. The Bogota study also notes that the private rates of return to training are much higher than the social rates of return, so the private incentives for participation are very high. More recent work also emphasizes the importance of prior schooling, suggesting that the impact of training in Bogota increases approximately 3 percent for every additional year of schooling but is negative for workers with fewer than eight

---

[24]Nevertheless, the efficacy of ORT in field settings is subject to a great deal of uncertainty (Jamison and Mosley, 1990).

years of schooling. This work also suggests that training gained working for one's present employer is more effective than training gained prior to joining the firm (Psacharopoulos and Vélez, 1992). The latter point, of course, does not necessarily mean that the social returns are higher (or lower) for training within firms than for alternatives; the study does not provide information with which to make an inference on this point. But another recent assessment does suggest that SENA is less successful than it might be in preparing workers in the skills employer need, particularly skills that enable an individual to adapt to changing needs over time (Zerda Sarmiento et al., 1992).

Studies of the returns to training programs in the region have not controlled well for what would have happened to trainees' earnings and occupation without training, nor for the characteristics of those who receive training. The studies implicitly assumed that both formal schooling and training were randomly distributed to members of the population, rather than that choices were made about how long the individuals went to school and for how long, if at all, they received training. The trainees in most of these programs actually had relatively high schooling levels and came from families with more educated parents; they also tended to have greater ability and motivation than those who did not enroll in training programs. Therefore, a careful evaluation of training programs needs to control for the preexisting characteristics of the trainees. Perhaps, for instance, individuals with greater motivation to succeed in labor markets obtained more schooling and benefitted more from training, and perhaps therefore the estimated positive interaction between schooling and training does not imply that training is more effective if individuals have more schooling, but instead that training is more effective if trainees have greater motivation for labor market success. Perhaps individuals with greater motivation or ability tend to obtain both more schooling and more training and receive higher earnings in part because of their greater motivation or ability (not just because of the greater training and schooling). Maybe . . . or maybe not. The point is that such subtleties cannot readily be ascertained on the basis of existing studies. Therefore, these studies provide much less persuasive evidence of the impact of training programs than their interpreters often claim.

Furthermore, as Riveros (1992a) notes, most evaluations of training programs in the region were undertaken within a context much different from, and more rigid than, today's—an outmoded context of substantial import substitution programs, in which future skill needs could be predicted relatively well as long as the basic macro strategy was maintained. Now and in the future, with the growing consensus on the need for market orientation and for integration into rapidly changing international markets, training programs need to be much more flexible and give workers more broad-based skills than was the case earlier. For instance, the formal centralized type of training offered in Chile by INACAP in the 1970s (as described in Chapter 3), with its inherent rigidity and dependence on relatively few large firms, was not able to respond quickly enough to the incentives for a changing production structure.

## Conclusions

Empirical evaluation of the impact of human resources in the Latin American and Caribbean region is difficult because only limited information is available and because of problems in constructing a counterfactual case for what the situation would have been with different human resources. Nevertheless, the combination of a priori reasoning and the aggregate and micro evidence that has been reviewed suggests the following major themes:

• There are not likely to be many quick fixes in the form of human capital investments that have large immediate effects on productivity, because of the long gestation period for most improvements in human resources; nevertheless, the cost effectiveness of many investments in terms of medium-term and long-term goals may be considerable.

• Quality of human resources is important and may be more important than quantity in some cases.

• Rates of return to human resource investments depend on the country's overall context and development strategy (macro stability, extent of markets, exposure to international competition, price incentives, regulations, discrimination); in an appropriate context, such rates of return tend to be relatively high.

• Rates of return to marginal human resource investments tend to be higher for females than for males.

• A relatively high initial human resource level for a given state of development is associated with relatively good macroeconomic performance in subsequent years through myriad channels (direct productivity effects, changes in expenditure patterns, inducement of further human resource investments, reduction of population pressures).

• The impact of the initial aggregate position of human resources holds for human resources related to health and nutrition as well as for those that are schooling related.

• For very low income populations, rates of return to improvements in health and nutrition (in terms of productivity gains) may be important and perhaps greater than the rates of return to improvements in education.

• For middle-income and higher-income populations, rates of return to improvements in education (in terms of productivity gains), even with controls for estimation problems, are likely to be considerable.

• In economies in which schooling is relatively limited, the highest rate of return may be to improvements in the quality and quantity of basic primary schooling; for countries with more extensive schooling experience, the rate of return may be higher for marginal investments in higher levels of schooling.

• Variations in schooling parallel a substantial portion of the income variance in economies in the Latin American and Caribbean region.

• Higher schooling also is associated with lower probability of a given worker being in poverty.

• Increasing the level of post-primary schooling facilitates adjustment by reducing the cost of acquiring new specific human capital (although with workers of lower schooling levels, the possible loss of previous specific human capital investments may outweigh gains from switching to new production activities).

• Evidence is relatively limited on returns to some human resource investments, such as training; given the substantial role that training has played in Latin America and the Caribbean, there would be high returns to more careful systematic analysis of training.

• There is evidence of important effects of human resources within the family, with parental (particularly maternal) schooling improving the health and nutrition of all family members.

• There is evidence that increasing schooling reduces fertility, perhaps through changing the opportunity cost of women using their time on child care instead of participating in the labor market.

# CHAPTER

# 3

## CONDITION OF HUMAN RESOURCES

Given the important impact of human resources on development in Latin America and the Caribbean, it is useful to ask the following questions: Are the region's human resource stocks and investment flows relatively low or high? Have the changes in these factors since the 1960s been relatively great or small? Have human resources deteriorated because of the debt crises and subsequent structural adjustments in many countries? How do these changes compare with international experience for different types of human resources—say, for schooling versus health? How do they compare for more disaggregated characterizations of human resources, such as primary versus secondary schooling? What is the nature of these comparisons for females versus males?

This chapter explores these issues using available aggregate indicators. It would not be very informative, however, to compare human resources across countries that differ considerably with regard to income, because human resources are in fact systematically associated with income. Moreover, the new economic growth models (see Box 2.1) emphasize that the state of a country's human resources is important in terms of future development prospects not in some absolute sense, but relative to what would be expected given the country's current state of development. The aggregate estimates in the preceding chapter are consistent with this emphasis. Furthermore, some characterizations of the region's human resources as being relatively poor make explicit comparisons with international experience (i.e., all countries in the world for which data are available). Urrutia (1991), for instance, surveys recent human resource experience in the region and concludes that "Latin America has consistently underinvested in education and basic health. Although the region made considerable progress in these two areas after 1950, progress was nevertheless insufficient and was slower than in East Asia."

Therefore, the comparisons emphasized here control for income by regressions of the relevant levels and changes in human resource investments on real per capita income, for all countries for which the data are available. The comparison for a given year for a given indicator for a particular country indicates how the value for that country differs from cross-country or international experience for that year, for a comparable level of per capita income. The comparison for the change between two years likewise indicates how the change in value for a particular Latin American or Caribbean country differs from the change in cross-country experience between those two years. The latter comparison, moreover, controls for fixed effects that are not controlled for in the cross-country comparisons for a given year, such as natural conditions and culture. Some of the estimates for a given year are for the difference between variables for males versus females; these estimates also control for unobserved country effects such as natural conditions and culture. This chapter builds primarily on these regressions, with their implications highlighted in figures and tables in the text. Such comparisons do have their limitations and must therefore be qualified, as discussed in Box 3.1, but they represent the best available approach for obtaining a systematic perspective on how levels and changes in human resource investments in the region, both generally and in particular countries, compare with international experience, controlling for per capita income.[1]

Of course, there is nothing magical or ideal about cross-country experience. It is merely the average international experience. Nevertheless, it does provide a benchmark against which to assess the region's experience so that legitimate generalizations about the region and particular countries can be made. For some human resource indicators, particular Latin American and Caribbean countries differ substantially from the cross-country experience. Such differences raise the following questions: Why do such differences exist? Are they acceptable because of the special conditions in these countries? Or might they indicate that human capital investments in these countries should be changed? The characterizations here were the basis for having ascertained in the previous chapter the extent to which the differences in aggregate human resources in these countries are associated with success in achieving various economic goals.

One reason for the differences in aggregate indicators of human resources across countries, even if there is control for real per capita income,

---

[1] Urrutia (1991) presents a useful summary of the performance of social indicators in Latin America and the Caribbean, but with a somewhat different emphasis than that of the present summary. For instance, his summary tends to focus on an earlier period, with the latest data being for 1985. It does not include gender differences in schooling, does not focus on control for real per capita income (and therefore the state of human resources relative to the level of development, as in the new neoclassical growth models), and does not statistically relate the condition of human resources in the region to human resource inputs and expenditures and to subsequent economic performance, as in chapters 2 and 4 of this study.

is that differences exist in the distribution of income and human resources. Urrutia (1991) suggests that distribution is a major factor in the aggregate differences across countries in the region: "In large measure, these [aggregate] health and education differences explain (or are explained by) the inequality in incomes." The only way that a country can have very high primary school enrollments, for instance, is to enroll almost all of the children of poor families in addition to those of middle and high-income families. Countries can have relatively high tertiary school enrollments, by contrast, by enrolling children almost exclusively from middle and high-income families. Likewise, differences in the infant mortality rates between otherwise similar countries are likely to stem substantially from differences in the access of poor families to adequate prenatal and postnatal health care. Thus, even though the available human resource measures for the comparisons in this chapter refer to averages for countries, they in part reflect underlying distributional patterns and changes in those patterns.

## Schooling

### Recent Attainment of Total Schooling

Table 3.1 and Figure 3.1 summarize the level of recent total schooling in Latin American and Caribbean countries compared with average international experience, controlling for per capita real income. Total schooling is represented by the expected grades of schooling for a synthetic cohort (hereafter "schooling"), based on enrollment rates at the primary, secondary, and tertiary levels.[2] Latin American and Caribbean countries have a diversity of experience but have recently tended, on average, to have greater schooling than the international experience, with 70 percent of the countries for which data are available standing above the international regression line.[3] Schooling recently has been particularly high relative to

---

[2] The expected schooling for a synthetic cohort in a year indicates the expected schooling if children experience the enrollment rates at all schooling levels for that year. For instance, for Brazil in 1987 the reported enrollment rates are 103 percent for the primary level, 39 percent for the secondary level, and 11 percent for the tertiary level. The numerators for the enrollment rates for the primary, secondary, and tertiary schooling levels are respectively the number of children 6 to 11, 12 to 17, and 20 to 24 years old. Therefore, the expected years of schooling for a synthetic cohort that faced the enrollment rates for these three schooling levels recorded for Brazil in 1987 is $9.07 = 1.03*6 + 0.39*6 + 0.11*5$.

[3] Nevertheless, the share of the total regional population above the international regression line is much smaller because Brazil, with its population currently greater than 150 million, is below the line.

## Box 3.1. Data Problems with International Comparisons of Human Resources

There are four problems in estimating relations between human resource investments and per capita income from cross-country data.

First, some data are not readily available (for instance, on training programs and on the quality of human capital investments and related social services).

Second, even for human resource investments for which data are available, there are still measurement problems, as illustrated by the data for the most emphasized human resource indicators—schooling and mortality rates/ life expectancies:

• The most commonly used data for investigating schooling are primary, secondary, and tertiary enrollment rates, as compiled by UNESCO from reports of the various ministries of education. There are several principal problems with these data: (a) Enrollment rates may reflect opening day enrollment rates and not regular attendance. (b) For many countries, only gross enrollment rates (enrollments of individuals of all ages) are available rather than net (age-appropriate) enrollment rates. For countries for which both gross and net enrollment rates are available, the ratios of the two vary considerably because of considerable differences across countries in late starting of school and in grade repetition. (c) Differences in starting ages and in duration of schooling levels make cross-country comparisons even more difficult. (d) Enrollment rates address only the quantitative, not the qualitative, dimension of schooling investments.

• Data on estimated life expectancies and on infant and child mortality have been used primarily for international comparisons of health and nutrition. These data are subject to the following comparability problems: (a) Definitions differ across countries. In some countries an infant must survive at least 24 hours before being counted a live birth rather than a late fetal death, which reduces the reported birth rate and infant mortality rate. Since the 24-hour restriction is more common for poorer countries, this difference in definition tends to lower the estimated inverse relation between per capita income and mortality. (b) There are different degrees of completeness of population data. The more developed countries usually base death rates and life expectancies on national registered deaths and official population estimates, which are believed to represent at least 90 percent of the births and deaths, particularly infant deaths occurring during the year. In contrast, registered data on deaths and infant deaths are estimated to be complete in only about 70 percent of Latin American countries, 18 percent of African countries, and 21 percent of Asian countries. The countries with incomplete, defective, or nonexistent vital registration data generally are those with higher mortality and lower per capita income. For these countries, mortality parameters are estimated using incomplete vital registration data or other mortality data collected in censuses or sample surveys. Because censuses are conducted infrequently, most of the values cited for these countries in the mid 1980s are in fact extrapolations from previous censuses rather than direct observations. Such data have obvious limitations that affect efforts to characterize short-run changes for such variables much more than efforts to represent longer-run changes. It is not clear exactly how the procedures for calculating such variables affect estimates of how particular Latin American and Caribbean country values differ from international values, since such biases depend on the nature of the estimation errors for all countries in the comparison. (c) A long life is not identical to a healthy life, although micro studies indicate that in the developing country context, there is a fairly strong positive association (see survey in Behrman and Deolalikar, 1988).

If the errors introduced by using such variables are independent of the right-side per capita income variables in the regressions, they do not cause any biases in the estimates of the regression coefficients. But these errors are likely to overestimate schooling and health for countries with lower per capita income. If so, then the cross-country estimates are likely to yield coefficients that understate the associations with real per capita income. It is nevertheless difficult to assess whether this is likely to result in a bias of where particular Latin American and Caribbean countries stand relative to the international regression line.

Third, the human resource measures generally available are only averages, not variances or other indicators of distribution. The means do, however, reflect some dimensions of the distributions. For instance, almost universal schooling enrollment rates usually imply that most children from poor families are enrolling, while lower enrollment rates imply that a proportionately larger number of children from poorer families are not enrolling.

Fourth, there are also problems with the right-side variables used to control for real per capita income, because of differences in data quality, coverage, definitions, and valuation. For instance, different procedures are used to translate domestic values into comparable international values. To make comparisons with broad international experience, this report uses World Bank data, which are available for almost all countries. For the 25 Latin American and Caribbean countries for which the World Bank and the IDB both have data for 1988, the correlation between per capita GDP/GNP from the two sources is 0.99. Therefore, the use of World Bank or IDB data to control for variation in per capita income does not affect the results. Another widely used representation of per capita product is based on purchasing power parity estimates, such as in Summers and Heston (1991). For the 25 Latin American and Caribbean countries, the correlations between the Summers and Heston (1991) data and those by the World Bank (1990) and IDB (1992) are 0.91 and 0.92, respectively. These high correlations do not address all problems in data quality, but do suggest that the differences between World Bank and IDB procedures (and between these two data sources and the Summers and Heston data) for converting data into a common currency do not affect the estimates importantly.

It is difficult to specify the net effect of these data problems on efforts to characterize how countries in Latin America and the Caribbean fare relative to other countries with similar per capita incomes. Because of such problems, international comparisons must be interpreted with caution.

*Sources:* Ahmad (1994), Behrman (1993a), Behrman and Rosenzweig (1994), Chamie (1994), Heston (1994), IDB (1992), Srinivasan (1994), Summers and Heston (1991), and World Bank (1990).

**Table 3.1.  Recent Schooling in Latin America and Caribbean Countries in Grades and Extent to Which Schooling Exceeds or Falls Short of 1987 International Experience**

| Countries | Schooling in Grades | Difference from International Experience |
|---|---|---|
| Dominican Republic | 11.8 | 4.5 |
| Honduras | 8.7 | 1.1 |
| Guatemala | 6.3 | −1.4 |
| Bolivia | 8.5 | 1.6 |
| El Salvador | 7.4 | −0.4 |
| Ecuador | 11.9 | 3.8 |
| Jamaica | 10.4 | 2.3 |
| Colombia | 10.9 | 2.6 |
| Costa Rica | 9.6 | 0.3 |
| Peru | 12.5 | 3.9 |
| Panama | 11.3 | 1.3 |
| Mexico | 11.1 | 1.7 |
| Brazil | 9.1 | −0.9 |
| Chile | 11.3 | 2.3 |
| Uruguay | 13.1 | 2.5 |
| Argentina | 13.0 | 2.3 |
| Venezuela | 11.1 | −0.7 |
| Trinidad and Tobago | 11.1 | −0.6 |

*Notes:* Schooling is the expected schooling for a synthetic cohort if children were to experience the enrollment rates at all schooling levels for that year.  Countries are listed in order of increasing per capita income for 1988 as given in IDB (1992a).
*Source:* Based on regression estimates by the author.

the international regression line in the Dominican Republic (4.9 grades above the regression line), Peru (3.9 grades), Ecuador (3.8 grades), Colombia (2.6 grades), Uruguay (2.5 grades), and Argentina, Chile, and Jamaica (2.3 grades). But schooling has been below the international regression line for Guatemala (−1.4 grades), Brazil (−0.9 grades), Venezuela (−0.7 grades), Trinidad and Tobago (−0.6 grades), and El Salvador (−0.4 grades). The differential schooling experience across Latin American countries, interestingly, does not seem to reflect the differential first grade repetition rates across countries relative to real per capita income within the region, as shown in Figure 3.2. Countries with relatively high repetition can have relatively high or relatively low schooling, and vice versa.

Recent estimates of the stock of schooling in 1987 among adults 15 to 64 years old also suggest that the region has a relatively schooled adult population in comparison with most of the developing world, including East Asia (Table 3.2). Thus, in terms of recent schooling and the schooling stock of adults, Latin America has relatively high schooling in comparison with other developing regions, including East Asia—not relatively limited schooling, as claimed by Urrutia (1991) and others. Of course, these schooling stocks vary considerably among countries in the region, as

**Figure 3.1. Expected Years of Schooling versus Real Per Capita Income, both for 1987**

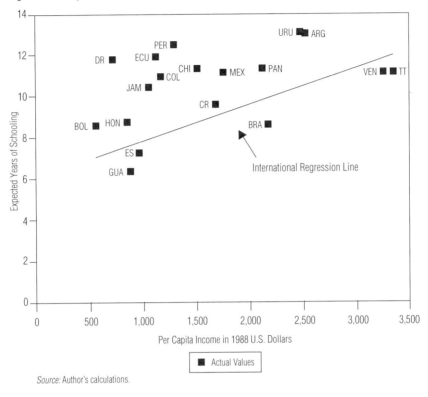

*Source:* Author's calculations.

would be anticipated from the variations in schooling among these countries. For Brazil, for example, Amadeo et al. (1993) estimate that the stock of schooling for adults 25 years of age and older averages 3.9 grades, 2.7 grades below the level predicted from cross-country regressions on real per capita income. In fact, Amadeo et al. (1993) suggest that Brazil may be diverging from the rest of Latin America and the Caribbean in terms of its human capital stock, because of that country's ongoing relatively limited schooling enrollments and relatively high repetition rates.[4]

Controlling for real per capita income clearly makes a considerable difference in characterizations of relative recent schooling among the

---

[4] Amadeo et al. (1993) estimate that: (a) Brazilian schooling enrollment rates for students age 6 to 11 are 74 percent, compared with 89 percent for high-income Latin American countries and 91.4 percent predicted by cross-country regressions on real per capita income; and (b) the percentage of repeaters in primary school in Brazil is 29 percent, compared with 18 percent predicted by cross-country regressions.

**Figure 3.2. First Grade Repetition Rates in Relation to GDP Per Capita, for Selected Countries, around 1990**

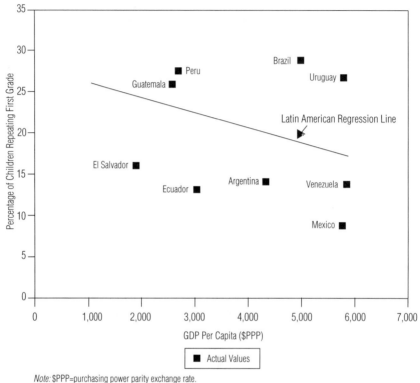

Note: $PPP=purchasing power parity exchange rate.
Source: Barros (1992).

Latin American and Caribbean countries. For instance, Trinidad and Tobago, Venezuela, and to a lesser extent, Brazil, all have greater levels of recent schooling than Bolivia, but Bolivia is the only one of these four countries that has schooling above the international experience once there is control for real per capita income. Likewise, Argentina, Ecuador, and Peru all have higher recent schooling that the Dominican Republic, but the Dominican Republic is a grade more above the international regression line than any other country in the region.

### Composition of Recent Schooling by Levels

Two countries with about the same per capita real income and the same total average schooling may have different compositions of schooling—one with more primary and the other with more post-primary enrollments.

#### Table 3.2.  Average Years of Schooling in Major Regions of the World
*(Per person between the ages of 15 and 64)*

|  | Level in 1987 (Grades) | | | |
| --- | --- | --- | --- | --- |
|  | Primary | Secondary | Tertiary | Total |
| Industrial | 6.2 | 2.6 | 0.7 | 9.5 |
| Developing | 3.5 | 0.8 | 0.1 | 4.5 |
| East Asia | 3.9 | 0.9 | 0.1 | 4.8 |
| South Asia | 2.7 | 1.0 | 0.1 | 3.8 |
| Latin America | 4.7 | 0.6 | 0.4 | 5.6 |
| Sub-Saharan Africa | 2.5 | 0.3 | 0.0 | 3.2 |
| Developed Europe | 4.8 | 1.0 | 0.3 | 6.0 |
| Middle East/North Africa | 3.4 | 1.0 | 0.3 | 4.7 |
| World | 4.0 | 1.1 | 0.2 | 5.5 |

*Source:* Dubey, Swanson, and Nehru (1992).

These different compositions may make a difference in distribution if children from poorer families are least likely to be disadvantaged at the primary level, and in growth if the rates of return are higher to primary than to post-primary school, as often is claimed (for instance, in Psacharopoulos, 1985). Within the region, moreover, relatively high recent schooling enrollment at the primary or secondary level is not necessarily associated strongly with relatively high schooling enrollment at the tertiary level.

Because the bivariate correlations of total schooling with primary and secondary schooling enrollment in the region, controlling for real per capita income, are greater than 0.8, the relatively high primary and secondary enrollments are quite strongly associated with relatively high overall schooling. But the bivariate correlations between tertiary schooling enrollment and total schooling and between primary and secondary enrollments are only 0.5; and those between tertiary enrollment and primary and secondary enrollments are only 0.2. Therefore, the fact that a country in the region has relatively high (low) primary and secondary schooling enrollments does not automatically mean that it has relatively high (low) tertiary enrollment. Different countries clearly tend to focus on different schooling levels. Therefore, it is of interest to consider schooling enrollment by levels.

Table 3.3 gives these enrollment rates and summarizes the extent to which recent enrollment rates at the primary, secondary, and tertiary levels in various countries exceed or fall short of the international regression lines. For recent primary school enrollment rates, the Dominican Republic (48 percent above international experience), Peru (30 percent), Ecuador (28 percent), Colombia (24 percent), and Mexico (21 percent) all are

**Table 3.3. Enrollment Rates in Latin America, with International Comparison, 1987**
*(Percent)*

| Countries | Primary | | Secondary | | Tertiary | |
|---|---|---|---|---|---|---|
| | Actual | Difference from International Regressions | Actual | Difference from International Regressions | Actual | Difference from International Regressions |
| | (1) | (2) | (3) | (4) | (5) | (6) |
| Haiti | 95 | 15 | 17 | −9 | — | — |
| Dominican Republic | 133 | 48 | 47 | 15 | 19 | 11 |
| Honduras | 106 | 19 | 32 | −2 | 9 | 0 |
| Guatemala | 77 | −10 | 21 | −14 | 9 | 0 |
| Bolivia | 91 | 8 | 37 | 8 | 17 | 9 |
| El Salvador | 79 | −9 | 29 | −7 | 18 | 8 |
| Ecuador | 117 | 28 | 56 | 18 | 30 | 20 |
| Jamaica | 105 | 16 | 65 | 27 | 4 | −6 |
| Colombia | 114 | 24 | 56 | 17 | 14 | 4 |
| Paraguay | 102 | 12 | 30 | −9 | — | — |
| Costa Rica | 98 | 2 | 41 | −7 | 25 | 13 |
| Peru | 122 | 30 | 65 | 23 | 25 | 15 |
| Panama | 106 | 6 | 59 | 6 | 28 | 15 |
| Mexico | 118 | 22 | 53 | 5 | 16 | 4 |
| Brazil | 103 | 3 | 39 | −15 | 11 | −2 |
| Chile | 103 | 9 | 70 | 25 | 18 | 7 |
| Uruguay | 110 | 7 | 73 | 15 | 42 | 28 |
| Argentina | 110 | 7 | 74 | 15 | 39 | 24 |
| Venezuela | 107 | −1 | 54 | −14 | 27 | 10 |
| Trinidad and Tobago | 100 | −9 | 82 | 14 | 4 | −13 |

*Source:* Based on regression estimates by the author.

more than 20 percent above the international regression line; at the other end of that spectrum, El Salvador, Guatemala, and Trinidad and Tobago all are 8 to 10 percent below. For recent secondary school enrollment rates, Chile (25 percent above), Peru (23 percent), Ecuador (18 percent), Colombia (17 percent), Argentina (15 percent), the Dominican Republic (15 percent), Uruguay (15 percent), and Trinidad and Tobago (14 percent) are all at least 10 percent above international experience; Brazil, Guatemala, and Venezuela all are 13 percent to 15 percent below. For recent tertiary enrollments, Uruguay (28 percent above), Argentina (24 percent), Ecuador (20 percent), Panama (15 percent), Peru (15 percent), and Costa Rica (13 percent) are all more than 10 percent above the international regression line; only Trinidad and Tobago (13 percent) is more than 10 percent below.

Figure 3.3 provides further information about the enrollment patterns across countries in enrollments at different schooling levels relative

**Figure 3.3. Percentage Deviation from Predicted Enrollments by Schooling Levels, 1987**

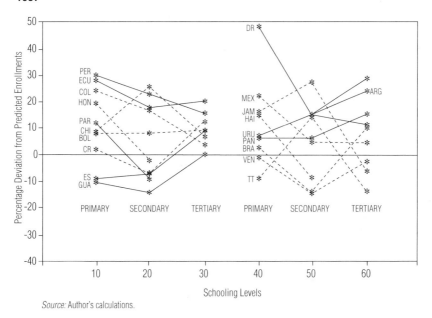

*Source:* Author's calculations.

to international experience, controlling for per capita income. For each country we have plotted the percentages above or below those predicted by international experience for recent primary, secondary, and tertiary enrollments. Only Bolivia has basically the same percentage of difference from (above) international experience for all three enrollment levels. The other countries differ from international experience by enrollment levels in one of the following patterns: (1) primary school enrollment relatively highest and tertiary enrollment relatively lowest (so lines in Figure 3.3 are downward sloping), as in Colombia, the Dominican Republic, Mexico, and Peru;[5] (2) secondary school enrollment relatively lowest (so lines are V shaped), as in Brazil, Costa Rica, Ecuador, Guatemala, and Venezuela); (3) primary school enrollment relatively lowest and tertiary enrollment relatively highest (so lines are upward sloping), as in Argentina, El Salvador, Panama, and Uruguay; or (4) secondary school enrollment relatively highest (so lines have an inverted V shape), as in Chile, Jamaica, and Trinidad and Tobago.

---

[5] Haiti, Honduras, and Paraguay may fall into this group or the next group, but the unavailability of information on their tertiary enrollments precludes knowing for certain.

With reference to the composition of schooling enrollments (given the total investment already discussed with regard to Figure 3.1), the first of these four groups probably is most consistent with productivity growth and more equal distribution (and the third group the least consistent) if the claims by those such as Psacharopoulos (1985) mentioned earlier are valid.[6] On the other hand, the fourth group may be most consistent (and the second group least consistent) with changing productivity and acquisition of new schools if secondary schooling becomes a more important bottleneck to development, as some commentators on human resources in East and Southeast Asia have claimed (such as Sussangkarn, 1988). For instance, Brunner (1989) argues that in the 1960s there were inadequate numbers of highly trained individuals in the East Asian region (only 1 percent of the population were professionals), so that the subsequent shift toward much greater training at the university level was warranted.

As noted earlier, there is reason on a priori grounds to suspect that the enrollments at different schooling levels are associated with a country's income distribution. It is difficult to examine to what extent the different enrollment rates are associated with income distribution, however, because reasonably comparable income distribution data are available for only six countries of the region: Brazil, Colombia, Costa Rica, Jamaica, Peru, and Venezuela (World Bank, 1992). Nevertheless, some bivariate correlations for these six countries are consistent with the hypothesized patterns. The income share of the bottom 20 percent of households is negatively correlated (r = −0.6) with the extent to which the tertiary enrollment rates exceed the levels predicted by the international regressions. The income share of the top 10 percent of households is negatively correlated (r = −0.5) with the extent to which primary and secondary enrollment rates each exceed the levels predicted by the international regressions. That is, relatively high income shares for the poorest quintile of households are associated with relatively low tertiary enrollment, and relatively high income shares for the richest decile of households are associated with relatively low primary and secondary enrollments.

Consistent cross-country evidence is even sparser for other considerations such as urban-rural, area, and ethnic differences. But systematic evidence from a few countries and anecdotes from others do suggest that rural residents, residents of poorer areas, and native ethnic groups receive relatively

---

[6] High primary school enrollment rates may reflect, in part, high grade repetition or enrollment of students who are older than normal primary ages because: (a) they started school late, and (b) the rates are bounded by zero below and by 100 percent (except for repetition and late starters) above.

less schooling (Box 3.2). If rural school costs are greater than urban school costs because of the smaller scale of operation, the greater difficulties in obtaining qualified teachers, and the higher opportunity cost of the students' time (they otherwise could be helping out on farms), then efficiency considerations alone would suggest greater schooling for those in urban areas. Concerns about equity and empowerment of the poor might work in the opposite direction. Estimates for the two largest countries in the region, Brazil and Mexico, suggest that schooling resources are allocated across areas with some consideration of equity as well as productivity issues (Box 3.3).

What are the implications of such enrollment patterns in the region for the stock of adult schooling? Table 3.2 indicates that in 1987 Latin America had relatively high stocks of primary and tertiary schooling relative to most of the rest of the developing world and the world total (although not relative to the industrial countries), but relatively low stocks of secondary schooling.

What is the relation between schooling levels and labor market experience? With regard to unemployment rates, the answer is not a simple monotonic relation, because those with more schooling not only face different labor demands but also have various employment alternatives. Those with little or no schooling are often from very poor households in which unemployment is a luxury they cannot afford. In Brazil, for instance, unemployment rates are lowest for illiterates, they increase with some schooling to reach a maximum for those with 5 to 8 years of schooling, and they then decrease with more schooling (Amadeo et al., 1993). This fact may mean that increasing basic schooling will increase unemployment among those at the lower end of the income distribution, if this rise in schooling is associated with changes that enable them to afford unemployment in lieu of employment in very low wage jobs.

### Composition of Recent Schooling by Gender

Schooling by gender is of interest because the rate of return to schooling females may be higher than that to schooling males (probably due to gender specialization in household production, including children's human capital development). Moreover, there appear to be systematic associations between gender gaps in schooling and important demographic and human resource outcomes such as fertility and infant and child mortality (as in, for instance, King, 1990 and 1991). Further, gender gaps in schooling are likely to cause gender gaps in earning capacity and thereby to contribute to inequalities in the distribution of access to economic resources.

Figure 3.4 and Table 3.4 (column 2) give recent gender gaps for total schooling (male minus female schooling levels for synthetic cohorts)

**Box 3.2. Schooling and Literacy Differences by Urban-Rural, Area, and Ethnic Group**

In every country in the region for which there are data, rural schooling levels are lower than urban levels. This, together with selective rural-urban migration, with the more-schooled likely to migrate, results in rural populations being much less schooled than urban ones. One indicator of rural-urban differentials in the stock of schooled adults is the difference in illiteracy rates for the population 15 years old and older (data from UNESCO and CELADE):

| Country | Year | Male | | Female | |
|---|---|---|---|---|---|
| | | Total | Rural | Total | Rural |
| Argentina | 1980 | 6 | 14 | 6 | 15 |
| Bolivia | 1976 | 24 | 37 | 49 | 69 |
| Brazil | 1985 | 21 | 45 | 23 | 48 |
| Chile | 1982 | 9 | 21 | 9 | 23 |
| Ecuador | 1982 | 13 | 22 | 19 | 33 |
| El Salvador (10+) | 1980 | 27 | 39 | 33 | 46 |
| Guatemala | 1973 | 46 | 60 | 62 | 78 |
| Honduras | 1974 | 41 | 52 | 45 | 57 |
| Nicaragua | 1971 | 42 | 64 | 43 | 67 |
| Panama | 1980 | 14 | 24 | 15 | 29 |
| Uruguay | 1985 | 6 | 11 | 5 | 8 |

There is considerable variance across countries in these urban-rural literacy gaps, from 3 percent for females in Uruguay to 25 percent for females in Brazil. But in most cases the gaps are 10 percent or more, indicating substantial differences in basic schooling. And generally the gaps are greater for higher schooling levels. With the exception of Uruguay, the gender differences in these urban-rural literacy gaps favor males by 1 to 7 percent.

Area differences in schooling and illiteracy rates also are very large in many countries. For Brazil, for example, the Northeast had illiteracy rates much higher and schooling attainment much lower than the other major areas:

in Latin America and the Caribbean relative to international regression lines that control for per capita income. These gaps generally are small in comparison with international experience, with negative values for all 14 Latin American and Caribbean countries for which data permit such calculations, including values more than a grade below the international regression line for the Dominican Republic (−2.5 grades), Peru (−2.0 grades), El Salvador (−1.4 grades), Jamaica (−1.4 grades), Chile (−1.1 grades), and Colombia (−1.1 grades). Columns 4 and 6 in Table 3.4 give the gender

| Area | Illiteracy Rate in 1987 | Mean Years of Schooling in 1990 |
|---|---|---|
| Northeast | 38 | 2.4 |
| North | 13 | 4.1 |
| Center-west | 17 | 3.9 |
| Southeast | 12 | 3.9 |
| South | 12 | 3.5 |

In urban Bolivia in 1990, children in the North (Cobija, Trinidad) had an estimated 0.3 grades less of schooling and children in the South (Sucre, Oruro, Potosi, Tarija) had an estimated 0.2 grades more of schooling than children in the central part of the country (La Paz, El Alto, Cochabamba, Santa Cruz), after controlling for parental schooling, family structure, family income, and language spoken.

Finally, schooling and other indicators of human resources tend to be lower for the 30 million indigenous people in the region than for the rest of the population. Because the indigenous population tends to live in the poorer and more rural areas, their lesser schooling is correlated with the lesser schooling of rural residents and poorer areas. In Guatemala, half of the population is estimated to be indigenous; wage earners in a national Guatemalan sample in 1989 who identified themselves as indigenous had a mean of 1.6 years of schooling, compared with 5.0 years for those who did not identify themselves as indigenous. Such patterns also hold in urban areas. In the major urban areas of Bolivia, where the indigenous population is estimated to be two-thirds of the total (higher than in any other country in the region, with only Guatemala and Peru also higher than 30 percent), children in households that speak Quechua and Aymará had an estimated 0.8 and 1.6 grades of schooling less than children in households that spoke Spanish in 1990, even after controlling for parental schooling, family structure, family income, area, and all residential community characteristics.

*Sources:* Amadeo et al. (1993); Behrman, Ii, and Murillo (1994); IBGE (1990); Nash (1992); Psacharopoulos (1993); and UNDP (1992).

gaps in enrollment rates for primary and secondary schooling levels (such information is not available for the tertiary level), again controlling for per capita income. These data reinforce the point that gender gaps favoring males in schooling in Latin America and the Caribbean are relatively small by international standards. Only for Guatemala at the primary level (by 2 percent) and for Peru at the secondary level (by 3 percent) do the gender gaps in these enrollment rates favor males by more than the international averages once there is a control for income.

**Box 3.3. Equity-Productivity Trade-offs in Distribution of Schooling across Areas in Brazil and Mexico**

For Brazil, Amadeo et al. report that recent state expenditure on schooling is positively correlated ($r = 0.6$) with the average income of the economically active population. Therefore, area disparities in total public expenditures tend to favor the richer states. Central government transfers to states for education are uncorrelated with state average incomes, so such transfers neither reduce nor increase inequalities of expenditures per student across states. Earlier estimates indicate that combined federal, state, and municipal allocations of teachers of differing schooling levels across rural and urban areas of Brazilian states are consistent with these governments making some trade-off between productivity and equity, but not with their weighing equity enough to make larger compensatory investments in poorer than in richer areas. Looking forward, Amadeo et al. (1993) predict increasing concentration of the unschooled in the poor Northeast (from 50 percent of the total in 1990 to 72 percent in 2010).

Recent estimates based on a model of government behavior underlying the distribution of federal schooling expenditures across states in Mexico for 1980 and 1990 suggest that the federal government allocates such resources with concern for both equity and productivity, and that the concern about equity probably increased over the decade. The estimates also suggest, with some ambiguity, a shift from putting negative weight on the indigenous population (represented by the proportion of the population that speaks an indigenous language) in 1980 to putting positive weight on the indigenous population. They also suggest that the tendency to favor states that supported the PRI in the 1980 election was reduced to nil by 1990.

*Sources:* Amadeo et al. (1993), Behrman and Birdsall (1988), Mello e Souza (1979), and Gershberg and Schuermann (1993).

The data also suggest some compositional differences among countries in the region: in five countries (Colombia, Ecuador, El Salvador, Jamaica, and Peru), the gender gaps in enrollment are more favorable for females at the primary level relative to international standards than at the secondary level, but the opposite holds for the other 11 countries for which such a comparison is possible.[7]

---

[7] For many countries in the region, however, the extent to which gender gaps in enrollment depart from international standards at the primary versus the secondary levels is not very large. Only for seven countries in the region is the absolute value of the difference as large as 5 percent; among these seven, in four cases females are favored more at the secondary than at the primary level.

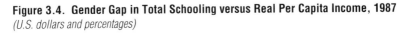

**Figure 3.4.  Gender Gap in Total Schooling versus Real Per Capita Income, 1987**
*(U.S. dollars and percentages)*

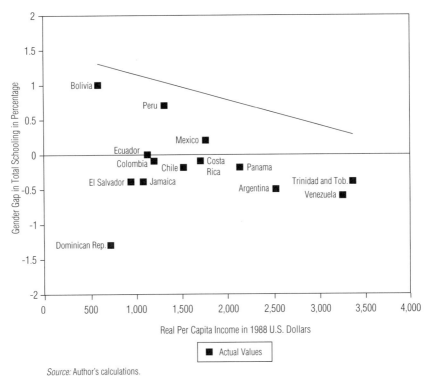

*Source:* Author's calculations.

Therefore, the prevalent tendency is for the gender gap favoring males in schooling to be relatively small in Latin America and the Caribbean compared with international experience, and even more so at the secondary school level.

Are there associations between these gender gaps and total schooling and enrollment rates in the region? Bivariate correlations (controlling for real per capita income) indicate the following: (1) the higher the total schooling, the smaller the gender gap in total schooling ($r = -0.6$); (2) the higher the total primary schooling enrollment rate, the lower the gender gap in primary schooling enrollment rates ($r = -0.5$); and (3) there is almost no association between total secondary schooling enrollment rates and the gender gap in such rates ($r = 0.1$). There is, then, some systematic inverse association between basic primary schooling and gender gaps, but this association does not carry over much to the secondary school level.

**Table 3.4.  Changes in Gender Gaps (Male–Female) in Schooling and in Primary and Secondary Enrollments, with International Comparison, 1987**

| Countries | Schooling (Grades) Actual | Schooling (Grades) Difference from International Regressions | Primary Enrollment Rate (%) Actual | Primary Enrollment Rate (%) Difference from International Regressions | Secondary Enrollment Rate (%) Actual | Secondary Enrollment Rate (%) Difference from International Regressions |
|---|---|---|---|---|---|---|
| | (1) | (2) | (3) | (4) | (5) | (6) |
| Haiti | — | — | 12 | −3 | 2 | −6 |
| Dominican Republic | −1.3 | −2.5 | −4 | −17 | −18 | −25 |
| Honduras | — | — | −4 | −16 | — | — |
| Guatemala | — | — | 14 | 2 | — | — |
| Bolivia | 1.0 | −0.3 | 12 | −1 | 4 | −3 |
| El Salvador | −0.4 | −1.4 | −4 | −16 | −2 | −8 |
| Ecuador | 0.0 | −1.0 | 2 | −9 | −2 | −8 |
| Jamaica | −0.4 | −1.4 | −2 | −13 | −4 | −10 |
| Colombia | −0.1 | −1.1 | −2 | −12 | 0 | −5 |
| Paraguay | — | — | 6 | −5 | 0 | −5 |
| Costa Rica | −0.1 | −0.9 | 2 | −6 | −4 | −8 |
| Peru | 0.7 | −0.2 | 4 | −6 | 8 | 3 |
| Panama | −0.2 | −0.8 | 4 | −2 | −8 | −11 |
| Mexico | 0.2 | −0.5 | 4 | −4 | 0 | −4 |
| Brazil | — | — | — | — | −12 | −15 |
| Chile | −0.2 | −1.1 | −2 | −11 | −2 | −16 |
| Uruguay | — | — | 2 | −3 | — | — |
| Argentina | −0.5 | −0.9 | 0 | −5 | −8 | −10 |
| Venezuela | −0.6 | −0.8 | 0 | −2 | −10 | −11 |
| Trinidad and Tobago | −0.4 | −0.6 | 0 | −2 | −6 | −7 |

*Source:* Based on regression estimates by the author.

## Changes in Total Schooling since 1965

Not only the recent levels of schooling but also the changes in schooling investments over time are of interest. Such changes are of particular interest given the economic crisis of the 1980s, during which some commentators suggested that human resources may have deteriorated considerably in the region (see Box 3.4). Figure 3.5 and Table 3.5 give the changes in schooling over the 1965–1987 period relative to international experience, controlling for nonlinear changes in per capita income. These changes were relatively high in the Dominican Republic (3.0 grades above the regression line), Ecuador (2.5 grades), Argentina (2.0 grades), Colombia (2.0 grades), Peru (2.0 grades), and Mexico (1.5 grades), but below the international experience in Jamaica (−1.8 grades), Brazil (−1.4 grades), Costa Rica (−1.2

grades), El Salvador (−1.2 grades), and Chile (−1.1 grades). Two-thirds of the 18 countries in the region for which such data are available had larger changes than those predicted by the international regression.[8] This result is striking, given some commentators' emphasis on the human resource costs of the 1980s.

A question of interest is whether countries with greater than predicted schooling growth rates in these decades had greater or lesser human resources than predicted by international experience in 1965, at the start of this period. The development literature has conjectures in both directions. Some authors say that there is an advantage to being relatively backward (Gerschenkron, 1962), while others contend that there is an advantage to having high human resources relative to per capita income (the new neoclassical growth model literature summarized in Box 2.1). The results for Latin America and the Caribbean in this period indicate more or less a standoff between these two possibilities. For ten countries the results are consistent with an advantage to backwardness, and for eight they are consistent with an advantage to having more initial schooling than predicted by international experience.

What are the implications of the changes in schooling investments for the stock of schooling for adults in Latin America and the Caribbean? Table 3.6 summarizes recent estimates for the major regions of the world for the 1960–1987 period. The average annual growth rate of this stock in the region was 2.0 percent, slightly below that in most other developing regions of the world, although higher than the world average and much higher than the industrial country average. Therefore, with respect to the stock of educated adults, Latin America and the Caribbean gained relative to the industrial world, but most of the rest of the developing world gained somewhat relative to Latin America and the Caribbean.[9] Because the region started this period with relatively low levels relative to the industrialized regions and with relatively high levels relative to other developing country regions, the position of Latin America and the Caribbean in the pattern of growth rates across regions reflects that regions with lower initial schooling stocks tended to have more rapid growth.

---

[8] Nevertheless, because Brazil had less growth in schooling investment in this period than predicted by international experience, the per capita performance of the region in this respect was substantially less positive than the experience of most countries.

[9] That most of the rest of the developing world gained relative to Latin America and the Caribbean is not inconsistent with the results in Table 3.5 because of the relatively low change in real per capita income in Latin America and the Caribbean.

## Box 3.4. The Impact of Economic Adjustment Programs on Human Resources of the Poor in Jamaica

A number of observers have claimed that recent economic recessions and associated macro structural adjustment programs in developing economies in Latin America and elsewhere have had substantial deleterious effects on the human resources of the poor in these societies. Therefore, they call for what Cornia, Jolly, and Stewart (1987, 1988) call "adjustment with a human face," i.e., with recognition of the possible impact of adjustment programs on the human resources of the poor, along with policies to limit such effects, and monitoring to be sure that such policies are successful. Despite confident assertions in such studies, however, considerable uncertainty remains about the impact of economic adjustment programs on health, nutrition, and schooling in developing countries.

The most visible of these studies are associated with UNICEF (Jolly and Cornia, 1984; UNICEF, 1984; Cornia, Jolly, and Stewart, 1987, 1988). These studies do not explicitly formalize the links between recession and/or economic adjustment and the human resources of the poor. Instead, they use secondary data to characterize some of the links to factors such as unemployment, the composition of government expenditures, and direct indicators of health, nutrition, and schooling.

The individual chapters in Jolly and Cornia (1984) provide a useful catalogue of trends but little information on changes stemming from recessions and economic adjustment programs. With a focus on possible negative impacts on children via recessions and economic adjustments, the authors appear to have pressed hard to find examples of deterioration in children's conditions but provide little direct evidence of it. To the contrary, Preston (1986), in his review of the Jolly and Cornia volume, stated that:

> What is remarkable is that the best data [on infant and child mortality] in most of the countries reviewed ... show continued improvements nearly everywhere. Nutritional status indicators also typically show improvement, and so do school enrollment figures, despite downturns in governmental expenditure on health and education in some countries (p. 376).

Preston (1986) therefore suggests that the appropriate conclusion, subject to conceptual and data difficulties, is that these studies indicate "how much can be achieved even in the face of unusual economic adversity—surely good news for social policy." He complains that instead of such emphasis, Jolly and Cornia (1984) have a "penchant for stressing the [few] negative trends... [which] receive the lion's share of attention in the introduction and summary." Thus, a set of studies that suggest little, or at least unproven, systematic impact of recession and economic adjustment on human resources is summarized as finding that adjustment policy usually multiplies negative recessionary impacts on the poor and vulnerable. Interesting in this connection are Jolly (1985) and the statements by Cornia in the summary to Jolly and Cornia (1984) that "the present crisis...has severely aggravated the situation of several social groups," "child welfare indicators...are unambiguous in pointing to a deterioration in child status," and "in most countries one observes...a serious deterioration in indicators of nutrition, health status, and school achievements."

The Jamaican experience regarding the impact of structural adjustment on social sectors and on the poor is one of the cases on which Cornia, Jolly, and Stewart (1987, 1988) base their conclusions; it has also been examined by Behrman and Deolalikar (1991). Detailed examination of the available data in the latter paper suggests that Cornia, Jolly, and Stewart (1987) overstate substantially the evidence of deterioration in the welfare of the poor in their summary of this case. Cornia and Stewart (1987) and Behrman and Deolalikar (1991) agree that the negative impact of the Jamaican structural adjustment was strongest in 1984 and 1985. Cornia and Stewart (1987) claim that the program in those years was "strongly deflationary," that "incomes per capita have been declining...since 1983," that "unemployment remained very high at 26 percent overall in 1984," that "educational expenditure per head of the population declined by 40 percent" (apparently for 1981–82 to 1985–86), and that hospital admissions of children suffering from malnutrition increased sharply in 1984 and 1985. But Behrman and Deolalikar (1991) raise questions about each of these assertions. Real GDP per capita, the consumer price index, the inflation rate, and the employment rate did not deviate significantly below the trend lines in 1984 and 1985. Educational expenditure per child age 5 to 14 declined by 8.6 percent between 1981–82 and 1985–86, not by the 40 percent that they claim (which apparently reflects the use of the general GDP deflator rather than the sector-specific deflator). Real food expenditures in 1984–85 increased significantly above the trend. Increases in the proportion of "malnutrition and/or gastroenteritis" cases among children admitted to the hospital fell from 23.5 percent to 19.0 percent from 1983 to 1984, which more than offset the increased shares for the separate categories of "malnutrition" (2.1 percent to 2.4 percent) and "gastroenteritis" (2.0 percent to 2.7 percent). This comparison between the UNICEF characterization of the Jamaican adjustment experience and that of Behrman and Deolalikar (1991) raises questions about the empirical foundations of the UNICEF claims.

*Sources:* Behrman and Deolalikar (1991); Cornia, Jolly, and Stewart (1987, 1988); Jolly (1985); Jolly and Cornia (1984); Preston (1986); and UNICEF (1984).

**Figure 3.5. Changes in Total Schooling versus Changes in Real Per Capita Income, 1965–87**

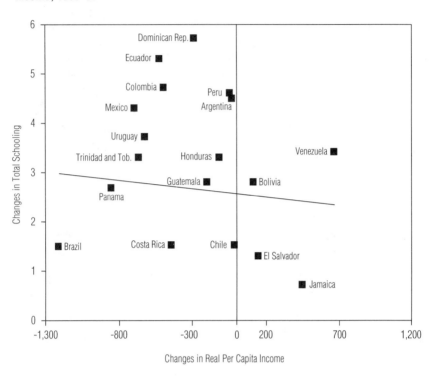

*Changes in Primary and Secondary School Enrollment Rates since 1965*

The changes in total schooling may be consistent with a wide range of compositional changes among enrollments at the primary, secondary, and tertiary levels. Table 3.7 gives the differences in the changes in primary, secondary, and tertiary school enrollments relative to those predicted by international experience, controlling for changes in real per capita income. The enrollment changes in the region clearly reflect a relative shift from primary to secondary and tertiary schooling.

For changes in primary schooling enrollment rates, 60 percent of the 20 countries for which the necessary data are available had increases less than those predicted by international experience, controlling for changes in real per capita income. Four countries in the region were more than 20 percent below the international prediction: Chile (40 percent below), Costa Rica (25 percent), Jamaica (25 percent), and El Salvador (23 percent). Another five were between 10 percent and 20 percent below the

**Table 3.5. Changes in Grades of Schooling in Latin America and Caribbean Countries, with International Comparison, 1965–87**

| Countries | Actual (Grades) | Difference from International Experience |
|---|---|---|
| | (1) | (2) |
| Dominican Republic | 5.7 | 3.0 |
| Honduras | 3.3 | 0.7 |
| Guatemala | 2.8 | 0.1 |
| Bolivia | 2.8 | 0.3 |
| El Salvador | 1.3 | −1.2 |
| Ecuador | 5.3 | 2.5 |
| Jamaica | 0.7 | −1.8 |
| Colombia | 4.7 | 2.0 |
| Costa Rica | 1.5 | −1.2 |
| Peru | 4.6 | 2.0 |
| Panama | 2.8 | −0.1 |
| Mexico | 4.3 | 1.5 |
| Brazil | 1.5 | −1.4 |
| Chile | 1.5 | −1.1 |
| Uruguay | 3.7 | 0.9 |
| Argentina | 4.6 | 2.0 |
| Venezuela | 3.4 | 1.1 |
| Trinidad and Tobago | 3.3 | 0.5 |

*Source:* Based on regression estimates by the author.

international prediction: Argentina, Brazil, Panama, Paraguay, and Uruguay. Only two countries were more than 20 percent above the international experience: the Dominican Republic (28 percent) and Haiti (26 percent). Another two were between 10 percent and 20 percent above: Colombia and Mexico.

For changes in secondary schooling enrollment rates, by contrast, 65 percent of the 20 countries for which the necessary data are available had increases greater than those predicted by international experience. Argentina, Trinidad and Tobago, and Peru had increases more than 20 percent above international experience, and another six countries—Chile, Colombia, Dominican Republic, Ecuador, Mexico, and Venezuela—had increases between 10 percent and 20 percent above. No countries in the region had increases more than 10 percent below the international experience.

For changes in the rates of tertiary schooling enrollment, also in contrast to those for primary schooling rates, more than 70 percent of the 18 countries for which the necessary data are available had increases greater than those predicted by international experience. One country—Uruguay—had an increase more than 20 percent above international experience, and another five—Argentina, Costa Rica, Ecuador, Panama, and

**Table 3.6.  Average Annual Growth of Years of Schooling in Major Regions of the World, 1960–87**
*(Per person between the ages of 15 and 64)*

|  | Percent per Year | | | |
|---|---|---|---|---|
|  | Primary | Secondary | Tertiary | Total |
| Industrial | −0.2 | 3.5 | 5.2 | 0.5 |
| Developing | 2.3 | 5.7 | 7.0 | 2.7 |
| East Asia | 2.2 | 5.7 | 5.4 | 2.7 |
| South Asia | 2.1 | 3.2 | 6.6 | 2.4 |
| Latin America | 1.5 | 5.8 | 7.1 | 2.0 |
| Sub-Saharan Africa | 3.3 | 8.4 | 10.2 | 3.7 |
| Developed Europe | 1.3 | 4.0 | 6.1 | 1.8 |
| Middle East/North Africa | 3.9 | 6.0 | 8.1 | 4.4 |
| World | 1.0 | 4.2 | 5.9 | 1.6 |

*Source:* Dubey, Swanson, and Nehru (1992).

Venezuela—had increases more than 10 percent above. But no countries in the region had increases more than 10 percent below the international experience.

In general terms, this relative shift from primary to secondary and tertiary school enrollments probably reflected greater inequality in access to schooling over time. What might be the implications of this shift for the stock of schooled adults in Latin America in comparison with the rest of the world? To recap, the growth rates by schooling levels for 1960–1987, as shown in Table 3.6, indicate that the secondary and tertiary schooling stock of adults in the region increased a little more rapidly than that of the rest of the developing world (and much more rapidly than in the industrial countries and the world as a whole). However, the primary schooling stock of adults in the region increased significantly more slowly than in most of the rest of the developing world (although still more rapidly than in the industrialized countries or than the world average). As noted earlier, Brunner (1989) argues that in the 1960s there were inadequate numbers of highly trained individuals in the region, so that the subsequent shift toward much greater training at the university level was warranted.

### Changes in Gender Gaps in Schooling since 1965

Gender gaps in schooling favoring males were reduced internationally, on average, by 0.4 grades in the 1965–1987 period after controlling for per capita income increases. Table 3.8 gives the differences from average international experience in the changes in these gender gaps for the 14 Latin

**Table 3.7. Changes in School Enrollment Rates in Latin America and the Caribbean, with International Comparison, 1965–87**
*(Percent)*

| Countries | Primary | | Secondary | | Tertiary | |
|---|---|---|---|---|---|---|
| | Actual | Difference from International Regressions | Actual | Difference from International Regressions | Actual | Difference from International Regressions |
| | (1) | (2) | (3) | (4) | (5) | (6) |
| Haiti | 45 | 26 | 12 | –7 | — | — |
| Dominican Republic | 46 | 28 | 35 | 14 | 17 | 9 |
| Honduras | 26 | 7 | 22 | 3 | 8 | –0 |
| Guatemala | 27 | 9 | 13 | –7 | 7 | –1 |
| Bolivia | 18 | –2 | 19 | 1 | 12 | 4 |
| El Salvador | –3 | –23 | 12 | –6 | 16 | — |
| Ecuador | 26 | 9 | 39 | 16 | 27 | 18 |
| Jamaica | –4 | –25 | 14 | –1 | 1 | –6 |
| Colombia | 30 | 13 | 39 | 17 | 11 | 2 |
| Paraguay | 0 | –17 | 17 | –6 | — | — |
| Costa Rica | –8 | –25 | 17 | –5 | 19 | 10 |
| Peru | 23 | 4 | 40 | 21 | 17 | 9 |
| Panama | 4 | –12 | 25 | 1 | 21 | 12 |
| Mexico | 26 | 10 | 36 | 12 | 12 | 3 |
| Brazil | –5 | –19 | 23 | –4 | 9 | –2 |
| Chile | –21 | –40 | 36 | 17 | 12 | 4 |
| Uruguay | 4 | –12 | 29 | 6 | 34 | 25 |
| Argentina | 9 | –10 | 46 | 28 | 25 | 17 |
| Venezuela | 13 | –9 | 27 | 14 | 20 | 14 |
| Trinidad and Tobago | 7 | –9 | 46 | 23 | 2 | –7 |

*Source:* Based on regression estimates by the author.

American and Caribbean countries for which data are available. Such gaps were reduced relative to international experience in half of these countries: the Dominican Republic (0.8 grades), Bolivia (0.5 grades), Jamaica (0.4 grades), Peru (0.4 grades), Trinidad and Tobago (0.4 grades), El Salvador (0.3 grades), and Venezuela (0.1 grades). For the others, the gender gap increased relative to international experience, with relatively large increases in Colombia and Argentina (0.5 grades) and Costa Rica (0.4 grades).

Underlying the relative changes by gender in schooling are, once again, some compositional changes. For primary school enrollment, gender gaps in the region were reduced more than international experience (controlling for per capita income changes) only in four of the 19 countries: Bolivia (8 percent), Peru (8 percent), El Salvador (4 percent), and Jamaica (2 percent); the gaps changed as much as international experience in Trinidad and Tobago; and they increased relative to international expe-

**Table 3.8. Changes in Gender Gaps (Male–Female) for Schooling and Primary and Secondary Enrollments, with International Comparison, 1965–87**

| Countries | Schooling (Grades) | | Primary Enrollment Rate (%) | | Secondary Enrollment Rate (%) | |
|---|---|---|---|---|---|---|
| | Actual | Difference from International Regressions | Actual | Difference from International Regressions | Actual | Difference from International Regressions |
| | (1) | (2) | (3) | (4) | (5) | (6) |
| Haiti | — | — | 0 | 6 | −2 | −3 |
| Dominican Republic | −1.3 | −0.8 | −4 | 2 | −18 | −18 |
| Honduras | — | — | −6 | 0 | — | — |
| Guatemala | — | — | 4 | 10 | — | — |
| Bolivia | −1.0 | −0.5 | −14 | −8 | −2 | −3 |
| El Salvador | −0.7 | −0.3 | −10 | −4 | −2 | −3 |
| Ecuador | −0.5 | 0.1 | −4 | 2 | −4 | −3 |
| Jamaica | −0.8 | −0.4 | −8 | −2 | −6 | −8 |
| Colombia | 0.0 | 0.5 | 2 | 8 | −2 | −1 |
| Paraguay | — | — | −6 | 0 | 0 | 1 |
| Costa Rica | −0.1 | 0.4 | 0 | 6 | −2 | 1 |
| Peru | −0.8 | −0.4 | −14 | −8 | 0 | −1 |
| Panama | −0.4 | 0.2 | −2 | 4 | −4 | −1 |
| Mexico | −0.5 | 0.1 | 0 | 6 | −8 | −2 |
| Brazil | — | — | — | — | 12 | −7 |
| Chile | −0.2 | 0.2 | −6 | 0 | 2 | −9 |
| Uruguay | — | — | 2 | 8 | — | 2 |
| Argentina | 0.0 | 0.5 | 2 | 8 | −2 | — |
| Venezuela | −0.5 | −0.1 | 0 | 7 | −8 | −11 |
| Trinidad and Tobago | −1.0 | −0.4 | −6 | −0 | −10 | −9 |

*Source:* Based on regression estimates by the author.

rience in the other 14 countries. For secondary school enrollment, gender gaps in the region were reduced more than international experience in 15 of the 17 countries in the Latin American and Caribbean region for which data are available (the two exceptions being Chile and Paraguay, with increases of less than 2 percent relative to international experience). Particularly large reductions in gender gaps in secondary school enrollment changes relative to international experience were experienced by the Dominican Republic (18 percent), Venezuela (11 percent), Brazil (9 percent), Trinidad and Tobago (9 percent), Jamaica (8 percent), and Mexico (7 percent). Thus, the region tended to have about average international reductions in gender gaps in schooling since 1965 compared with international experience, but with relatively limited gains for females compared with males for primary schooling and relatively large gains for females for secondary schooling.

## Health, Nutrition, Life Expectancy and Mortality

### Recent Life Expectancies at Birth

Life expectancy at birth is often used as a summary measure of health and nutrition conditions. The better a country's health and nutrition conditions, the longer a person's expected life in that country. Figure 3.6 plots recent life expectancies at birth versus real per capita income for countries in the Latin American and Caribbean region for which data are available (also see Table 3.9 for data by gender). Costa Rica and Jamaica have the highest life expectancies at birth in the region, and Haiti and Bolivia by far the lowest. Since life expectancies are positively correlated with per capita income across countries (as indicated by the international regression lines in the figure) it is therefore interesting to ask how life expectancies in particular countries compare with predictions based on international experience, given their per capita income levels.

Life expectancy at birth for females in 1988 in the following countries was at least five years above the levels predicted by international regressions that control for nonlinear effects of per capita income: Jamaica (14.1 years above the regression line), Costa Rica (12.9 years), Chile (11.8 years), Colombia (9.5 years), the Dominican Republic (9.1 years), Mexico (8.5 years), Uruguay (8.3 years), Panama (7.8 years), Paraguay (7.5 years), Ecuador (6.8 years), El Salvador (6.8 years), Honduras (6.3 years), and Argentina (6.1 years). It was near the predicted level for Haiti (0.1 years above), and was below the line for Bolivia (–2.0 years). Life expectancy at birth for males in 1988 in the following countries was at least five years above the levels predicted by international regressions that control for nonlinear effects of per capita income: Jamaica (13.7 years above the regression line), Costa Rica (12.9 years), Chile (8.7 years), the Dominican Republic (8.4 years), Colombia (8.2 years), Panama (8.1 years), Paraguay (7.2 years), Ecuador (6.5 years), Honduras (5.7 years), Uruguay (5.7 years), and Mexico (5.6 years). It was less than a year above in Brazil (0.9 years), and was below in Haiti (–0.8 years) and Bolivia (–3.8 years). In comparison with international experience, controlling for per capita income, life expectancies in the Latin American and Caribbean region are relatively high, despite considerable diversity and the relatively low levels in Bolivia and, to a lesser extent, in Haiti.

### Gender Gaps in Life Expectancies at Birth

In every country in Latin America and the Caribbean for which data are available, female life expectancies at birth exceed those for males, so the

**Figure 3.6. Life Expectancy at Birth versus Real Per Capita Income, 1988**

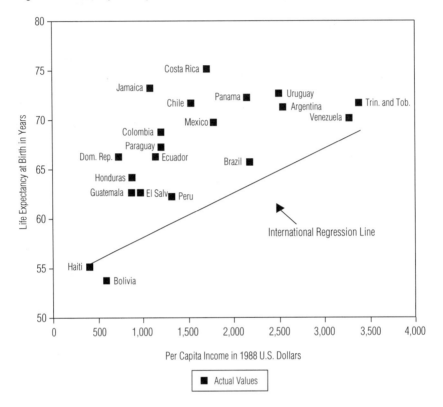

gender gaps (defined, consistent with our earlier use in regard to schooling, as male minus female) are negative. As can be seen from Table 3.9, for about two-thirds of the countries in the region, these gender gaps in life expectancies are four or five years,[10] but they are much greater in El Salvador (nine years) and somewhat greater in Chile, Mexico, and Uruguay (seven years) and in Argentina and Venezuela (six years). There is some debate regarding the extent to which such gender gaps reflect biological gender differences rather than behavioral differences. But the substantial increases in life expectancies in the region and elsewhere in recent decades suggest that behavioral factors are quite important.

Because gender gaps in life expectancies at birth are related to per capita income, it again is of interest to ask how recent gender gaps in life

---

[10] For Nicaragua, which is not included in the figure because of the absence of income data, the gap is reported to be three years (World Bank, 1990).

**Table 3.9. Female and Male Life Expectancies at Birth, with International Comparison, 1988**

| Countries | Female | | Male | |
| --- | --- | --- | --- | --- |
| | Actual | Difference from International Regressions | Actual | Difference from International Regressions |
| | (1) | (2) | (3) | (4) |
| Haiti | 57 | 0 | 53 | −1 |
| Dominican Republic | 68 | 9 | 64 | 8 |
| Honduras | 66 | 6 | 62 | 6 |
| Guatemala | 65 | 5 | 60 | 4 |
| Bolivia | 56 | −2 | 51 | −4 |
| El Salvador | 67 | 7 | 58 | 1 |
| Ecuador | 68 | 7 | 64 | 7 |
| Jamaica | 75 | 14 | 71 | 14 |
| Colombia | 71 | 10 | 66 | 8 |
| Paraguay | 69 | 8 | 65 | 7 |
| Costa Rica | 77 | 13 | 73 | 13 |
| Peru | 64 | 2 | 60 | 2 |
| Panama | 74 | 8 | 70 | 8 |
| Mexico | 73 | 9 | 66 | 6 |
| Brazil | 68 | 2 | 63 | 1 |
| Chile | 75 | 12 | 68 | 9 |
| Uruguay | 76 | 8 | 69 | 6 |
| Argentina | 74 | 6 | 68 | 5 |
| Venezuela | 73 | 2 | 67 | 1 |
| Trinidad and Tobago | 74 | 3 | 69 | 3 |

*Source:* Based on regression estimates by the author.

expectancies for various countries in the region compare with those predicted from international experience (Table 3.10, column 1.) The general tendency in the region is for gender gaps in life expectancies to favor females more than predicted by international experience—this is true in four-fifths of the 20 countries for which data permit such a calculation. This tendency is particularly evident in El Salvador (favoring females by 5.5 years more than predicted), Mexico (3 years), and Uruguay (2.5 years). Within the region, females are favored less than predicted by international experience only in Colombia (1.3 years less than predicted), Haiti (0.9 years), and Panama (0.3 years), with Costa Rica having the same gender difference as predicted by international experience.

As noted earlier, it is frequently conjectured that aggregate measures of human resources are associated with the distribution of income and political power. The unavailability of roughly comparable income distribu-

**Table 3.10. Gender Gaps (Male–Female) in Life Expectancies at Birth in 1988 and Changes since 1965 in Latin America and the Caribbean, Controlling for Level or Changes in Real Per Capita Income**

| Country | Gender Gap (Male–Female) in Life Expectancy at Birth in 1988 | Change in Life Expectancies since 1965 | | Changes in Gender Gap in Life since 1965 |
|---|---|---|---|---|
| | | Female | Male | |
| | (1) | (2) | (3) | (4) |
| Haiti | 0.9 | 0.5 | 0.2 | −0.2 |
| Dominican Republic | −0.7 | 1.5 | 1.3 | −0.2 |
| Honduras | −0.6 | 5.5 | 5.2 | −0.2 |
| Guatemala | −1.5 | 5.5 | 3.3 | −2.2 |
| Bolivia | −1.8 | −0.6 | 0.2 | 0.8 |
| El Salvador | −5.5 | 1.4 | −3.8 | −5.2 |
| Ecuador | −0.4 | 1.6 | 0.3 | −1.2 |
| Jamaica | −0.4 | −1.6 | −1.9 | −0.2 |
| Colombia | 1.3 | 0.5 | 0.3 | −0.2 |
| Paraguay | −0.3 | −7.4 | −6.7 | 0.8 |
| Costa Rica | 0.0 | 1.5 | 1.3 | −0.2 |
| Peru | −0.3 | 2.5 | 2.2 | −0.2 |
| Panama | 0.3 | −0.4 | −0.6 | −0.2 |
| Mexico | −3.0 | 2.6 | −0.6 | −3.2 |
| Brazil | −0.7 | −0.3 | −0.5 | −0.2 |
| Chile | −3.1 | 2.5 | 2.2 | −0.2 |
| Uruguay | −2.5 | −5.4 | −4.7 | 0.8 |
| Argentina | −1.5 | −4.6 | −3.8 | 0.8 |
| Venezuela | −1.1 | −1.7 | −2.9 | −1.2 |
| Trinidad and Tobago | −0.1 | −2.4 | −2.7 | −0.2 |

*Source:* Based on regression estimates by the author.

tion data for many countries in the region limits the extent to which this conjecture can be empirically explored. But it is worth noting that there is a −0.6 bivariate correlation between the extent to which the gender gap in recent life expectancies at birth exceeds that predicted by international experience and the recent income share of the bottom quintile of households in the countries for which such data are available.

### *Long-Run Changes in Life Expectancies at Birth since 1965*

Life expectancies at birth have increased worldwide since 1965, even controlling for per capita income growth: by 8.8 years for males and 9.6 for females. In most of the developing world, including Latin America and the Caribbean, these changes are part of the demographic transition in which the age structure of the population changes from one in which by far the largest groups are the youngest groups to one in which most age groups from 0 to 60 now have nearly equal population sizes. That is, the population age pyramid for the region is in the midst of changing from one with a very broad base in the youngest ages in the 1950s to one projected, in another 40 years, to have a narrower base similar to that of, say, England's. That means that the number of young dependents per working age population unit is declining substantially, although the number of elderly dependents per working age population unit is rising. With such changes, of course, there are concomitant changes in relative demands on schooling systems and in the nature of health problems, with the latter shifting away from infants and children and toward the health problems of adults and the elderly.

Table 3.10 (columns 2 and 3) indicates how life expectancies at birth in Latin American and Caribbean countries have changed relative to this international experience. About half the Latin American and Caribbean countries had improvements in male life expectancies at birth since 1965 greater than the international experience, controlling for changes in per capita income, with relatively large increases in Honduras (5.2 years greater than the international regression), Guatemala (3.3 years), Chile (2.2 years), and Peru (2.2 years) and with relatively small increases in Paraguay (–6.7 years vis-à-vis the international regression line), Uruguay (–4.7 years), Argentina (–3.8 years), El Salvador (–3.8 years), Venezuela (–2.9 years), and Trinidad and Tobago (–2.7 years). A larger proportion of Latin American and Caribbean countries—about two-thirds—had improvements in female life expectancies at births since 1965 greater than the international experience. Honduras and Guatemala had the largest improvements in female life expectancies, about five years greater than the international experience, with Chile, Mexico, and Peru showing improvements of about 2.5 years relative to international experience. Only a third of the countries had improvements in female life expectancies at birth less than the international experience, but in three contiguous southern countries, these improvements were substantially less: Paraguay (7.4 years less), Uruguay (5.4 years less), and Argentina (4.6 years less).

### Changes in Gender Gaps in Life Expectancies at Birth since 1965

These patterns suggest that the region has had changes in the gender gaps of life expectancies at birth since 1965 in comparison with international experience. Table 3.10 (column 4) gives these changes. For 80 percent of the Latin American and Caribbean countries for which data are available, life expectancies at birth increased more for females than for males in comparison with international experience—with El Salvador (5.2 years) and Mexico (3.2 years) being especially noteworthy in this respect.

## Recent Infant Mortality Rates

Initial increases in life expectancy at birth, from low levels, typically have been dominated by reductions in infant mortality rates. Further increases, after higher levels of life expectancies have been attained, tend to be the result of reduced mortality rates for older adults. Therefore, it is of interest to consider the infant mortality rates in Latin America and the Caribbean to gain some insight into their importance for the relatively high life expectancies noted earlier. Table 3.11 and Figure 3.7 give recent infant mortality rates per 1,000 live births in the region versus per capita income, with the international regression line for reference. The rates vary substantially across countries, with more than one in 10 live births in Haiti and Bolivia ending in infant death at one extreme, and at the other extreme between one and two infant deaths per 1,000 live births in Chile, Costa Rica, Jamaica, Panama, Trinidad and Tobago, and Uruguay. The infant mortality rates are, however, strongly inversely associated with total life expectancy at birth (r = –0.9).

The international regression line in the figure indicates a definite downward tendency for infant mortality as per capita income increases. Part of the variation across countries in the region stems from variations in per capita income, but a substantial proportion of the variation in recent infant mortality experience remains even when controlling for per capita income.

It is noteworthy that three-fourths of the countries in the region have infant mortality rates below the international regression line. Some have rates substantially below international experience, particularly Jamaica (55 deaths per 1,000 live births below), Chile and Costa Rica (46 deaths per 1,000 below), and Colombia, Panama, Paraguay, and Trinidad and Tobago (about 35 deaths per 1,000 below). At the other extreme, Haiti is 45 and Bolivia is 20 deaths per 1,000 live births above the international experience. We should also note that among countries with fairly close recent per capita incomes and life expectancies at birth, there are some cases in which the infant mortality rates differ a fair amount. For instance, Venezuela has relatively high infant mortality in comparison with Trinidad and Tobago, as does Honduras relative to Guatemala and El Salvador. This pattern implies that Venezuela has relatively high infant and lower adult mortality rates in comparison with Trinidad and Tobago, as does Honduras relative to Guatemala and El Salvador.

## Declines in Infant Mortality Rates since 1965

Infant mortality rates have strongly declined worldwide since 1965: by 49 deaths per 1,000 live births even with control for changes in per capita

Table 3.11.  Infant Mortality Rates per 1,000 Live Births in 1988 and Changes in Infant Mortality Rates in 1965–88 in Latin America and Caribbean, Actual and Relative to International Experience

| Countries | Infant Mortality Rates per 1,000 Live Births, 1988 | | Changes in Infant Mortality Rates per 1,000 Live Births, 1965–1988 | |
|---|---|---|---|---|
| | Actual | Relative to International Experience | Actual | Relative to International Experience |
| | (1) | (2) | (3) | (4) |
| Haiti | 116 | 24 | −62 | −13 |
| Dominican Republic | 63 | −22 | −47 | 2 |
| Honduras | 68 | −13 | −60 | −11 |
| Guatemala | 57 | −23 | −55 | −6 |
| Bolivia | 108 | 20 | −52 | −3 |
| El Salvador | 57 | −23 | −63 | −13 |
| Ecuador | 62 | −14 | −50 | −2 |
| Jamaica | 11 | −66 | −38 | 12 |
| Colombia | 39 | −35 | −47 | 1 |
| Paraguay | 41 | −33 | −32 | 16 |
| Costa Rica | 18 | −46 | −54 | −6 |
| Peru | 86 | 14 | −44 | 5 |
| Panama | 22 | −34 | −34 | 13 |
| Mexico | 46 | −17 | −36 | 12 |
| Brazil | 61 | 5 | −43 | 3 |
| Chile | 20 | −48 | −81 | −32 |
| Uruguay | 23 | −27 | −24 | 24 |
| Argentina | 31 | −18 | −27 | 22 |
| Venezuela | 35 | −3 | −30 | 21 |
| Trinidad and Tobago | 16 | −21 | −26 | 22 |

Source: Based on regression estimates by the author.

income. Among Latin American and Caribbean countries, relatively large declines have been experienced in Chile (a reduction of 81 infant deaths per 1,000 live births) and Honduras (a reduction of 72 deaths per 1,000 births); and there have been relatively small declines in the three contiguous southern countries of Argentina, Paraguay, and Uruguay (reductions of about 25 infant deaths per 1,000 live births).

## Recent Gender Differences in Risk of Dying by Age 5 per 1,000 Births

In recent international experience, the risk of dying by age 5, on the average, controlling for per capita income, is 14 deaths per 1,000 births higher for males than for females. That is, the gender gap favors females. Table 3.12 gives the recent mortality rates per 1,000 live births for females and males and the difference between these rates, as well as the deviations from international

**Figure 3.7. Infant Mortality Rates versus Real Per Capita Income, 1988**

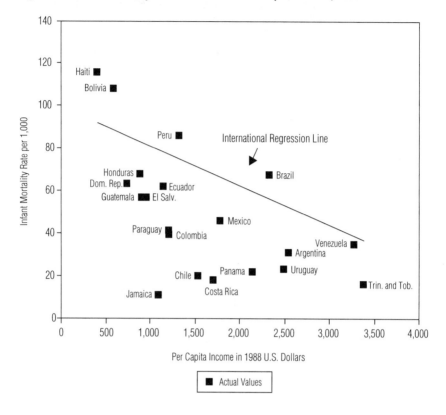

experience. The risk of dying by age 5 is also higher for males than for females in Latin America and the Caribbean—from four deaths per 1,000 births for Costa Rica, Nicaragua, and Trinidad and Tobago, to 18 and 21 deaths per 1,000 births for Bolivia and Haiti. But this risk is higher than predicted for males for only 40 percent of the countries in the region (for countries for which there are data). For Haiti (seven more deaths per 1,000 births for males than females) and Bolivia (five more), the experience has been particularly unfavorable to males. At the other extreme, the mortality experience has been relatively unfavorable for females in Jamaica (eight more deaths), Costa Rica (seven), the Dominican Republic (six), and Ecuador and Mexico (five).

### Recent Urban-Rural and Area Differences in Infant and Child Mortality and Health

The region has a wide range of rural-urban infant and under-5 mortality rate differentials (Table 3.13). In some countries, the rural rates are lower

**Table 3.12. Gender Differences in Mortality Rates by Age 5 per 1,000 Live Births in Latin America and the Caribbean, with International Comparison, 1988**

| | Mortality Rates by Age 5 per 1,000 Live Births | | | | | |
| | Female | | Male | | Male–Female | |
| Countries | Actual | Difference from International Regressions | Actual | Difference from International Regressions | Actual | Difference from International Regressions |
|---|---|---|---|---|---|---|
| | (1) | (2) | (3) | (4) | (5) | (6) |
| Haiti | 14 | 12 | 16 | 19 | 21 | 7 |
| Dominican Republic | 73 | −40 | 80 | −46 | 7 | −6 |
| Honduras | 71 | −37 | 85 | −36 | 14 | 1 |
| Guatemala | 63 | −44 | 77 | −42 | 14 | 1 |
| Bolivia | 14 | 22 | 16 | 27 | 18 | 5 |
| El Salvador | 63 | −42 | 77 | −41 | 14 | 1 |
| Ecuador | 74 | −25 | 81 | −31 | 7 | −5 |
| Jamaica | 10 | −91 | 14 | −100 | 4 | −8 |
| Colombia | 20 | −67 | 25 | −74 | 5 | −7 |
| Paraguay | 44 | −54 | 56 | −54 | 12 | −0 |
| Costa Rica | 18 | −64 | 22 | −71 | 4 | −7 |
| Peru | 11 | 11 | 11 | 8 | 9 | −3 |
| Panama | 21 | −49 | 29 | −51 | 8 | −3 |
| Mexico | 51 | −29 | 57 | −34 | 6 | −5 |
| Brazil | 62 | −7 | 75 | −4 | 13 | 3 |
| Chile | 20 | −67 | 25 | −74 | 5 | −7 |
| Uruguay | 22 | −39 | 28 | −43 | 6 | −4 |
| Argentina | 30 | −29 | 40 | 29 | 10 | 0 |
| Venezuela | 36 | −6 | 45 | −6 | 9 | 0 |
| Trinidad and Tobago | 15 | −25 | 20 | −29 | 5 | −4 |

*Source:* Based on regression estimates by the author.

than the urban rates (Colombia, the Dominican Republic, and Trinidad and Tobago), while in other countries, rural rates are much higher than urban rates (Bolivia, Brazil, Mexico, Peru). The urban-rural infant mortality rates varied little in Bolivia, Colombia, and Paraguay in comparison with other countries (Table 3.14).

For access to health care, the indicators tend to be better for urban areas (exceptions include polio and DPT immunizations in Trinidad and Tobago and measles immunizations in the Dominican Republic).

## Training

Training is a very important form of human resource investment, with some advantages over basic schooling and child health and nutrition in

**Table 3.13.  Urban vs. Rural Variability of Health Indicators**

| Country | Survey Year | Area | Infant Mortality Rate[a] | Under 5 Mortality Rate | Immunizations[b] | | | | Child Global Malnutrition[c] | Access to Maternal Care at Birth[d] |
|---|---|---|---|---|---|---|---|---|---|---|
| | | | | | BCG | Measles | Polio3 | DPT3 | | |
| Dominican Rep. | 1986 | Urban | 69 | — | 58 | 18 | 31 | 40 | 10 | 95 |
| | | Rural | 66 | — | 53 | 19 | 26 | 32 | 17 | 83 |
| Guatemala | 1987 | Urban | 65 | 99 | 64 | 75 | 62 | 60 | 26 | — |
| | | Rural | 85 | 130 | 47 | 67 | 49 | 43 | 37 | — |
| Bolivia | 1985 | Urban | 79 | 114 | 69 | 74 | 65 | 56 | 11 | 58 |
| | | Rural | 112 | 168 | 53 | 70 | 46 | 44 | 16 | 18 |
| El Salvador | 1988 | Metropolitan | 42 | 42 | 86 | 86 | 88 | 59 | — | 88 |
| | | Urban | 40 | 63 | 85 | 82 | 66 | 65 | — | 65 |
| | | Rural | 56 | 74 | 72 | 79 | 61 | 61 | — | 34 |
| Ecuador | 1987 | Urban | 52 | 65 | — | — | — | — | — | — |
| | | Rural | 77 | 112 | — | — | — | — | — | — |
| Colombia | 1990 | Urban | 29 | 36 | — | — | — | — | — | — |
| | | Rural | 23 | 33 | — | — | — | — | — | — |
| Colombia | 1986 | Urban | 39 | 48 | 52 | 41 | 44 | 44 | 10 | — |
| | | Rural | 41 | 58 | 50 | 35 | 41 | 41 | 15 | — |
| Paraguay | 1990 | Urban | 32 | 43 | 86 | 64 | 62 | 64 | 10 | — |
| | | Rural | 38 | 38 | 51 | 51 | 43 | 42 | 22 | — |
| Peru | 1991/ 1992 | Urban | 47 | 67 | 93 | 76 | 75 | 75 | 6 | — |
| | | Rural | 90 | 131 | 81 | 63 | 53 | 53 | 18 | — |
| Mexico | 1987 | pop. <2,500 | 79 | 104 | — | — | — | — | — | 67 |
| | | 2,500–19,999 | 62 | 78 | — | — | — | — | — | 80 |
| | | 20,000 + | 40 | 48 | — | — | — | — | — | 80 |
| | | Metropolitan | 29 | 32 | — | — | — | — | — | 80 |

**Table 3.13.  (continued)**

| Country | Survey Year | Area | Infant Mortality Rate[a] | Under 5 Mortality Rate | Immunizations[b] | | | | Child Global Malnutrition[c] | Access to Maternal Care at Birth[d] |
|---|---|---|---|---|---|---|---|---|---|---|
| | | | | | BCG | Measles | Polio3 | DPT3 | | |
| Brazil | 1986 | Urban | 76 | 88 | 82 | 88 | 90 | 86 | 10[e] | 92 |
| | | Rural | 107 | 121 | 59 | 75 | 72 | 65 | 16[c] | 58 |
| Trinidad and Tobago | 1987 | Urban | 36 | 41 | — | 52 | 59 | 85 | 5 | 96 |
| | | Rural | 28 | 30 | — | 38 | 88 | 88 | 8 | 96 |

[a] Number of infants, per thousand live births, who die before reaching one year of age.
[b] Percentage of children immunized. For Bolivia, Brazil, Colombia (1990), Guatemala, Paraguay, and Peru, figures are for the 12–23 month age group. For Colombia (1986), Dominican Republic, El Salvador, and Trinidad and Tobago, figures are for the under 5 age group.
[c] Refers to 0–59 month age group in most cases, although the age group varies for a few countries. Child global malnutrition is expressed as a percentage of the child population (usually those under 5 years of age, although age groups vary in some cases) who are two or more standard deviations from the average weight for their age.
[d] Percentage of births occurring in hospitals, clinics, or other professional medical establishments.
[e] Brazilian malnutrition figures refer to the Northeast only.
*Source:* Psacharopoulos et al. (1992, Table 5.1) as calculated from Westinghouse Demographic and Health Surveys, with the exception of El Salvador (1988), which was conducted by the Salvadoran Demographic Association with the assistance of the U.S. Center for Disease Control.

**Table 3.14. Regional Variability of Infant Mortality Rates per 1,000 Live Births**

| Country | Survey Year | High | Region | Low | Region |
|---------|-------------|------|--------|-----|--------|
| Guatemala | 1987 | 119 | Central | 48 | North |
| Bolivia | 1986 | 96 | Altiplano | 84 | Llanos |
| Ecuador | 1989 | 67 | Cotopaxi | 18 | Galapagos |
| Colombia | 1990 | 40 | Pacific | 23 | Bogota |
| Paraguay | 1990 | 42 | North | 28 | Greater Asuncion |
| Peru | 1992 | 103 | Inca | 30 | Lima |
| Mexico | 1977–87 | 74 | Northeast | 40 | North Central |
| Brazil | 1986 | 142 | Northeast | 44 | Southern |
| Venezuela | 1986 | 53 | T.T. Amazons | 17 | Distrito Federal |

Sources: Psacharopoulos et al. (1992, Table 5.3) based on data from the Westinghouse DHS surveys except Brazil, Ecuador, and Venezuela. Brazil: IMR are for infant classification of two years and under. IBGE, *Perfil Estatístico de Crianças e Mães no Brasil; Aspectos de Saúde e Nutrição das Crianças no Brasil 1989.* Brazil: IBGE, 1992. Ecuador: INEC, *Yearly Vital Statistics;* Ecuador: INEC, 1989. Mexico: See 1987 Mexico DHS for complete breakdown of regions. Many states were left out of regional tabulation. Venezuela: *Venezuela Poverty Study: From Generalized Subsidies to Targeted Programs.* World Bank Report No. 9114–VE, June 1991.

that the gestation lags before productivity is affected are relatively shorter for training. Enrollments in publicly financed national training systems in Latin America grew tenfold between 1955 and 1985, and in the late 1980s public spending on training accounted for as much as 0.5 percent of GNP (Jiménez, Kugler, and Horn 1989). Aggregate data, however, are not available to summarize the condition of training programs in the region in the same manner as we summarized schooling attainment and indicators of health and nutrition. Therefore, this section summarizes the conditions of training only in Brazil, Chile, and Colombia.

## Brazil

There are two major vocational education and training institutions in Brazil: the national industrial apprenticeship service, SENAI *(Serviço Nacional de Aprendizagem Industrial)*; and SENAC, the commercial counterpart of SENAI.[11]

SENAI was created in the early 1940s and since then has had a prominent role in training workers. Enrollment in SENAI in 1991 stood at about 950,000, and the cumulative total enrollment since 1970 is more than nine million. Management of SENAI is the responsibility of the National Confederation of Industries (CNI) and the local federations of industries in each Brazilian state. SENAI maintains very close relations with

[11] This summary is based on Barros (1992).

firms and employer associations, and some of its courses are offered within firms or are firm specific. The main source of SENAI's funding is a 1 percent tax on the payroll of all firms (1.2 percent for enterprises with more than 500 workers). Firms can be exempted from the tax if they sign agreements to have SENAI provide specific training services, which have grown relatively quickly.

Training includes long courses (880 to 960 hours per year), sometimes combined with apprenticeships and shorter courses (45 to 180 hours) designed to enhance qualifications of workers in specific occupations. Over time, a shift has occurred from long courses and apprenticeships toward short courses. The great majority of SENAI students in the short courses are employed workers sent to SENAI by their firms. The schooling level of SENAI students when they enroll is high relative to that of the general population.

About 70 percent of students in the long SENAI courses with an apprenticeship (CAI, *Curso de Aprendizagem Industrial*) were employed one month after completing the course, with about 60 percent of those with jobs after one month using skills learned at SENAI. A number of months later about 80 percent were working, although the percentage of those using skills learned at SENAI dropped to 42 percent.

The evolution of occupations and wages suggests that the graduates of SENAI who had shifted away from using specific skills learned at SENAI were able to use their general education to perform different tasks. About 50 percent of the students in the very short course (CEP, *Curso de Especialização Profissional*) were employed at the start of the course, and about 80 percent were employed one month after the course ended. But only 50 percent of those employed one month after the course were using skills learned in the course, and this percentage fell to 35 percent a number of months later. Amadeo et al. (1993) note that this is a low proportion, given that the students are supposed to learn a certain task or occupation. About 90 percent of the students in courses for employed adults were employed at the start of the course, and about the same percentage were employed a month after it ended. But only 18 percent of those students were using skills learned in the course one month thereafter—a very low percentage, given the objective of learning specific skills.

The majority of students in the long courses continue with other studies after finishing the SENAI courses, as do a substantial number of those in the short courses. The subsequent evolution of students' occupations generally is good, with increases over time in the share of graduates who are promoted (although fewer CEP night students are promoted). Likewise, the graduates tend to experience wage increases (although not the graduates from the courses for employed adults). The graduates are more likely to work in medium-sized and large firms—particularly in electronics, metallurgy, metalworking, and transport equipment—than are workers on average.

SENAC is the analogue of SENAI for the service and commercial sectors. Funding is similar, with a 1 percent payroll tax on firms in the service sector. But exemptions for firm-specific training are not common. SENAC also is much more closely associated with the federations of commerce and much less closely associated with individual firms. Therefore, SENAC's clients are not the firms and their employees, but the students themselves. Data on SENAC are much more scarce than data on SENAI. The students are largely females younger than 20 with high levels of schooling (in 1989, 88 percent had completed primary school and 54 percent had completed secondary school). In contrast to SENAI, most students were not working during the course, and many had never worked before. The wages of employed graduates have been relatively low, with only 23 percent receiving more than three times the minimum wage. During the 1980s, in contrast with SENAI, SENAC increased the relative emphasis on longer courses and on more hours per student.

## Chile[12]

Since the 1950s, Chile has consistently recognized that training has positive benefits and requires government support to be effective. In the 1950s, because of a concern in Chile about worker training, CORFO *(Corporación de Fomento de la Producción)* entered into a technical cooperation agreement with the government of the United States. One direct effect of this agreement was the creation of SERCOTEC *(Servicio de Cooperación Técnica.)* From 1960 to 1966, SERCOTEC's Department of Professional Formation trained about 2 percent of the Chilean work force.

In 1966, these expanding training activities led the Chilean government to establish an autonomous organization, INACAP (*Instituto Nacional de Capacitación*) in which training activities were centralized. INACAP received technical assistance and resources from Germany, England, and other developed countries in designing its programs. From the beginning, INACAP directed its training efforts primarily toward the lowest levels of the occupational pyramid, with courses that concentrated on the agriculture, mining, and manufacturing sectors. The principal objective of these courses was to develop individuals without qualifications into

---

[12] This description is from Paredes, Riveros, Balmaceda, Manzur, and Núñez (1993), who discuss worker training in Chile in more detail.

mid-level skilled workers. INACAP also began to develop technical training, particularly for the mechanical and electrical industries, in cooperation with various national universities.

A basic change in the extent of training centralization took place in the 1970s. In 1973, with the change in government and the shift toward a national development strategy that depends much more on the private sector, INACAP was reorganized. The primary shift was away from centralized provision of training by the state to decentralized training oriented toward the needs of enterprises, in response to the perception that the centralized system had not provided trainers who matched the demands of the productive sectors.

In keeping with this change, SENCE *(Servicio de Capacitación y Empleo)* was created in 1976 in the Ministry of Labor as a coordinating and supervising agency, and in 1977 INACAP was placed on a self-financing footing and its preferential treatment as a state training agency was eliminated. SENCE was designed to subsidize and supervise private training programs, to supervise the provision of labor market information through government and private employment offices, and to establish technical norms. Since 1988, it has also administered an apprentice program. SENCE recognizes and supervises a number of established training organizations (OTE, *Organismos Técnicos de Ejecución*), including INACAP, some universities, professional institutes, technical training centers, and technical and professional schools. These organizations are financed by tuition payments. SENCE also recognizes seven (as of the end of 1991) nonprofit private sector and regional enterprise associations (OTIR, *Organismos Técnicos Intermedios*) designed to promote training for their member firms. The OTIRs are not allowed to train workers themselves but must contract with an OTE for training. The OTIRs are funded by members' contributions, which the government counts as training costs, with tax benefits; the OTIRs are required to spend at least 80 percent of these funds on training.

In Chile, the government subsidizes decentralized training through several programs. Four types of state-subsidized training programs are discussed below.

The first and largest types of training programs are for workers in enterprises. The number of annual participants in these programs grew from about 23,000 in 1977 to almost 100,000 in 1980, and to almost 200,000 in 1990. The subsidized expenditure per participant increased from about US$80 in 1977 to a peak of US$158 in 1981. This declined to US$80 in 1986, and increased again to US$97 in 1990. There are restrictions on the use of these subsidies; i.e., a ceiling on the hourly cost of training per participant (about US$5 in 1992), which limits the prices of the OTE. The maximum subsidy is 100 percent of the value of training costs for low-wage workers and 50 percent of value of training costs for workers receiving more than 10 minimum wages (a minimum wage was about US$100 per month in 1992). The purpose of this differential is to direct subsidized training toward lower-skilled workers. Firms also receive a tax deduction of up to 1 percent of payroll (or three minimum wages over the same time period, whichever is greater) for the cost of training from an OTE or developed by the firm itself, if it has the prior approval of SENSE.

Second, there are also training scholarships financed from the national budget for SENCE-approved training for those not working in firms. These scholarships are for the unemployed, for those searching for work for the first time, and for independent workers registered in municipal employment offices. The scholarship recipients are trained by an OTE that wins an open contract competition based importantly on costs. The number of scholarship recipients increased from about 33,000 in 1977 to a peak of almost 52,000 in 1980; this number declined to about 20,000 for the 1981–1986 period and to less than 15,000 for 1986–90. The expenditure per participant increased from US$86 in 1977 to a peak of US$125 in 1981; this declined to a trough of US$61 in 1985 and increased to a little more than US$80 for 1986–90. The decline starting in 1981 reflected shifts in the award procedures toward stiffer criteria.

Third, Chile has an apprentice program for workers under 21 years of age who are not subject to the minimum wage (in fact, the subsidy is eliminated if they receive more than two minimum wages) and are under contract for a maximum of two years. To date this program has been very small, covering only 2,324 apprentices in the 1988–1991 period. This is also a subsidized program in that a percentage of the remuneration paid to apprentices (with a limit of 60 percent of the minimum wage per apprentice and with a 10 percent limit on the share of workers qualifying as apprentices in the firm's total work force) is treatable as training for tax purposes.

Fourth, the government recently has instituted a subsidized youth training program to deal with the special problem of youth (see Box 3.5).

### Colombia

Colombia's SENA *(Servicio Nacional de Aprendizaje)* is one of the world's largest national training systems.[13] SENA was founded by 1957,

---

[13] This discussion of SENA draws heavily on Jiménez, Kugler, and Horn (1989) and on Zerda Sarmiento et al. (1992).

with an initial enrollment of 2,000, which grew to more than 500,000 by 1980 (these enrollment figures count individuals more than once if they enroll in more than one SENA module). In 1980, the cost to SENA was equivalent to about 13 percent of the cost of total recurrent central government expenditures on schooling. Initially SENA was directed toward the urban formal sector, but in the mid 1970s it began also to orient activities toward the informal sector, microenterprises, and rural areas. SENA is administratively linked to the Ministry of Labor but is financially independent; beginning in 1982, its funds have come from a 2 percent payroll tax on all private and public enterprises (before 1982, smaller firms were excluded).

SENA offers a wide variety of long and short courses. The long courses (more than 2,000 hours) include apprentice programs for skill training for youth, promotional programs for advanced skills training after apprenticeships, and complementary programs for adults who want to upgrade existing skills to apprenticeship levels. The short courses (averaging about 200 hours) include qualifying courses to introduce new but relatively low levels of skills. The short courses have been growing relatively rapidly, in part because apprenticeships have declined (9 percent of trainees in 1975, 2 percent in 1990) as formal schooling has expanded, and in part in response to shifts in employment toward services and commerce. At least in Bogota, the probability of receiving training is higher if an individual has more years of schooling, is older, has a father with more schooling, was born in an urban area, is female, works in the public sector, and is a participant in the social security system (Psacharopoulos and Vélez, 1992).

Future job growth is likely to occur disproportionately in smaller businesses. Therefore, self-employment/entrepreneur development and training offered by SENA may also prove to be of value.

The Carbajal Foundation in Colombia has been in operation since 1961, providing training and credit to small entrepreneurs. The target audience is small businesses with 10 or fewer employees. The program offers three complementary services: training, technical assistance, and credit. The foundation attributes the positive impact of its program principally to the training component. To obtain credit, microentrepreneurs pay a fixed fee to attend business courses, and subsequently receive six to eight visits from consultants. There is also a subprogram targeted toward retailers. The foundation's program is being replicated in a number of other countries in the region, using materials adapted to local conditions (Mazza, 1992).

## Box 3.5. Youth Training Program in Chile

Chilean structural adjustment produced disproportionately high rates of youth unemployment and created a new class of *marginales* who have gone many years without employment and are difficult to integrate into the economy in the normal course of events. After the commercial and financial opening of the economy and the reduction in the size and role of the state, the economy began to recover. But the labor market was characterized by notable skills mismatching. The expansion of economic activity took place largely with more trainable (older) workers. In the 1960s the unemployment rate for people age 20 to 24 years was only 3 percent greater than for people older than 24 (9.7 percent against 6.4 percent), but in the 1980s the youth unemployment rate was double that of the older group (22.4 percent against 11.6 percent). The relatively high youth unemployment created two major concerns. First, training and postformal education are channeled primarily through formal employment, with the result that youth unemployment that may lead to persistent, even structural, skills mismatch is not addressed by the system. Second, there are negative social consequences, given the positive correlation between youth unemployment and poverty. A special youth training program (YTP) was deemed necessary because of these concerns. Half of the public resources for the program were obtained locally, and half from the IDB. The program began in 1992.

The YTP's goal for its first four years has been to provide short-term (no longer than one year) training for 100,000 young people. The target population, estimated to be about 200,000, includes people 15 to 24 years old with low family income who are no longer in formal schooling. In its first year of operation, the program trained 40,000 youths at a cost of about US$23 million.

The YTP was designed to avoid three common problems of training activities in developing countries: (1) the creation of an inefficient government bureaucracy with excessive expenditures; (2) broad but rather inefficient cover-

## Conclusions

This chapter has elaborated on available information about levels and changes in human resources in Latin America and the Caribbean, using international comparisons and supplementing the data with details about the experiences of particular countries. International comparisons have limitations because of data problems, including the shortage of information on training and on the quality of human resource investments; and also because of the great diversity across countries in the region. Subject to such caveats, the analysis presented here suggests that:

age that does not allow the targeting of specific groups; and (3) the lack of strong links between the needs of business and the capabilities created through training.

To deal with the first and third problems, the YTP follows a practice used in Chile since the mid 1970s—an open bidding process for private firms to design and implement training courses. Applicants to conduct the training are selected on the basis of the price and the quality of the course, i.e., instruction and on-the-job experience for the students. Private training firms account for 66 to 90 percent of first year trainees (with some variation across area); municipalities and universities account for the remainder. To enhance the connection between the YTP and the labor market, experience ("job practice") in production units is required, thereby enabling trainees to learn on technology currently in use. To provide the right incentives and to ensure consistency between demand for and supply of human resources, the YTP selects private training institutions according to the percentage of trainees for whom a job practice is guaranteed. Although there is still no evaluation of ex post skills mismatching, the opinion of some entrepreneurs is that the program design has reduced this problem. The fact that 20 to 35 percent of the courses outside of Santiago have area-related components also suggests that efforts are being made to tailor programs to local labor market needs.

In order to target YTP's benefits to labor market entrants and to avoid inducing youth to quit formal schooling, only a small monetary subsidy is awarded. This subsidy amounts to less than one-third of the minimum wage during the training class period, with slightly higher levels during the job practice. In addition, trainee selection is carried out at the municipal level, to enable more appropriate targeting and to reduce the need for a large bureaucracy. Preliminary evidence shows that more than 90 percent of the trainees are from low and low-middle income families, and that more than 5 percent are from families in extreme poverty.

*Source:* Prepared by Ricardo Paredes.

• With regard to recent levels of human resource investments and stocks in Latin America and the Caribbean, most countries in the region tend to fare a little better than international experience, controlling for per capita income. This positive comparison holds for schooling investments and schooling stocks and for indicators of health and nutrition (no systematic data are available to make such comparisons for training). This generalization contrasts sharply with that of some commentators, such as Urrutia (1991), who claim that Latin America and the Caribbean have underinvested in human resources relative to other regions. Looking forward, this generalization suggests relatively positive prospects for many countries in the region, if high levels of human resources for a given level of development lead to above average subsequent performance, as suggested by the new neoclassical economic growth models.

• With regard to changes in aggregate human resources in the past quarter century, the region has fared about as well as or a little better than international experience, controlling for per capita income changes. This fact is striking, given that the region usually is thought to have suffered more than most of the rest of the world (although perhaps not more than Sub-Saharan Africa) in the "lost decade" of the 1980s.

• Gender gaps favoring males in schooling are relatively small in comparison with international experience, despite relatively small reductions over the past quarter century. Gender gaps favoring males in life expectancies are also relatively small, in part because of relatively large gains for females in the past quarter century. If the total returns to female human resources are higher than those to male human resources (because of the greater impact of female human resources on sociodemographic outcomes, in addition to their impact on economic productivity), then the fact that gender gaps favoring males are relatively small augurs well for the potential of the region.

• At more disaggregated levels, human resource investments in the region tend to favor urban over rural areas, the better-off over the poorer, and those of European descent over others. Such differences may have costs in terms of both alleviating poverty and increasing productivity.

• Individual countries have had diverse experiences, associated in part with differences in income distribution (with higher primary schooling enrollments and higher life expectancies in countries in which the income share of the bottom quintile of households is greater and that of the top decile is smaller). Countries with relatively high schooling do not necessarily have relatively high life expectancies; there is, in fact, only a 0.3 correlation between how much a country's recent schooling differs from the international regression line and how much its recent female life expectancy differs from that line.

Likewise, countries with relatively high changes in schooling since 1965 have not necessarily had significant related changes in life expectancies since 1965 (r = −0.02). But there are some patterns regarding which countries in the region have tended to be among the best and worst performers in schooling and life expectancies, in recent levels and in changes since 1965. Table 3.15 gives the five countries most above and the five countries most below the international regression lines for the recent levels and changes since 1965 in schooling and female life expectancy at

**Table 3.15.  Countries with Recent Human Resource Levels and Growth Most or Least Above the Levels Predicted by International Experience**

|  | Schooling | | Change in Schooling since 1965 | | Female Life Expectancy at Birth | | Changes since 1965 in Female Life Expectancy at Birth | |
|---|---|---|---|---|---|---|---|---|
|  | (1) | | (2) | | (3) | | (4) | |
| Countries most above international experience | 1. | Dominican Republic | 1. | Dominican Republic | 1. | Jamaica | 1–2. | {Honduras |
|  | 2. | Peru | 2. | Ecuador | 2. | Costa Rica |  | {Guatemala |
|  | 3. | Ecuador | 3–5. | {Peru | 3. | Chile | 3. | Mexico |
|  | 4. | Colombia |  | {Colombia | 4. | Colombia | 4–5. | {Chile |
|  | 5. | Uruguay |  | {Argentina | 5. | Dominican Republic |  | {Peru |
|  |  |  |  |  |  |  |  |  |
| Countries most below international experience | 1. | Guatemala | 1. | Jamaica | 1. | Bolivia | 1. | Paraguay |
|  | 2. | Brazil | 2. | Brazil | 2. | Haiti | 2. | Uruguay |
|  | 3. | Venezuela | 3–4. | {Costa Rica | 3. | Brazil | 3. | Argentina |
|  | 4. | Trinidad and Tobago |  | {El Salvador | 4. | Peru | 4. | Trinidad and Tobago |
|  | 5. | El Salvador | 5. | Panama | 5. | Venezuela | 5. | Venezuela |

*Note:* The top group includes the five highest countries (in decreasing order), and the bottom group includes the five lowest countries (in increasing order).  For schooling, for example, the Dominican Republic is most above and Guatemala is most below the international regression line.
*Source:* Based on regression estimates by the author.

birth.[14]  The countries most above the international regression lines are Colombia, the Dominican Republic, and Peru—each of which is in the top five for three of the four human resource level and growth indicators.[15]  Among the countries farthest below the international regression lines are Brazil and Venezuela, each of which is in the bottom five for three of the four human resource level and growth indicators.

This chapter suggests that the current condition of human resources in terms of aggregate indicators is relatively good in a number of respects, but that there are also a number of reasons to suspect that current human resource investments in the region are less than optimal. These reasons include:

• The relatively good condition of the aggregate human resource indicators in the region, compared with international experience, in part

---

[14] The deviations from international regressions for the recent levels and the changes in life expectancies at birth are highly correlated in the region for females and males ($r = 0.95$ for the levels, $r = 0.90$ for the changes since 1965), so only the former are included in the table.
[15] Peru is in the bottom five for the fourth indicator.

reflects merely the persistence of human resource stocks in a period in which real per capita incomes have declined substantially. Had income growth been better in the past decade, the relative human resource conditions might have appeared less satisfactory, controlling for (higher) income, even by the crude indices for which data are available.

• At some more disaggregate levels for which reasonably comparable data are available, such as the stock of secondary schooling, the region lags behind international experience. The limited secondary schooling stock among adults in the region is likely to limit possible future growth in economies that are more integrated into rapidly changing world markets.

• In terms of public support for human resources, the region has, on average, fared less well in recent comparisons with international experience than it did earlier (Chapter 4). This fact may have a negative effect on the future condition of human resources.

• Some major changes are occurring in the region (as discussed further in Chapter 4), such as the demographic and nutritional transition and the spread of AIDS, which are profoundly changing the composition of health service needs, even though the effects of these changes are not yet apparent in the aggregate statistics. Delivery of services related to health, for example, has not yet adjusted sufficiently.

• If the region is to succeed in its aspirations for rapid economic growth, greater human resource investments are needed to facilitate this growth.

• Human resource investments in the poorer members of society are an effective means of improving the welfare and increasing the productivity and income of many such individuals (as discussed in Chapter 2). This fact is relatively important in Latin America and the Caribbean, given the region's relatively great income inequalities and the associated high incidence of poverty.

Such factors point to the need to improve human resource investments in Latin America and the Caribbean.

# CHAPTER

# 4

# DETERMINANTS OF HUMAN RESOURCE INVESTMENT

Evidence points to the importance of human resource investments for future outcomes in Latin America and the Caribbean (Chapter 2). Therefore, it is important to ask exactly what determines the level of human resource investments in the region, and more specifically, how do policies affect the region's human resources? These questions lay the foundation for considering (Chapter 5) how best to invest in the region's human resources.

Government human resource investment policies are of particular interest for purposes of this book. In this chapter, we first discuss several simple analytical considerations regarding these policies. We then summarize the limited available aggregate and micro evidence about the actual determinants of human resources investments in the region, with particular emphasis on policies.

## Preliminary Points on Policies Related to Human Resource Investments

Government policies can increase human resource investments in two major ways: (1) through increasing the private marginal benefits of such investments by increasing complementary investments, improving the quality of related services, improving labor markets (including the lessening of discrimination), and reducing risk (through greater macro and international stability); and (2) through reducing the private marginal costs of such investments by increasing the accessibility and reducing the user charges of human resource-related public services, subsidizing human resource investments, increasing inducements for private providers to expand those services, facilitating arrangements that lessen the opportunity cost of time for such investments, and improving capital markets. The fact that governments can increase human resource investments through such mechanisms, however, does not necessarily mean that they should do so or that they should use all of these mechanisms. And the fact that returns to certain human resource investments are high does not necessarily mean that governments should have policies that favor those particular human resource investments. Private incentives may be sufficient.

To think about what governments should do, it is necessary to consider the policy objectives and the best means to pursue those objectives. Unfortunately, empirical studies—and how they are interpreted in designing human resource investment policy—often ignore such simple considerations. As a result, the interpretations of and justifications for certain policies can be quite misleading.

### Policy Objectives and Distortions

Policy changes should be made if market or policy failures cause distortions between private and social incentives, and if the marginal costs of policy changes in terms of direct resources and added distortions are likely to be less than the marginal benefits. Four major sources of distortions between private and social incentives are considered below:

*Technological externalities.* Technological externalities are effects of one entity on another that are not transferred through markets, such as those resulting from general knowledge or the control of contagious diseases. Because these externalities are not transferred through markets, competitive markets do not always create the right incentives for the production and use of goods and services that have externalities.

*Increasing returns to scale over the relevant range.* If there are increasing returns to scale over the relevant range, producers can gain from restricting supplies so that the marginal benefits to users are greater than the marginal costs to the producers. Examples include the production of some drugs for national markets that are protected from international competition by trade barriers, and the provision of health services in small remote communities. An extreme example of increasing returns to scale is a public good—that is, a good or service that can be provided to one individual without there being less for others; e.g., basic scientific knowledge.

*Missing or imperfect markets.* Individuals may not be able to produce, consume, or invest efficiently, in the sense of equating marginal benefits with marginal costs, because of critical missing markets. One important example is the region's private capital markets, which often will not lend, or lend much, for human resource investments. Another example is the absence of adequate insurance markets, which results in risk-averse individuals being unwilling to invest in human resources, since they cannot protect themselves adequately by diversifying and pooling risks.

*Policy-induced distortions.*    Most policies, whatever the motivation for their introduction and however well they attain their avowed objectives, introduce distortions between social and private marginal costs and benefits. Examples include: regulations that preclude entry of, or discriminate against, private providers of educational and health services; the pricing of educational and health services below their social marginal costs; and public pay schedules for employees in human resource-related service provision that bear little relation to their productivity.

Because substantial components of social costs are distortions introduced by policy interventions, there is some presumption that, from the point of view of efficiency and productivity, there is a policy hierarchy in which more direct price interventions are ranked more highly.[1] For example, direct subsidies for schooling are likely to cause fewer distortions than will increasing the marginal benefit to schooling through subsidizing the production of goods and services, which will create work for more-schooled individuals (who will in turn increase the returns to all other factors used in such production). The art of good policy in regard to efficiency and productivity objectives, in the uncertain real world in which policymakers operate, is to (1) be clear about the nature of the market or policy distortion that may warrant policy change, and (2) select a policy that is as high as possible in the policy hierarchy (taking into account the possibility that no policy may be better than some policy, since all policies might have high marginal social costs). Policies that are high in the policy hierarchy, in addition to having lower distortionary costs, also are likely to be more transparent and thus less subject to unobserved abuse by government officials or beneficiaries.

### Policy Objective 1: Increase Productivity

Increasing productivity is one of the major policy objectives in the region. Such an objective suggests that policy changes should be made if (1) there are market or policy failures that cause distortions; and (2) the marginal costs of policy changes in terms of direct resources and added distortions are likely to be less than the marginal benefits, given the imperfect information about a rapidly changing economic environment and given the behavior of individuals in various private and public entities.

Policy interventions for productivity and efficiency reasons relate to important positive technological externalities, including those resulting

---

[1] Of course, there may be costs to policies in addition to distortion costs; for example, important political costs. For a discussion of such a policy hierarchy, see Corden (1974).

from activities such as the control of contagious diseases. Since technological externalities are not transferred through markets, as are pecuniary
externalities, competitive markets generally do not create the right incentives for goods and services that have benefits largely in the form of externalities. Social benefits may also exceed private benefits in this case because
of marginal income or wealth taxes.

Figure 2.1B illustrates such motives for possible policy interventions
if the dashed line represents the social marginal benefits and the solid line
represents the private marginal benefits, with the marginal costs (both private and social) still given by the solid upward-sloping line.[2] In this case
the private equilibrium is with human resources equal to H*, which is a
lower level of human resource investments than the social equilibrium of
H** because of positive externalities (more explicit examples of which are
discussed later). Therefore, on productivity/efficiency grounds, policies
may be warranted to increase private human resource investments by shifting the private marginal benefits curve up or the private marginal cost
curve down (or some combination), so that the incentives would be for an
individual to invest in close to the socially optimal level of human resources. But policies usually have some costs, so the social marginal cost
curve may be greater than the private marginal cost curve. If the social
marginal cost curve is sufficiently greater than the private curve, in fact,
the social equilibrium investment might be lower than the private one
even if there are positive externalities on the benefit side.

There are also important questions about efficiency and productivity
in the supply of goods and services related to human resource investments.
Efficiency questions pertain to the choice and level of outputs, the choice
and level of inputs, and the use of given inputs to produce outputs. If
supply is efficient, various goods and services related to human resource
investments are provided to the point at which the marginal social benefits
of the last unit of each equals the marginal social costs of producing the
last unit of each, inputs are used to the point at which the value of the
social marginal product equals the marginal social costs of each, and inputs
are fully employed.

The basic policy issues on the supply side pertain to how to create a
policy environment such that human resource-related services are pro-

---

[2] Yet another possibility is that human resource investments are risky, individuals are risk
averse, private markets do not exist for sharing such risks, but socially such risks can be
pooled. In this case, there is no difference between the private and the social expected marginal benefit curves, but due to risk aversion, individuals on their own invest less than would
be indicated by the expected marginal benefits (which do not incorporate the disutility effects of risk aversion).

vided as efficiently as possible, subject to some constraints such as concerns about distribution. How can supply provision be organized so that providers are responsive to individual and social demands to provide the right quantities and qualities of these services and to use the right combination of inputs to produce these outputs (in light of the true marginal social costs of these inputs)—all in a world in which information about the nature of demands and production processes is quite imperfect? Pricing issues for such services and for the inputs that are used in them pertain to how to create incentives for the socially desirable supply, given the equity objectives and the possibility of market failures from externalities and from economies of scale.

Such concerns may mean that prices should differ from what free market prices would be. But these concerns are unlikely to mean that prices should differ from market prices as much as they often do for the provision of social services and for the cost of related inputs in most countries in the region (especially for services that are "free" in monetary terms, although not in total terms). It is sometimes claimed that the products of and inputs into these services need to be priced differently from those of other goods and services because it is difficult to measure the quality of these services. Although this point may have some merit in regard to comparison with the price of wheat or rice, it is not clear why the difficulty of measuring the quality of such services is greater than the difficulty of measuring the quality of many other goods and services traded in markets in most economies. In any case, major policy questions for the supply side relate to which institutional forms, and which price and information policies, are likely to make the provision of services related to health and education relatively efficient under real world conditions. Policy failures in the region have been frequent in the sense that policies have introduced distortions regarding the supply of relevant goods and services.

Good information is important both for good policy formulation and for the development of institutions that can efficiently provide services related to education and health investments. Good information is critical, for instance, for decisions about the cost effectiveness of various types of education and health policies and about where resources should be directed. Moreover, good information about the nature and impact of such services is critical for consumers to be able to make intelligent choices about different types of educational and health-related services. But on a priori grounds, there is reason to believe that private entities do not adequately provide many types of information, especially if it has public good characteristics; that is, that at zero or very low marginal social costs, additional people can obtain information without reducing the information held by others. No incentives exist for private entities to disseminate such information to the point at which the price equals the very low (or zero) marginal social costs. Therefore, government collection, analysis, and provision (or subsidization) of information is likely, a priori, to increase efficiency.

Governments can increase the dissemination of information in a number of ways. One way is to monitor the performance of various providers of services related to human resource investment and then publicize the results (such as data on the value added of various schools, training institutions, hospitals, and clinics). Another way is to subsidize new activities directly related to human resource development, such as the development of innovative teaching methods, because the private incentives to undertake such activities are likely to be inadequate as a result of risk aversion and the public good nature of the information derived. Yet another way to increase dissemination of information is to create incentives for suppliers of human resource-related services to integrate with those who demand such services so that the right kinds of human resources are produced; linking training programs to employers is a pertinent example. Still another way is to have open bidding for the private provision of human resource services.

Because substantial components of social costs consist of distortions introduced by policy interventions, there is some presumption, from the point of view of efficiency and productivity, of a policy hierarchy in which more direct price interventions are ranked more highly. For instance, direct subsidies for schooling are likely to cause fewer distortions than would an attempt to shift the marginal benefit curve by subsidizing the production of goods and services, which will create work for more-schooled individuals (thus shifting the private benefit curve and increasing the returns to all other factors used in such production). The art of good policy in regard to efficiency and productivity objectives—in an uncertain real world with the many other constraints that policymakers must also consider—is to focus on policies that are high up in the policy hierarchy (and to consider the possibility that no policy at all might be better than actually having a policy, since all relevant policy options might have high marginal social costs). Policies high up in the policy hierarchy, in addition to having fewer distortionary costs, are likely to be more transparent and thus less subject to unobserved abuse by either government officials or beneficiaries.

*Policy Objective 2: Improve the Distribution of Opportunities and Outcomes*

A second major policy objective pertains to the distribution of opportunities and outcomes. With regard to opportunities, it might be stated that all citizens should have opportunities to improve their command over resources through self-betterment and hard work. With regard to the distribution of outcomes, it might be stated that all citizens have the right to an existence above some poverty line and to have certain basic needs satisfied. The concern with opportunities, however, is not identical to the concern with outcomes. For some members of society—the very young, the very old, and the disabled—guaranteeing equal opportunities may not guarantee the satisfaction of basic needs. But for many others, the concerns with opportunities and with outcomes are related. Indeed, in most societies, human resource investments play a central role in efforts to both establish greater equality of opportunities and ensure satisfaction of basic needs. Human resource investments help ensure more equal opportunity because the poor have only one economic asset to sell—their own labor time; therefore, a promising strategy to improve their command over resources is to enrich the value of their time, and increase what it will command in the labor market, through human resource investments.[3] And such investments by definition help ensure the satisfaction of basic needs such as health, nutrition, and education.

The question of opportunities can enter through either the marginal benefits or the marginal costs. For instance, unequal access to the labor market or other opportunities for certain racial, ethnic, or language groups or for females may be reflected in lower marginal benefits for such individuals, and therefore in lower equilibrium human resource investments, all else being equal. If the returns to human resource investments for poorer families are systematically lower privately than socially, because of higher discount rates stemming from the immediate pressures of poverty, then the marginal benefits for individuals from poorer families are lower than for otherwise identical individuals from richer families. If the costs of human resource investments are higher for poor than for rich individuals because of less access to resource markets, then the marginal cost curve is higher for poorer than for richer individuals and the equilibrium human resource investment is lower, all else being equal. If poorer individuals in more remote areas must travel farther to obtain services of equal quality, again the marginal costs tend to be higher and the equilibrium human resource investment lower. If there is gender division in household tasks, with girls specializing in sibling care or boys specializing in agricultural production, the marginal costs and the equilibrium human resource investments may differ by gender.

---

[3] Other possibilities would be to redistribute other assets to the poor. But this is often not a politically palatable alternative.

In the interest of equalizing opportunities, policies could be adopted to ensure more equal access to labor market opportunities, to capital markets, and to social services. These policies could work through increasing marginal benefits and reducing marginal costs for the poorer members of society. Or they could work through legal requirements for minimal human resource investments, such as compulsory schooling levels. But the probable success and the implications of various policy alternatives vary substantially. The most attractive of these alternatives are likely to increase both efficiency and opportunities for the poor. Examples include the reduction of discrimination in labor markets[4] and in access to social services, and the reduction of capital market imperfections.

Other policies to help provide equal opportunities for the poor, however, may create efficiency costs by introducing distortions. For instance, policies to subsidize the cost of social services related to education, health, and nutrition induce the poor to make more use of such services but may also increase distortions between private and social costs. General subsidized provision of such services, moreover, is also likely to: benefit the middle and upper classes more than the poor unless the subsidized service is an inferior good or has very low income elasticity of demand; place large strains on the public budget if it is widely used (which often leads to a deterioration of quality); encourage population growth by reducing the private costs of children; and discourage private suppliers of the good or service. In the real world, in which information is imperfect and individuals respond to incentives, it generally is difficult to restrict the beneficiaries of policies by regulations. Therefore, policies that are of interest only to the poor (for instance, workfare programs at low wages, subsidies for foods consumed primarily by the poor) may be attractive.

Regulations and legal requirements regarding human resource investments are also options. Consider, for instance, the effort to mandate minimum human resource investments, such as minimum schooling levels. If such efforts are to have any meaning, they must mandate higher levels than would occur in their absence. But if the mandated levels are above the privately optimal levels, then the private incentives are to evade the mandated levels. Such policy options need to be evaluated with an awareness of the expense and difficulty of monitoring such behavior.

A further issue in thinking about policy choices is the fact that certain policies are motivated by paternalism—an attitude that conflicts with

---

[4] Such a policy would tend to increase the marginal benefits for some of the poor and therefore their human capital investments. But it might also increase the opportunity cost of the time of the poor for such investments and thus increase marginal costs, with some offsetting effects.

the democratic recognition of differences in tastes among affected individuals. Two examples are useful.

First, certain behaviors sometimes are characterized as "bad" by other members of society—for instance, dropping out of school or consuming tobacco, alcohol, or too much red meat. But it is often not clear whether these behaviors are bad because of important negative externalities or because policymakers or other elites think they know what is best for others. To the extent that there are serious negative externalities or unexploited positive externalities, there can be an efficiency-based reason for considering policy interventions. If consuming alcohol, for instance, incites violence or driving that endangers others, then these serious negative externalities may warrant policy interventions to lessen or eliminate such behavior. If any of these behaviors stems from the (economically unwarranted) lack of publicly available information about the negative effects of these behaviors, then enhancing the dissemination of information may indeed increase the public good and therefore warrant policy intervention. If individual consumption behaviors impose a burden on the rest of society because they cause health conditions the care of which entails large social costs beyond the private costs, then policy changes may be warranted (although in this case, from an efficiency perspective, the appropriate policy change may be to alter the pricing of curative health care so that the private and social incentives are the same). On the other hand, if informed individuals make behavioral decisions that lessen their health or reduce their life expectancy (say, through eating "too much" red meat) with no externalities, there are no efficiency reasons for policy interventions.[5]

A second example of paternalism is a policy intervention designed to change people's preferences instead of (or beyond) just providing information. Family planning programs, for instance, may disseminate information about family planning alternatives. The dissemination of such information clearly may be warranted from an efficiency point of view (depending on the exact marginal social cost and benefit calculation). But such programs may also attempt to change people's preferences by disseminating the view, for example, that two children per family is the desirable maximum. This may be effective in reducing the number of children

---

[5]There are further difficult questions regarding which individuals should be considered responsible for decisions affecting only themselves. How old should they be? Should society use restrictions other than age to decide who is capable of making such decisions? For individuals whom society deems incapable of assuming such responsibilities, who should make such decisions? To what extent does society have an interest in such people beyond or different from that of their families and communities? Such questions, however, do not vitiate the basic point in the text.

that people have, but to the extent that people's preferences have been altered, it becomes very difficult to assess whether they are better off, and thus whether such policies increase efficiency in the economic sense. Ignoring such issues is not likely to lead to better policy, from either an efficiency or a distributional perspective.

Thus, there are a number of important considerations in devising policies to improve equity and efficiency: the role of market failures; possible trade-offs between productivity/equity and distributional considerations; the incentives and distortions introduced by policies, as well as the related helpful notion of a policy hierarchy; the need to be concerned with quality as well as quantity of social services; budget constrains; policy distortions; targeting to desired recipients; the problems of policy design and monitoring, given imperfect and changing information; and the dangers of paternalistic behavior disguised as superior knowledge about what is good for certain groups of people.

## Determinants of Schooling

Chapter 2 suggested that schooling has a substantial impact on a number of outcomes of interest in the Latin American and Caribbean region. Chapter 3 discussed the levels and changes in schooling in the region. This chapter will consider the determinates of schooling, first on an aggregate level and then on the basis of micro studies.

### Aggregate Indicators of Schooling Inputs

#### Recent Levels of Schooling Inputs

Aggregate quantitative indicators of inputs into schooling are quite limited. Table 4.1 shows the available data for three such indicators—primary school pupils per teacher, the percentage share of central government expenditure devoted to schooling, and central government expenditure on schooling as a percentage of GNP—as well as how each differs from the levels predicted by international experience. Figures 4.1A and 4.1B plot the first and third of these indicators against real per capita income, with the international regression lines indicated as well.

These indicators should be interpreted with caution. The available evidence suggests, for example, that the pupil-to-teacher ratio does not strongly affect learning (see the following subsection); therefore, a low ratio may be an index of inefficiency, with too many personnel devoted to teaching, rather than an indicator of a rich learning environment. Also, the

**Table 4.1.  Recent Schooling Inputs in Latin America and the Caribbean, with International Comparison, 1988**

| Countries | Primary Pupils/Teacher | | % Central Government Expenditure on Schooling | | % GNP that Central Government Spends on Schooling | |
|---|---|---|---|---|---|---|
| | Actual | Difference from International Experience | Actual | Difference from International Experience | Actual | Difference from International Experience |
| | (1) | (2) | (3) | (4) | (5) | (6) |
| Guatemala | 35 | −0.8 | — | — | — | — |
| Bolivia | 27 | −11.7 | 18.4 | 5.3 | 2.9 | −0.4 |
| El Salvador | 45 | 9.6 | 17.1 | 4.3 | 1.9 | −1.4 |
| Costa Rica | 31 | 1.1 | 16.2 | 3.8 | 4.5 | 1.0 |
| Peru | — | — | 15.3 | 2.7 | 2.2 | −1.2 |
| Panama | — | — | 15.6 | 3.5 | 5.4 | 1.8 |
| Mexico | 32 | 2.5 | 7.4 | −4.9 | 2.1 | −1.5 |
| Brazil | — | — | 4.8 | −7.3 | 1.2 | −2.4 |
| Chile | — | — | 12.0 | −0.5 | 4.0 | 0.5 |
| Uruguay | — | — | 7.1 | −4.8 | 1.7 | −2.0 |
| Argentina | — | — | 6.9 | −5.0 | 1.5 | −2.2 |
| Venezuela | — | — | 19.6 | 8.0 | 4.3 | 0.5 |
| Trinidad and Tobago | 24 | 2.5 | — | — | — | — |

*Source:* Based on regression estimates by the author.

available aggregate data on expenditures refer only to central government expenditures, not to total government expenditures, to say nothing of combined private and government expenditures. Because countries in the region appear to vary considerably with respect to the proportion of total schooling expenditures that originate from the central government, comparisons across countries have to be made with care. In Brazil, for instance, central government expenditures accounted for only 23 to 36 percent of total government expenditures in the 1960–1982 period (Amadeo et al., 1993). In fact, in 1989 Brazil's total public expenditures on schooling as a percentage of GNP were at the median of a group of seven countries in the region with relatively high expenditures on schooling, even though its recent central government expenditures as a share of GNP have been relatively low.[6] The data for some other countries, such as Mexico, are subject to similar limitations.

[6]Barros (1992, Table 4.1.1) gives the following total public expenditures on schooling as percentage shares of GNP in 1989: Argentina 3.1, Brazil 3.7, Chile 3.6, Costa Rica 4.4, Mexico 3.8, Uruguay 3.1, and Venezuela 4.2.

**Figure 4.1A. Primary Pupils/Teacher versus Real Per Capita Income, 1988**

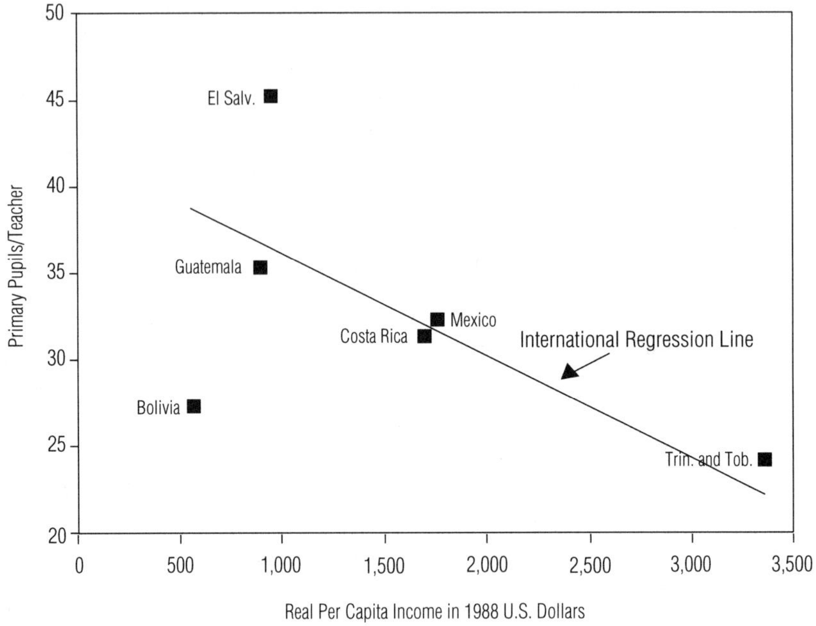

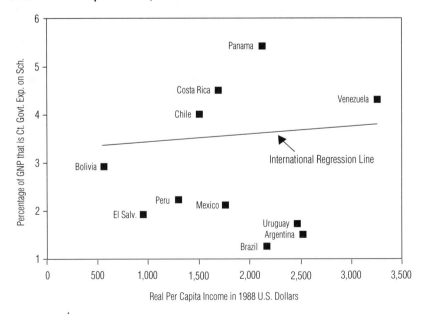

**Figure 4.1B. Percentage of GNP that is Central Government Expenditure on Schooling versus Real Per Capita Income, 1988**

These schooling input indicators are positively associated across countries with real per capita income. But there is considerable variation within the region, controlling for real per capita income. Among the six countries for which data on primary pupils per teacher are available, only in Bolivia (with 12 students fewer per teacher than international experience) and in Guatemala (barely) are the number of students per teacher less than predicted by international experience. In Bolivia the high number of recorded teachers apparently reflects the considerable power of the teachers union, which leads to overstaffing (many "ghost" teachers on the payroll rarely show up in the classroom); the union also enforces the arcane requirement that specialists teach specialized subjects even at fairly basic levels in remote areas. Among the four countries with more students per teacher than international experience, only in El Salvador (with 10 students more per teacher) is the actual number greater than international experience by more than three students per teacher. Thus, these comparisons primarily raise questions about overstaffing in Bolivia, and perhaps about understaffing in El Salvador.

Recent data on central government expenditures on schooling as a percentage of total central government expenditures and as a percentage of total GNP are available for 11 countries in the region. For about half of these countries, schooling shares of total central government expenditures were greater than the international regression line. Therefore, on average, there were not higher shares devoted to schooling even though there were higher schooling investments (see Chapter 3), nor were there lower shares devoted to schooling because central government expenditures on schooling in the region were squeezed relative to international experience as part of the large adjustment efforts in the 1980s. These 11 countries, nevertheless, had substantial variance in the shares of government expenditures on schooling relative to what was predicted by international experience. Venezuela (8 percent above the predicted level) and Bolivia (5 percent above) have had relatively high shares of central government expenditure on schooling. Brazil (7 percent below), and Argentina, Mexico, and Uruguay (5 percent below) have had relatively low shares. These figures must be interpreted with care, however. The relatively high shares for Bolivia reflect the relatively high number of "ghosts" on the teacher payroll rather than investments in schooling. And the relatively low shares for Brazil and Mexico reflect relatively great decentralization of public schooling expenditures to state and local levels in these two very large countries.

Although the schooling share in total central government expenditures in the region has been, on average, similar to international experience, central government expenditures on schooling as a share of GNP have been less than international experience in seven of the 11 cases because total government expenditures have tended to be smaller shares of GNP than the international experience. Central government expenditures on schooling as a percentage of GNP have been at least 2 percent less than international experience in Argentina, Brazil, and Uruguay, and at least 1 percent less in El Salvador and Mexico. Only for Costa Rica and Panama, at the other end of the spectrum, have these shares been at least 1 percent more than international experience.

The correlations among these three schooling input indicators are significant because of their relation to real per capita income. But the correlations are fairly small once there is control for per capita income (that is, 0.5 for the two expenditure share measures and about −0.3 for each expenditure share measure with primary pupils per teacher). The extent to which the number of primary pupils per teacher exceeds the level predicted by international experience in the region has negative bivariate correlations of −0.7 to −0.8 with the secondary enrollment rates, with total schooling and with gender gaps favoring males in primary and secondary enrollment rates and in total schooling (all controlling for real per capita income). These correlations suggest that schooling success in quantitative terms, especially for females, is associated somewhat with lower pupil-to-teacher ratios.

The extent to which the schooling share of central government expenditures of GNP in the region exceeds the level predicted by international experience has a positive correlation of 0.8 to 0.9 with tertiary enrollment, but negative (and much smaller) correlations with primary and secondary enrollment rates (again, controlling for real per capita income). This fact suggests that relatively high central government schooling expenditures in the region are associated with inefficient (because the returns have been higher to primary and secondary schooling) and inequitable (because the beneficiaries of tertiary schooling are concentrated among better-off families) schooling allocations. But none of these recent schooling input indicators is very strongly associated with the measures of schooling success discussed in Chapter 3 if there is control for per capita income. In fact, with such control, none of these indicators has significant coefficient estimates in regressions that determine the various measures of recent schooling investment in the region. This lack of significance must be interpreted with care because of the relative scarcity of observations and the imperfect nature of schooling input and output measures, but it does suggest that resources devoted to schooling in the region are not allocated very effectively, judging by the fact that they do not have significant impact on the available schooling outcome measures.

*Medium-Run Changes in Indicators of Schooling Inputs*

Table 4.2 gives the change in these indicators over the medium run, with and without control for changes in real per capita income. Half of the six countries in the region for which there are data increased the number of primary pupils per teacher relative to international experience in the 1965–1987 period, with relatively large increases of 10 for Costa Rica and El Salvador. At the other end of the spectrum, Mexico's drop of 7 relative to international experience is most noteworthy.

In international experience, the change in the schooling share of total central government expenditures is not significantly related to the change in real per capita income. But eight of the 11 countries in the region for which data are available had a greater drop in the schooling share of total central government expenditures in the 1972–1988 period than predicated. Particularly large drops were experienced by Argentina (11 percent less than international experience), Bolivia (9 percent less), Costa Rica (9 percent less), and Peru (6 percent less). At the other end of the spectrum, only Venezuela (3 percent more) had an increase more than 1 percent above international experience; Chile and Uruguay also were slightly above international experience.

Also during the period, 8 of the 11 countries in the region had decreases in the GNP share of central government expenditures on schooling relative to international experience. Argentina and Chile had relative decreases more than 2 percent of GNP greater than predicted by international experience, and Peru had a greater than 1 percent decrease. The mechanisms among these countries differed, however, with Chile having a relatively positive increase in the schooling share of central government expenditures and a fall in the share of central government expenditures as a share of GNP, and Argentina and Peru having just the opposite.

Judging by shares of central government expenditures on schooling, therefore, the medium-run experience through the late 1980s was a slippage in the region relative to international experience, presumably due in large part to the debt and restructuring problems of the 1980s. Is there evidence that such slippage negatively affected relative schooling attainment in the region? Simple regressions of the changes in various schooling attainment measures since 1965 show no significant relation to changes in the central government share of schooling expenditure (all controlling for changes in real per capita income). This lack of significance again raises questions about how effectively such expenditures have been allocated. Nevertheless, the change of schooling was 0.14 grades smaller and the changes in primary and secondary schooling enrollment rates were 1.6 percent and 1.4 percent less, respectively, for every increase of one in the

**Table 4.2.  Changes in Schooling Inputs in Latin America and the Caribbean, with International Comparison**

| Countries | 1965–1987 Change in Primary Pupils/Teacher | | 1982–1988 Change in % Central Government Expenditure on Schooling | | 1972–1988 Change in % GNP that is Central Government Expenditure on Schooling | |
|---|---|---|---|---|---|---|
| | Actual | Difference from International Experience | Actual | Difference from International Experience | Actual | Difference from International Experience |
| | (1) | (2) | (3) | (4) | (5) | (6) |
| Guatemala | 2 | 4.5 | — | — | — | — |
| Bolivia | −1 | −1.5 | −12.9 | −9.4 | −0.1 | 0.1 |
| El Salvador | 11 | 10.1 | −4.3 | −1.0 | −0.8 | −0.7 |
| Costa Rica | 4 | 9.5 | −12.1 | −9.3 | −0.8 | −0.9 |
| Peru | — | — | −8.3 | −5.3 | −1.6 | −1.5 |
| Panama | — | — | −5.1 | −2.5 | −0.3 | −0.5 |
| Mexico | −15 | −6.9 | −9.0 | −6.2 | 0.2 | −0.1 |
| Brazil | — | — | −3.5 | −0.9 | −0.2 | −0.4 |
| Chile | — | — | −2.3 | 0.6 | −2.2 | −2.2 |
| Uruguay | — | — | −2.4 | 0.0 | −0.7 | −0.9 |
| Argentina | — | — | −13.1 | −10.7 | −2.4 | −2.6 |
| Venezuela | — | — | 1.0 | 3.1 | 0.9 | 0.6 |
| Trinidad and Tobago | −10 | −3.0 | — | — | — | — |

*Source:* Based on regression estimates by the author.

primary-pupil-to-teacher ratio in the region. These significant associations, although based on only six countries, suggest some positive impact of reducing class size over time.

The fact that the region performed, on average, about as well as international experience with regard to the changes in schooling attainment measures summarized in Chapter 3, despite some deterioration in relative central government schooling expenditures, suggests some combination of the following: (1) compositional changes in central government expenditures that led to more efficient use of these resources; (2) deterioration in physical capital stock because of lack of maintenance, in order to keep salary and other current expenditures relatively high; (3) deterioration in the quality of schooling although the quantity was maintained; (4) reduction in the prices of some critical inputs, such as teachers' real salaries, so that real expenditures were more or less maintained despite the declining shares of such expenditures; and (5) shifts in the composition of total expenditures on schooling from the central government to other levels of government and to the private sector. Available information unfortunately does not permit the identification of the relative importance of each of these different possibilities.

Given the emphasis by some on the differential importance of schooling levels, and given the widespread perception that the beneficiaries of subsidies to tertiary schooling are largely the middle and upper classes (see Chapter 2 and Table 5.1), it is also of interest to ask about the levels and changes in the share of total central government schooling expenditures directed toward tertiary schooling (Table 4.3). The cross-country variations in these shares within the region for 1985 are considerable, from 13 percent in Cuba and 18 percent in Ecuador at the low end, to more than 40 percent in Costa Rica and Venezuela at the high end. The patterns in the movement of these shares over the last two decades also vary substantially across countries, with substantial downward declines in Argentina (from a peak of about 30 percent in 1975), Brazil (from a peak of about 60 percent in 1970), and Chile (from a peak of about 38 percent in 1970), and with significant increases in Costa Rica, Cuba, Mexico, and Venezuela. Thus, countries in the region vary considerably in both the level and the changes of their relative central government emphasis on tertiary schooling, with possible greater knowledge-related externalities but also probable more regressive income distribution implications, in comparison with lower schooling levels.

### Other Evidence of Schooling Determinants

*Determinant 1. Family background (including parental schooling and income) is important, but perhaps with diminishing effects over time.*

Studies for Brazil, Nicaragua, Panama, and Peru report significantly positive effects of parental schooling on child schooling (Birdsall, 1985; Heckman and Hotz, 1986; King and Bellew, 1988; Wolfe and Behrman, 1987). The estimated magnitudes range from an additional 0.1 to 1.1 grades of schooling for children for every additional grade of schooling of the parents. These estimates generally suggest a stronger association with maternal than with paternal schooling. The Nicaraguan estimates, however, suggest that parental schooling is representing in part some unobserved dimensions of family background; in standard estimates the coefficient of maternal schooling is 0.45, but it drops to 0.11 with adult sibling control for childhood family background. The estimates for both Panama and Peru indicate diminishing effects of parental schooling over time. For Peru, for instance, the impact on females (males) of an additional year of mother's schooling was 0.33 years (0.29) for the 1925–1939 birth cohort and 0.12 years (0.18) for the 1960–1966 cohort. Parallel

**Table 4.3. Public Tertiary Schooling Expenditure as Percentage of Total Central Government Schooling Expenditures in Latin America and the Caribbean, 1960–1985**

| Country | 1950 | 1970 | 1975 | 1980 | 1985 |
|---|---|---|---|---|---|
| Dominican Republic | 11 (1951) | 21 | 22 (1976) | 24 | 21 |
| Guatemala | — | 13 | 20 (1976) | 18 (1979) | — |
| Ecuador | 19 (1951) | 10 | 11 | 16 | 18 (1984) |
| Colombia | 17 (1961) | 24 | 11 (1973) | 24 | 22 |
| Costa Rica | — | 11 | 24 | 26 | 41 |
| Peru | 4 (1949) | 17 (1968) | 16 (1974) | — | — |
| Mexico | 1 | 10 | 13 | 27 | 29 |
| Brazil | 10 (1951) | 59 | 24 | 30 (1978) | 21 (1984) |
| Chile | 8 | 38 (1969) | 25 | 33 | 20 (1984) |
| Argentina | — | 21 | 30 | 23 | 19 (1984) |
| Venezuela | 17 (1951) | 26 | 37 | 35 | 43 |
| Cuba | — | — | — | 7 | 13 |

*Source:* Brunner (1989, Table 78), as compiled from various UNESCO annual statistical yearbooks.

estimates for father's schooling are $0.13$ $(0.25)$ and $0.07$ $(0.10)$ years. These results suggest, very significantly, that the expansion of public schooling weakened the intergenerational links over time.

Family income (or proxies for it) generally has a significant positive effect on schooling of children in studies for Brazil, Chile, Nicaragua, and Peru (Behrman and Wolfe, 1987a, b; Birdsall, 1985; Farrell and Schiefelbein, 1985; King and Bellew, 1988). Estimates for Brazil, for instance, imply that child schooling attainment increases by 5 to 8 percent for a 10 percent increase in income. Within the framework of Chapter 2, income enters into human resource investment determination only if capital market access is positively associated with income, or if household discount rates are negatively associated with income (because the pressure of poverty means that immediate survival takes precedence over investments), or if schooling is in part consumption rather than just investment. The fact that income is significant for schooling attainment suggests that at least one of these factors is relevant. This finding is important because imperfect capital markets are one reason that policy interventions to support human resource investments may be warranted on efficiency grounds. But in part, income appears to be representing other dimensions of family background or of the community, such as the quality of local schools, because the estimated impact of income declines substantially with control for unobserved family background (using adult sibling data) or for the quality of local schools. The Peruvian estimates, the only ones for which separate estimates are given by birth cohorts, also suggest a declining income effect over time, again possibly because of expansion of the schooling system.

*Determinant 2. Evidence (although limited) suggests that households, rich and poor alike, highly value access to and improved quality of schooling.*

A study for rural Peru uses the cost of travel time and of time not working while in school to infer price elasticities for the demand for secondary schooling (Gertler and Glewwe, 1990). The estimates indicate that price elasticities increase as prices rise and that they do not differ much by income, except that they are lower for the top quarter by income than for the lower three quarters. Within the sample, price elasticities for the lower three quarters of households increase from about 0.1 to 0.4 as prices increase, while those for the highest quarter of households are about 0.1 for all prices. This means that if schooling costs to households were to increase 10 percent, enrollers from the bottom three quarters of households would decline by 1 to 4 percent (depending on the initial price), and those from the top quarter of households would decline by about 1 percent. Therefore, the enrollment declines induced by increased prices would be fairly limited (particularly starting from initial low prices), but would be regressive in that they would be less for the top quarter of households than for others.

Price elasticities alone, however, do not show whether households are better or worse off with a policy that increases schooling fees and uses those fees to improve school quality or expand the number of schools. Therefore, the Peru study estimates whether households in areas without a local secondary school would be willing to pay to cover the costs of operating a local school. The estimates suggest that households at all income levels are willing to pay more than the costs of operating a new school to reduce travel time from two hours to zero, although none is willing to pay that amount to reduce travel time from one hour to zero. Although the analysis is crude, it suggests that the welfare of residents in villages that are fairly remote from secondary schools would improve with local secondary schools, even if they had to pay the full costs of operating such schools.

*Determinant 3. Some specific measured inputs have limited impact on school achievement, but school effectiveness could be considerably improved through appropriate incentives.*

There is some evidence that a few specific school characteristics affect schooling attainment and achievement (cognitive achievement scores) in Latin America and the Caribbean. In Peru, for instance, the number of grades offered in a school, and secondarily, the availability of reading or math books (or both) significantly increased the years of schooling for most cohorts of females and males (King and Bellew, 1988). For Brazil, studies suggest that the quality of teachers (measured by their schooling or salaries) positively affects schooling attainment, as suggested in Chapter 2 (Birdsall, 1985, Box 2.2); and that the availability of basic textbooks, instructional materials, and better facilities improves cognitive achievement (Armitage et al., 1986; Harbison and Hanushek, 1992). There are important zonal or geographical variations in Brazilian schooling quality that are associated with variations in schooling attainment, although quality improvements may induce more—or less—schooling of children in poor households (Box 4.1). In Nicaragua, the availability of textbooks has an important impact on children's ability to learn mathematics, particularly in rural areas (Jameson et al., 1981).

What is striking about the currently available empirical evidence, however, is how little really is known about which specific characteristics improve schooling achievement. A recent summary of 96 studies of educational production functions highlights this point (Table 4.4). Among the six variables summarized here, none has statistically significant positive effects for more than two-thirds of the studies, and only half of them (facilities, teacher education, and expenditure per student, with the last based on relatively few studies) have significant positive effects in half of the studies. The teacher-pupil ratio, which is widely used as an index of the quality of schooling, has a significant coefficient in half of the studies, but the sign is the opposite of that presumed in half of these cases.

What do such results suggest? Certain specific inputs into schooling—namely, instructional materials (not included in Table 4.4), teacher education, and facilities—appear to have fairly a widespread impact. For some of these inputs, the returns to improvements may be quite high (see the discussion of grade repetition, below). Several studies also provide evidence that school effects are much larger than the effects of specific identifiable inputs. For reasons that are not clear from the available quantitative studies, some schools are much better than others at teaching students. Therefore, there is the potential to substantially increase the effectiveness of school systems if better practices are widely adopted. But the lack of knowledge of exactly what constitutes better practices makes it unlikely that directives or regulations from above will lead to substantial improvements. What is needed are incentive systems that induce better practices by rewarding schools (and teachers and staff) that do well; these rewards should be linked to improvements in schooling.

The apparent limited effectiveness of teachers' salaries, as shown in Table 4.4, might be seen as evidence against such a strategy. But these results are from experiences in which teachers' salaries were generally linked not to performance, but to credentials and tenure. Therefore, the limited extent to which teachers' salaries are linked to schooling achieve-

**Box 4.1. Zonal Disparities in Schooling within Brazil:
the Role of Schooling Quality**

There are striking zonal disparities in schooling attainment and illiteracy between the Northeast and all other zones of Brazil. Almost 40 percent of the
population in the Northeast is illiterate, but in all other zones illiterates number
less than 20 percent. The average number of years of schooling for the Northeast is only about 60 percent of the average for the other zones.

   These zonal disparities in schooling attainment raise concern because the
overall schooling level of the Brazilian population is very low compared to
other Latin American countries with similar per capita income. Average schooling in Brazil is close only to that of the poorest South American country, Bolivia. As a consequence, the indicators for the relatively educated Southeast of
Brazil are barely better than those for Bolivia and worse than those for Peru and
Colombia. The indicators for the Northeast are far worse than for any country
in South America.

   Because the supply of schools in Brazil does not seem to be a major
bottleneck in schooling, public attention has turned to the quality of public
primary education. The low quality of public primary education is considered
to be the fundamental cause of extremely high repetition and dropout rates and
of the low schooling attainment of the Brazilian population.

   To what extent are the zonal disparities in schooling attainment the result of concomitant zonal disparities in the quality of schooling? To address this
question, we consider the zonal variations in two measures of quality of schooling: time spent in school and cost per pupil.

   The first two figures and the table present estimates of the average time
spent in school, by state. They reveal that, on average, Brazilian children spend
slightly less than 4 hours per day in lower primary public schools (first to fourth
grade). They also reveal differences in the average time spent in school between
the Northeast and the other zones. All states in the Northeast are far below
average except for Bahia (BA), Maranhão (MA), and Sergipe (SE). On average,
northeastern children spend 10 percent less time in school than children in the
Southeast.

   Next, we consider zonal variability in the cost per pupil for state and
municipal primary schools. In Brazil, primary schooling is mainly a responsibility of the municipalities, with state governments supplementing the cost when
necessary. The table and the last two figures present the cost per pupil in state
and municipal schools by state. In all states, the cost per pupil in state schools
tends to be greater than in municipal schools, which is consistent with the general impression that state schools tend to be better than municipal schools.
More importantly, the zonal disparities in expenditures per student are extremely pronounced. The cost per pupil in state schools in the Northeast is a
third that of similar schools in the Southeast. The differential between these
two zones for municipal schools is even greater: the cost per pupil in the Northeast is a seventh of the cost in the Southeast.

In summary, the evidence clearly indicates that zonal disparities in quality of schooling are strongly correlated with zonal disparities in schooling attainment. This finding corroborates the hypothesis that limited school quality in Brazil has strong negative effects on schooling attainment of children in both urban and rural areas of the Northeast. These zonal disparities may indicate that unequal access to public services could be a major cause of the difficulties in bringing about economic and social integration between the Northeast and the rest of Brazil. Therefore, improvements in the quality of public schooling for northeastern children must be a priority for reducing zonal disparities in Brazil.

Not all types of improvements in quality, however, will increase the schooling attainment of poor children. One can differentiate between two types of improvements in the quality of schooling by which type tends to increase schooling attainment for children from poor families and reduce the degree of inequality in schooling opportunities. A change in quality increases the schooling attainment of poor children if it releases family resources. On the other hand, if the change requires a concomitant increase in family resources in order to be utilized, it may exclude poor children from the schooling process. Let us assume that for each level of resources committed by families, there is an optimum amount for each dimension of the quality of schooling. At levels below this optimum, increases in quality release family resources and increase schooling attainment; at levels above the optimum, increases in quality demand extra family resources and may lead to a decrease in the schooling attainment of poor children. Thus increases in quality may either release or demand extra family resources.

A change in quality of schooling of the release type most benefits poor children if it substitutes for family resources. In this case, greater quality would help not only to increase the schooling level of poor children but also to reduce the degree of inequality of opportunities. Examples would be the public provision of transportation for all children to and from school, as well as free school materials.

A change in quality of schooling of the demand type most benefits children from high-income families and may be prejudicial against poor children, since it increases the demand for family resources and therefore reinforces the role of family background. In this case, inequality in opportunities increases. For instance, let us suppose that schools opted for a more advanced curriculum. To implement this, they contract better-qualified teachers and require students to work harder. One would expect an increase in the repetition rate for children whose parents, because of their low schooling level or because of a binding budget constraint, would not be able to help their children with homework or pay for extra classes. Another example would be a compulsory increase in the number of hours that children have to stay in school, forcing children who have to combine work and study to drop out. In both examples, the increase in quality has a positive impact only if families also increase the amount of resources they devote to their children's schooling. In these cases, minimal requirements have been raised, making schooling more expensive, and perhaps too expensive

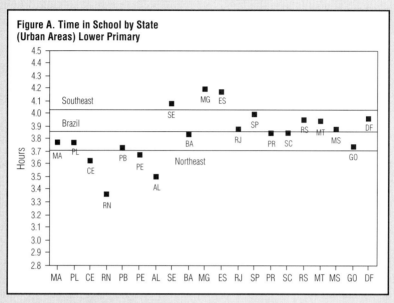

Figure A. Time in School by State (Urban Areas) Lower Primary

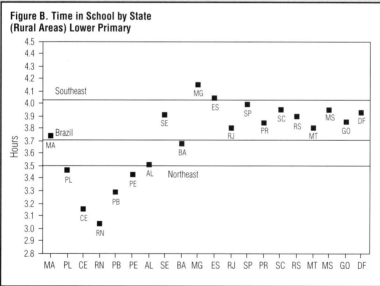

Figure B. Time in School by State (Rural Areas) Lower Primary

for poor families. Therefore, improved schooling services may make schools more inaccessible for poor children, leading to a decrease in schooling attainment and consequently to an increase in the degree of inequality in schooling opportunities.

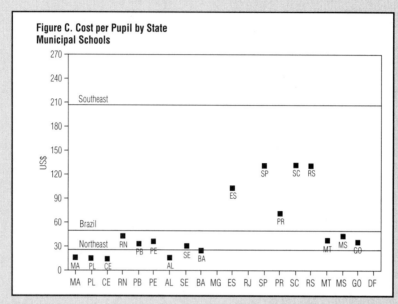

Figure C. Cost per Pupil by State
Municipal Schools

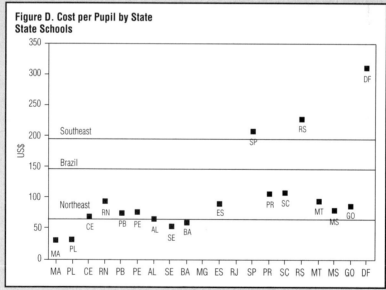

Figure D. Cost per Pupil by State
State Schools

To increase the schooling attainment of poor children, therefore, one should design changes in quality of schooling that release family resources, not increase the demand for those resources.

**Table A. Zonal Disparities in Cost per Pupil and Time Spent in School**

| | Cost Per Pupil Per Year (US$) | | Time in School | | GDP Per Capita (US$1988) |
|---|---|---|---|---|---|
| | State | Municipal | Lower Urban | Primary Rural | |
| Brazil Average | 146 | 52 | 3.9 | 3.7 | 2,241 |
| North Zone | 63 | 35 | 3.8 | n.a. | 1,401 |
| Acre (AC) | 49 | 49 | 3.7 | n.a. | 2,035 |
| Amapa (AP) | 98 | 32 | 3.9 | n.a. | n.a. |
| Amazonas (AM) | 81 | 44 | 3.8 | n.a. | n.a. |
| Para (PA) | 53 | 27 | 3.8 | n.a. | 1,109 |
| Rondonia (RO) | 208 | n.a. | 3.7 | n.a. | n.a. |
| Roraima (RR) | 144 | n.a. | 4.0 | n.a. | n.a. |
| Northeast Zone | 67 | 29 | 3.7 | 3.5 | 918 |
| Alagoas (AL) | 67 | 21 | 3.5 | 3.5 | 895 |
| Bahia (BA) | 62 | 28 | 3.8 | 3.7 | 1,226 |
| Ceara (CE) | 67 | 22 | 3.6 | 3.2 | 778 |
| Maranhão (MA) | 33 | 23 | 3.8 | 3.7 | 564 |
| Paraiba (PB) | 74 | 36 | 3.7 | 3.3 | 628 |
| Pernambuco (PE) | 77 | 37 | 3.7 | 3.4 | 1,102 |
| Piaui (PI) | 33 | 22 | 3.8 | 3.4 | 472 |
| Rio G. do Norte (RN) | 98 | 42 | 3.4 | 3.0 | 858 |
| Sergipe (SE) | 57 | 32 | 4.1 | 3.9 | 943 |
| Southeast Zone | 194 | 209 | 4.0 | 4.0 | 3,217 |
| Espirito Santo (ES) | 89 | 107 | 4.2 | 4.0 | 1,914 |
| Minas Gerais (MG) | n.a. | n.a. | 4.2 | 4.1 | 1,850 |
| Rio de Janeiro (RJ) | 306 | 266 | 3.9 | 3.8 | 3,352 |
| São Paulo (SP) | 203 | 138 | 4.0 | 4.0 | 3,993 |
| South Zone | 143 | 109 | 3.9 | 3.9 | 2,382 |
| Parana (PR) | 107 | 63 | 3.9 | 3.8 | 2,037 |
| Rio G. do Sul (RS) | 227 | 138 | 3.9 | 3.9 | 2,738 |
| Santa Catarina (SC) | 106 | 139 | 3.9 | 4.0 | 2,344 |
| Center-West Zone | 84 | 40 | 3.8 | 3.9 | 1,949 |
| Distrito Federal (DF) | 308 | n.a. | 3.9 | 3.9 | 4,498 |
| Goias (GO) | 84 | 38 | 3.7 | 3.8 | 1,277 |
| Mato Grosso (MT) | 91 | 39 | 3.9 | 3.8 | 1,788 |
| Mato G. do Sul (MS) | 75 | 45 | 3.9 | 3.8 | n.a. |

n.a. = not available.

*Source:* Prepared by Ricardo Paes de Barros, Rosane Silva Pinto de Mendonça, and James Alan Shope for this report based in part on material in Albuquerque (1991), Albuquerque and Villela (1991), Barros and Mendonça (1992), Fletcher and Costa Ribeiro (1987), IBGE (1990), and Ministry of Education of Brazil (1990).

**Table 4.4. Summary of Educational Production Functions for Developing Countries**

|  | Percentage Distribution | | | |
|---|---|---|---|---|
|  | Positive Significant Effect | Negative Significant Effect | Insignificant Effect | Number of Studies |
| Teacher/pupil ratio | 26 | 26 | 48 | 31 |
| Teacher education | 55 | 3 | 42 | 64 |
| Teacher experience | 34 | 4 | 62 | 47 |
| Teacher salary | 29 | 14 | 57 | 14 |
| Expenditure per pupil | 50 | 0 | 50 | 12 |
| Facilities | 66 | 8 | 26 | 35 |

*Source:* Based on summary of 96 studies in Harbison and Hanushek (1992, Table 2.2), updated to include their own results.

ment in such a context does not provide insight regarding what would happen with institutional structures in which teachers' salaries were linked to performance. There are difficult questions about how to measure teachers' performance without introducing distortions, but it seems likely, on the basis of evidence to date, that efforts to tie teachers' salaries to performance might produce a high efficiency gain. Likewise, there are difficult questions regarding how to make schools more responsive to demands, but it appears that the potential gains may be considerable.

*Determinant 4. Studies (although limited) suggest that private schools may be more effective than public schools.*

Most schooling at the primary and secondary levels in Latin America and the Caribbean occurs in public schools that are free or almost free. But there are at least two major reasons to promote more education in private schools. First, more private education would reduce the pressures on government budgets and thereby help to maintain fiscal balance. Second, private schools a priori would likely be more efficient because administrators and teachers have incentives that make them more responsive to students and their parents than teachers in public schools.

Simple comparisons of test scores between private and public schools, however, do not provide an empirical test of the second point unless students of all income levels are assigned randomly to schools. Comparisons of family background for students in private versus public secondary schools in Brazil, Colombia, and the Dominican Republic suggest, however, that students in private schools have substantially better family situations than do students in public schools, with family incomes almost twice as high, a higher percentage of fathers with white collar occupations, and roughly twice as many mothers with post-primary schooling (Jiménez, Lockheed, and Paqueo, 1991; de Mello e Souza and da Silva, 1992). Recent studies for Colombia and the Dominican Republic control for family background by estimating achievement relations for private and for public secondary school students, and then using the average characteristics of the public school students to estimate achievement for private school students who have these characteristics.[7] The results suggest that for a given family background, Colombian students score 13 percent higher on math and verbal achievement scores and Dominican Republic students score from 31 percent to 47 percent higher on math achievement scores if they are in private rather than public schools. The unit costs, moreover, tend to be substantially lower in the private than in the public schools (although not in private schools in the Dominican Republic that are authorized to give Ministry of Education examinations). Therefore, the private schools tend to be much more cost effective than public schools—60 percent more in Colombia and 100 percent more in the Dominican Republic in schools not authorized to give Ministry of Education examinations (although private schools that are authorized to give these examinations are about as effective as public schools).

Why do the private schools perform better? One important factor in the Dominican Republic appears to be better access to textbooks. In studies for other developing areas, another factor seems to be the practice of recruiting teachers with lower formal qualifications and giving them more in-service training, as well as promoting better teaching practices regarding homework, testing, and classroom discipline. But such observed school characteristics account for only part of the difference between private and public school performance. An important policy implication may be the advisability of mimicking the entire incentive structure of private schools, including decentralization and mechanisms such as the voucher system used in Chile that encourage schools to be more responsive to the needs of students and parents. Also, because there have been so few studies that control for selectivity of students into different schools, much valuable information about improving policies would result from undertaking further investigations of the relative effectiveness of private versus public schools at different schooling levels and in different contexts.

---

[7] The family background characteristics include income of head of household (for Colombia), mother's schooling, and father's occupation. The procedure described in the text assumes that all relevant family background characteristics are highly correlated with these characteristics, which may be a strong assumption. Similar studies undertaken for the Philippines, Tanzania, and Thailand have also had similar results.

*Determinant 5. Grade repetition is a problem and an opportunity.*[8]

Every year, more than 17 million children start the first grade in Latin America and the Caribbean. About 40 percent of the children start school "on time"—that is, at the legal age of 5 to 7 years, although with substantial variance across countries (Table 4.5, column 1). But almost all children eventually start school—93 percent for the region. Therefore, access to primary school does not seem to be a major problem in most of the region, although it may be in a few countries such as Haiti, and to a lesser degree, Colombia, the Dominican Republic, El Salvador, and Guatemala (Table 4.5, column 2).

The degree of repetition, however, is striking, particularly for the first grade. Latin America and the Caribbean have a first grade repetition rate of 42 percent and an overall primary grade repetition rate of 29 percent, according to recent estimates based on a special UNESCO/ OREALC survey. Official estimates have been only about half as high.[9] The survey rates imply that more than seven million first graders and more than 19 million primary grade students are repeaters in the region every year. More than US$4 billion is spent each year to teach these primary school repeaters (under the assumption that the unit cost is a little more than US$200).[10]

Although the region has the highest repetition rates of any major region in the world, there is, of course, substantial variance across countries. The highest rates (more than 50 percent) are estimated for Brazil, Colombia, the Dominican Republic, Guatemala, Haiti, and Honduras, and the lowest (10 percent or lower) are reported for Chile, Jamaica, and Trinidad and Tobago (Table 4.5, column 3). The rates have been slowly declining, from almost 50 percent for first grade repeaters in 1980 to 42 percent in 1988. Repetition affects students from all socioeconomic

---

[8] The initial part of this discussion draws on Schiefelbein and Wolff (1992), to which interested readers are referred for more detail.

[9] These estimates are much higher than official estimates for four apparent reasons: (1) Students stop attending school to work and are counted as dropouts, but then begin again in the next year in the same grade without being counted as repeaters. (2) Teachers do not give high priority to filling out forms on repetition and tend to systematically underreport repeaters. (3) Some students who pass but are not very mature are encouraged to reenroll in the same grade the subsequent year but are not counted as repeaters. (4) Parents may present their children as new students in new schools if they have been forced out of previous schools because of behavioral problems, or if they have moved to another district.

[10] This is the value used in Schiefelbein and Wolfe (1992). Values ranging from US$30 for low-income areas of rural Northeast Brazil to US$195 in Southeast Brazil are reported in Hanushek, Gomes-Neto, and Harbison (1992).

**Table 4.5.  School Access and First Grade Repetition Rates in
Latin America and the Caribbean**
*(Percent)*

|  | 1990 School Access | | 1988 First Grade Repetition Rates |
|---|---|---|---|
|  | On time | Ever |  |
|  | (1) | (2) | (3) |
| Haiti | 1 | 44 | 61 |
| Dominican Republic | 76 | 76 | 58 |
| Honduras | 83 | 93 | 53 |
| Guatemala | 52 | 72 | 55 |
| Bolivia | 61 | 90 | 33 |
| El Salvador | 65 | 73 | 54 |
| Ecuador | 82 | 100 | 33 |
| Jamaica | 82 | 100 | 6 |
| Colombia | 43 | 83 | 52 |
| Paraguay | 100 | 100 | 33 |
| Costa Rica | 43 | 99 | 22 |
| Peru | 66 | 97 | 38 |
| Panama | 82 | 99 | 28 |
| Mexico | 96 | 100 | 33 |
| Brazil | 69 | 92 | 53 |
| Chile | 40 | 98 | 10 |
| Uruguay | 43 | 100 | 15 |
| Argentina | — | — | 31 |
| Venezuela | 76 | 95 | 28 |
| Trinidad and Tobago | 100 | 100 | 0 |

*Source:* Schiefelbein (1992, tables 1 and 2).

groups, but mostly those from lower-income remote rural households whose parents had less schooling, and whose first language is an indigenous one. Most repeaters are boys, although the gender gap appears to be declining over time.

Some repetition does not necessarily indicate a problem. Almost any school system will have some students who are not yet mature enough to be promoted, or who have a variety of learning disabilities and would benefit sufficiently from repetition to make it economically efficient. Also, some households might intend to keep a child in school for the entire year if health, weather, harvests, and labor markets are normal, but then withdraw the child if the family faces difficulties and reenroll him/her the following year. Likewise, the absence of repetition is not necessarily an indication of a good school system, since a school might automatically promote all students whether or not they have learned anything.

The repetition rate in the Latin American and Caribbean region, however, suggests that there is a major problem, that the achievement of students is inadequate. For Brazil, for instance, Amadeo et al. (1993)

claim that the greatest problem is not a lack of schools (about 90 percent of each cohort has school access) but a lack of sufficient school quality to induce students to stay in school and to progress on time through the grades. That is, repetition and dropouts constitute the most serious problems. Amadeo et al. claim that high repetition rates limit school access, delay entrance, and have high resource costs, and that improved school quality, which makes schooling more attractive and cheaper, will therefore induce increased schooling attainment. Of particular interest is improved quality that also reduces the costs to families, such as free school materials and transportation, financed in part by redistributing resources from richer to poorer schools (Box 4.1).

Information is quite imperfect regarding which strategies are likely to be most cost effective in improving schooling quality, as noted earlier. But a recent study (Hanushek, Gomes-Neto, and Harbison, 1992) of northeastern rural Brazil using longitudinal data on students suggests that there may be potential for substantial gains. This study estimates that some quality improvements, namely in textbooks and writing materials, may have a 10-to-1 immediate payback by increasing achievement (in value-added terms) and promotion rates, thereby saving the resources that otherwise would go to teaching more repeaters (who learn at much less cost if they are promoted than if they repeat grades). Although this study has its limitations,[11] it certainly suggests that we should look more deeply into the possible gains from improving promotion rates through improving some dimensions of school quality.

*Determinant 6. Other possible schooling innovations have been tried*

Many other innovations have been tried in the region, with varying degrees of apparent success. But relatively few have been systematically evaluated and the results widely disseminated. One exception is radio education for mathematics in rural Nicaragua. Comparisons suggest that the achievement gains per unit cost were almost 50 percent higher from radio education than from textbooks, which tend to be higher than those from most other interventions (Lockheed and Hanushek, 1988). This radio intervention, moreover, probably has additional gains from lessening the negative effects of local school monopolies in rural areas. There probably would be high returns to public subsidies for systematically evaluating other innovations and disseminating the results.

---

[11] There are some technical questions about the nature of the sample, the attrition that takes place in it, and the specification and estimation of the relations in the study—all of which might change the estimates a fair amount.

## Health and Nutrition Determinants

### Aggregate Indicators of Health and Nutrition Inputs

#### Recent Levels of Inputs Related to Health and Nutrition

Data for three widely available indicators of health personnel and for one indicator of nutrition are summarized in Table 4.6. For each indicator, the table shows both the value for a recent year and the degree to which that value differs from predictions based on international experience (controlling for per capita real income). Figures 4.2A–D plot these data against real per capita income.

These health input indicators, not surprisingly, tend to improve as per capita income increases. Population per physician and population per nurse (broadly defined) both tend to be lower with higher real per capita income, while the percentage of births attended by health personnel and daily calorie supply per capita tend to be greater.

The region has a relatively high number of physicians per capita; all 20 of the countries for which the data are available have lower population per physician than predicted by international experience. Nevertheless, individual countries differ from average international experience by varying amounts, with Trinidad and Tobago and Venezuela being much closer to international experience than other countries in the region.

The number of nurses per capita in the region also tends to be high relative to international experience, although not as high as the number of physicians per capita. Of the 17 countries in the region for which these data exist, 13 have more nurses per capita than the international regression line. The four exceptions (with fewer nurses per capita than international experience) are Argentina, Bolivia, Brazil, and Haiti.

The percentages of births attended by health staff, in contrast to physicians and nurses per capita, are close to international experience on average, once there is control for real per capita income; eight countries in the region are below the international regression line and nine are above. The percentages of births attended by health staff are particularly low relative to international experience in Ecuador, El Salvador, Guatemala, Haiti, and Paraguay (all more than 15 percent below the international prediction, with Paraguay and Guatemala more than 30 percent below), and are relatively high in Chile, Costa Rica, and Jamaica (all more than 30 percent above the international regression line).

The daily calorie supply per capita in the region is also above international experience in half the cases (more than 300 calories per day above in Argentina, Mexico, and Paraguay) and below international experience in

**Table 4.6.  Recent Health and Nutrition Physical Inputs in Latin America and the Caribbean, with International Comparison**

| Countries | Population per Physician 1984 | | Population per Nursing Person 1984 | | Percentage Birth Attended by Health Staff, 1985 | | Daily Calorie Supply Per Capita, 1986 | |
|---|---|---|---|---|---|---|---|---|
| | Actual | Difference from International Experience | Actual | Difference from International Experience | Actual | Difference from International Experience | Actual | Difference from International Experience |
| | (1) | (2) | (3) | (4) | (5) | (6) | (7) | (8) |
| Haiti | 7,180 | −6,093 | 2,290 | 335 | 20 | 1 | 1,902 | −382 |
| Dominican Republic | 1,760 | −9,831 | 1,210 | −543 | 57 | 10 | 2,477 | 101 |
| Honduras | 1,510 | −9,310 | 670 | −990 | 50 | 1 | 2,068 | −351 |
| Guatemala | 2,180 | −8,462 | 850 | −789 | 19 | −31 | 2,307 | −122 |
| Bolivia | 1,540 | −10,704 | 2,480 | 649 | 36 | −9 | 2,143 | −198 |
| El Salvador | 2,830 | −7,551 | 930 | −677 | 35 | −16 | 2,160 | −283 |
| Ecuador | 820 | −8,885 | 610 | −916 | 27 | −26 | 2,058 | −422 |
| Jamaica | 2,040 | −7,663 | 490 | 1,036 | 89 | 36 | 2,590 | 110 |
| Colombia | 1,240 | −8,154 | 660 | −828 | 51 | −3 | 2,542 | 44 |
| Paraguay | 1,450 | −7,972 | 1,000 | −493 | 22 | −32 | 2,853 | 357 |
| Costa Rica | 960 | −6,146 | 450 | −761 | 93 | 32 | 2,803 | 178 |
| Peru | 1,040 | −7,678 | — | — | 55 | −1 | 2,246 | −273 |
| Panama | 980 | −4,474 | 390 | −620 | 83 | | 2,446 | −273 |
| Mexico | 1,240 | −5,641 | 880 | −304 | — | — | 3,132 | 494 |
| Brazil | 1,080 | −4,336 | 1,210 | 204 | 73 | 7 | 2,656 | −65 |
| Chile | 1,230 | −6,555 | 370 | −924 | 97 | 38 | 2,579 | −8 |
| Uruguay | 520 | −3,571 | — | — | — | — | 2,648 | −149 |
| Argentina | 370 | −3,249 | 980 | 172 | — | — | 3,210 | 396 |
| Venezuela | 700 | −640 | — | — | 82 | 4 | 2,494 | −464 |
| Trinidad and Tobago | 1,080 | −270 | 260 | −229 | 90 | 11 | 3,082 | 117 |

*Source:* Based on regression estimates by the author.

half (more than 300 calories per day below in Ecuador, Haiti, Honduras, and Venezuela). Thus, these four indicators suggest that for the region on average, and particularly for countries such as Ecuador and Haiti, the composition of health-related inputs is skewed toward physicians and associated expensive curative care for relatively small elites rather than toward more basic health services and nutrition.

These indicators of health and nutrition inputs are associated across countries in the region, although in large part because of associations with real per capita income. With control for real per capita income, the only bivariate correlations as large as 0.5 in absolute magnitude are between the percentages of births attended by health staff and daily calorie supply per person (0.7), and population per nurse person (−0.6). The correlations also indicate that there is a positive association among higher numbers of

**Figure 4.2A.  Population per Physician versus Real Per Capita Income, 1988**

**Figure 4.2B.  Population per Nursing Person versus Real Per Capita Income, 1988**

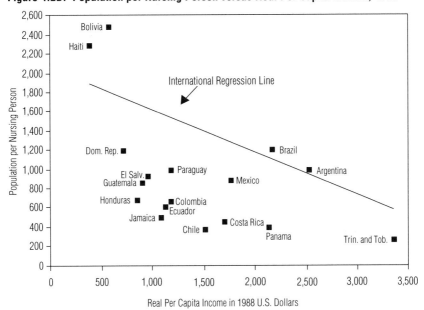

**Figure 4.2C.  Percentage of Births Attended by Health Staff versus Real Per Capita Income, 1988**

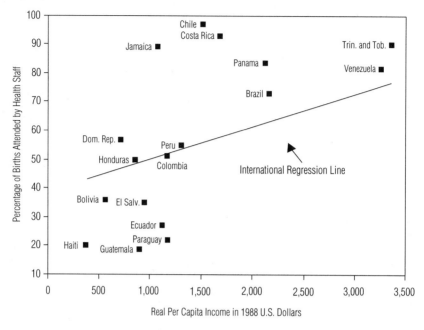

**Figure 4.2D.  Daily Calorie Supply Per Capita versus Real Per Capita Income, 1988**

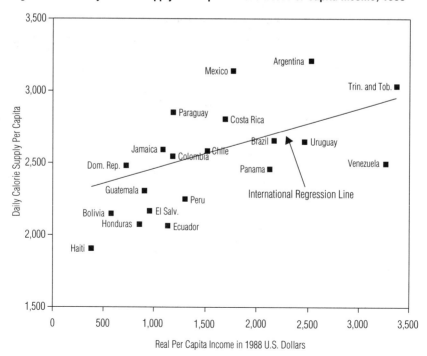

nurses per population, higher percentages of births with health staff in attendance, and higher daily calorie supply per person even after controlling for real per capita income—but that each of these three indicators is negatively associated with number of physicians per population. That is, countries with relatively high numbers of physicians per capita, controlling for real per capita income, tend to have relatively low values of the other three indicators (and vice versa). Thus, such countries tend to have inputs that are associated more with expensive curative medicine and less with basic preventive medicine.

Do these health and nutrition inputs relate to health and nutrition outcome indicators such as life expectancies and infant and child mortality rates? The answer to this question is positive, in part because of the cross-country associations among real per capita real income, health and nutrition inputs, and health and nutrition outcomes. It is also positive if there is control for per capita real income, as in Table 4.7. This table gives the significant coefficient estimates from multivariate regressions for the region's recent life expectancies at birth, infant mortality rates, risk of dying by age five, maternal mortality rates, and rates of low birth weight. The right-side variables in each regression include the four indicators under discussion. The patterns in these estimates are striking.

For none of the health and nutrition outcomes in the table is the population per physician significantly nonzero even at the 10 percent level. But the other three indicators all have a number of significant coefficient estimates that indicate that having more of them improves health and nutrition outcomes, even with control for per capita real income. An increase of 1,000 people per nurse is significantly associated with the following: lower life expectancy (by 6.2 years); higher infant mortality rates (by 34 infants per 1,000 live births); higher risk of dying by age five, particularly for males (45 to 50 children per 1,000 live births); and higher levels of maternal deaths (by 138 per 1,000 births). There is no significant impact on the percentage of births with low birth weight.

An increase of 10 percent in the proportion of births attended by health staff is associated with a significant increase in life expectancy at birth (by 0.7 years) and reductions in the following: infant mortality (by 2.3 children per 1,000 live births); the risk of dying by age five (by 2.7 children per 1,000 live births, and somewhat more for males); and (with less precision) maternal mortality (by 23 mothers per 1,000 live births). Again, there is no significant impact on low birth weight.

An increase of 100 calories per day per capita is significantly associated with an increase in life expectancy at birth (by 0.6 years) and reductions in the following: infant mortality rate (by 3.9 per 1,000 live births); the risk of dying by age five (by 4.6 per 1,000 live births and again,

**Table 4.7.  Estimated Effects of Indicators of Health and Nutrition Inputs on Measures of Health and Nutrition in Latin America and the Caribbean**

| | 1984 Population (1,000) Per | | Percentage Births Attended by Health Staff, 1985 | Daily Calorie Supply Per Capita, 1986 |
|---|---|---|---|---|
| | Physician | Nurse person | | |
| Life expectancy at birth, 1988 | | | | |
| Total | — | −6.2 | 0.069 | 0.0057 |
| Female | −0.26** | −6.2 | 0.068 | 0.0051 |
| Male | — | −6.1 | 0.070 | 0.0063 |
| Infant mortality rate per 1,000 | | | | |
| live births, 1988 | — | 34 | −0.23 | −0.039 |
| Risk of dying by age five/ | | | | |
| 1,000 live births, 1988 | — | 47 | −0.27 | −0.046 |
| Female | — | 45 | −0.23* | −0.044 |
| Male | — | 50 | −0.31 | −0.049 |
| Male–female | — | 4.9 | −0.085 | −0.005** |
| Maternal mortality per 100,000 | | | | |
| live births, 1980 | 16** | 138 | −2.3** | 0.21** |
| Low birth weight (%), 1985 | −0.81** | — | — | −0.008** |

*Note:* All included point estimates are significantly nonzero at the 5 percent level except those indicated by * are significantly nonzero at the 10 percent level and those indicated by ** are significantly nonzero at the 20 percent level.
*Source:* Based on regression estimates by the author.

somewhat more for males); and the percentage of births with low birth weight (by 1 percent), with a puzzling, somewhat imprecisely estimated increase of 21 in maternal mortality rates per 100.

Of course, all of these aggregate indices of health and nutrition outcomes and inputs in the region are crude, so interpretations of their associations must be qualified. Still, the results in Table 4.7 suggest that for basic health (as reflected in life expectancies at birth, infant and small-child mortality rates, and maternal mortality), basic nursing services, health care at birth, and basic nutrition are important positive factors. Countries in the region with better performance regarding these inputs, controlling for real per capita income, tend to have better basic health outcomes than would be expected on the basis of their real per capita incomes. In contrast, however, countries with more physicians per capita than expected given the countries' per capita income do not have any systematically different basic health outcomes, although they may have differences in morbidity experiences that are not reflected in the aggregate life expectancy and mortality data.

In addition to the four physical indicators of health and nutrition inputs covered in Tables 4.6 and 4.7, there are data for 10 or 11 countries in the region on central government expenditures on health and on housing, amenities, social security, and welfare (hereafter, "other health-related expenditures"). Table 4.8 gives these data, both as shares of total central government expenditures and as shares of GNP, as well as the actual expenditures and the difference between these expenditures and those predicted by international regressions, controlling for real per capita income. These data are subject to the same limitations as are data for the shares of central government expenditures on schooling discussed above—namely, they do not include expenditures at other levels of government or private expenditures, nor do they adjust for differences in relative prices across countries—so they must be interpreted with caution.

Recent central government health expenditures and other health-related expenditures in the region tend to be high relative to international experience, exceeding the international regression line in seven out of 11 cases for the former and in seven out of 10 cases for the latter. For the share of central government expenditures on health, Costa Rica and Panama are particularly noteworthy, with actual expenditures more than 10 percent above the international regression line; Mexico, at the other end of the spectrum, is almost 5 percent below the line. For the share of other health-related expenditures in total government expenditures, Uruguay is 33 percent above the international regression line, Chile is 26 percent above, Bolivia is 17 percent, Argentina is 15 percent, and Costa Rica is 13 percent; Mexico, again, is farthest below that experience but less than 5 percent below. The relatively high central government share of other health-related expenditures largely reflects the social security systems. In a number of cases, not surprisingly, these large shares in total government expenditures also imply relatively large shares of GNP. Central government health expenditures are more than 3 percent of GNP above predicted levels in Costa Rica and Panama. Central government health-related expenditures are more than 3 percent of GNP above predicted levels in Chile (more than 9 percent above), Uruguay (more than 6 percent), and Costa Rica (more than 3 percent). These patterns suggest substantial fiscal pressures stemming from central government health and health-related expenditures in a number of countries in the region.

What effects do such expenditure patterns have on measured health and nutrition? If there is control for real per capita income, simple bivariate correlations suggest that central government health expenditures are positively associated with life expectancies at birth (a correlation of 0.7 and somewhat higher for males) and negatively associated with infant and child mortality and low birth weight (correlations of about –0.6). But central government expenditure shares of other health-related services have correlations as large as 0.5, in absolute value, only with low birth weights (about –0.6). Moreover, in simple regressions with the health measures discussed in Chapter 3 and used Table 4.8, neither the central government expenditure

**Table 4.8. Central Government Expenditures on Health and Health-Related Services as Percentage Shares of Total Government Expenditure and GNP, with International Comparison, 1988**

| Countries | Central Government Health Expenditures | | | | Central Government Other Health-Related Expenditures | | | |
| | As % of Total Central Government Expenditures | | As % of GNP | | As % of Total Central Government Expenditures | | As % of GNP | |
| | Actual | Difference from International Experience | Actual | Difference from International Experience | Actual | Difference from International Experience | Actual | Difference from International Experience |
| | (1) | (2) | (3) | (4) | (5) | (6) | (7) | (8) |
| Bolivia | 1.9 | -2.9 | 0.3 | -0.9 | 25.6 | 17.0 | 4.0 | 1.7 |
| El Salvador | 7.1 | 2.0 | 0.8 | -0.6 | 4.4 | -6.0 | 0.5 | -2.6 |
| Costa Rica | 19.3 | 13.7 | 5.4 | 3.7 | 26.7 | 13.2 | 7.5 | 3.3 |
| Peru | 5.8 | 0.5 | 0.8 | -0.7 | — | — | — | — |
| Panama | 16.7 | 10.8 | 5.7 | 3.8 | 16.0 | 0.8 | 5.5 | 0.6 |
| Mexico | 1.1 | -4.6 | 0.3 | -1.5 | 9.3 | -4.5 | 2.6 | -1.7 |
| Brazil | 9.5 | 3.6 | 2.4 | 0.4 | 24.2 | 8.9 | 6.1 | 1.1 |
| Chile | 6.3 | 0.8 | 2.1 | 0.4 | 39.2 | 26.4 | 13.1 | 9.2 |
| Uruguay | 4.8 | -1.3 | 1.1 | -0.9 | 49.5 | 33.1 | 11.7 | 6.3 |
| Argentina | 2.1 | -4.1 | 0.5 | -1.6 | 32.0 | 15.4 | 6.0 | 1.4 |
| Venezuela | 10.0 | 3.4 | 2.2 | -0.2 | 11.7 | -7.2 | 2.6 | -4.0 |
| Trinidad and Tobago | — | — | — | — | — | — | — | — |

*Note:* Health-related expenditures include housing, amenities, social security, and welfare.
*Source:* Based on regression estimates by the author.

**Figure 4.3A.  Percentage Central Government Expenditure on Health versus Real Per Capita Income, 1988**

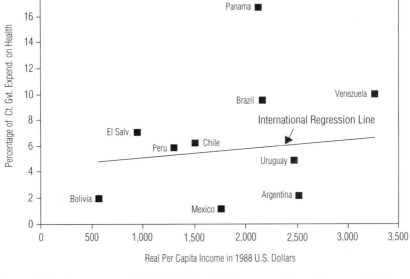

**Figure 4.3B.  Percentage of GNP that is Central Government Expenditure on Health versus Real Per Capita Income, 1988**

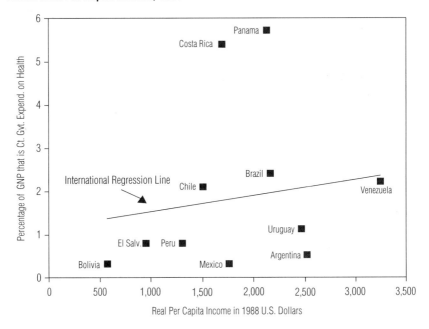

shares on health nor on health-related services have significant coefficient estimates. Therefore, in contrast to the indicators of physical health and nutrition inputs, the central government expenditure patterns, particularly in the other health-related category, do not seem related to basic health measures such as life expectancies at birth and infant, child, and maternal mortality rates. In terms of these health and nutrition measures, it would thus seem that reallocations of central government expenditures more toward basic health and nutrition inputs would be well advised.

*Longer-Run Changes in Health and Nutrition Inputs*

Table 4.9 gives the changes in the ratio of population per physician, the population per nurse, and the daily calorie supply per capita since 1965, as well as the changes in these three indicators with control for changes in real per capita income. The population-to-physician ratio increased in the region compared with international experience; for all 20 countries (although much less for Haiti and Trinidad and Tobago than elsewhere), the increase was greater than predicted by international experience, controlling for changes in real per capita income. The region thus tended to move substantially toward international experience regarding population per physician in the two decades after 1965, although it still had relatively low population-to-physician ratios in the 1980s.

Population per nurse also tended to increase in the region relative to international experience, although Guatemala and Haiti had substantial reductions. Daily calorie supply per capita increased less in 70 percent of the countries in the region than predicted by international experience, with Argentina, Chile, Haiti, Peru, and Uruguay all having changes of more than 300 calories per day below international experience (and only the Dominican Republic having a change of more than 300 calories per day above). Therefore, in the two decades after 1965, the predominant tendency in the region was for deterioration in these health and nutrition input indicators relative to international experience, presumably because of the budgetary imbalances and debt problems and resulting stringencies in many countries.

It is nevertheless striking that, controlling for changes in real per capita income, the changes in health and nutrition inputs were not associated with changes in health and nutrition outcomes.[12] Resources apparently were used more effectively (as indicated in the recent regressions in

---

[12] None of the bivariate correlations is as high as 0.3 in absolute value.

**Table 4.9. Changes in Health and Nutrition Physical Inputs in Latin American and the Caribbean, with International Comparison**

| Countries | Changes in Population per Physician, 1965–84 | | Changes in Population per Nursing Person, 1965–84 | | Changes in Daily Calorie Supply Per Capita, 1965–86 | |
|---|---|---|---|---|---|---|
| | Actual | Difference from International Experience | Actual | Difference from International Experience | Actual | Difference from International Experience |
| | (1) | (2) | (3) | (4) | (5) | (6) |
| Haiti | −6,820 | 317 | −1,060 | −7,433 | −98 | −380 |
| Dominican Republic | 60 | 7,273 | −430 | 2,769 | 605 | 327 |
| Honduras | −3,860 | 2,757 | −860 | 2,093 | 105 | −182 |
| Guatemala | −1,510 | 5,184 | −7,400 | −4,415 | 280 | −6 |
| Bolivia | −1,760 | 4,901 | −1,510 | 1,461 | 274 | −15 |
| El Salvador | — | — | −370 | 2,379 | 301 | 6 |
| Ecuador | −2,180 | 4,908 | −1,710 | 1,438 | 118 | −159 |
| Jamaica | 50 | 5,514 | 150 | 2,615 | 359 | 52 |
| Colombia | −1,260 | 5,617 | −230 | 2,830 | 368 | 88 |
| Paraguay | −390 | 6,670 | −550 | 2,586 | 226 | −51 |
| Costa Rica | −1,050 | 5,096 | −180 | 2,575 | 437 | 148 |
| Peru | −610 | 5,311 | — | — | −79 | −376 |
| Panama | −1,150 | 5,076 | −1,210 | 1,579 | 191 | −94 |
| Mexico | −840 | 5,650 | −100 | 2,800 | 488 | 205 |
| Brazil | −1,420 | 5,398 | −1,890 | 1,146 | 254 | −20 |
| Chile | −890 | 4,787 | −230 | 2,327 | −13 | −313 |
| Uruguay | −360 | 5,121 | — | — | −163 | −459 |
| Argentina | −230 | 4,316 | 370 | 2,436 | 0 | −315 |
| Venezuela | −510 | 2,655 | — | — | 173 | −171 |
| Trinidad and Tobago | −2,860 | 1,669 | −300 | 1,760 | 585 | 276 |

*Source:* Based on regression estimates by the author.

Table 4.7) without large losses, at least in terms of the basic indicators of life expectancies at birth and infant, child, and maternal mortality.

Table 4.10 gives the changes over the 1972–1988 period (for the 11 countries for which data are available) in central government expenditures on health and on other health-related services, as shares of both total governmental expenditures and GNP (without and with control for changes in real per capita income). About half the countries had greater increases in central government expenditure shares than predicted by international experience, and about half had smaller increases. The cuts in government expenditures on health and on health-related services, therefore, were not particularly severe relative to international experience during this period, despite frequent statements to the contrary. They also were not as extensive as the changes in the indicators of physical health and nutrition inputs summarized in Table 4.9.

**Table 4.10. Changes in Central Government Expenditures on Health and Health-Related Services as Percentage Shares of Total Government Expenditure and of GNP, with International Comparison, 1972–88**

| Countries | Central Government Health Expenditures | | | | Central Government Other Health-Related Expenditures | | | |
| | As % of Total Central Government Expenditures | | As % of GNP | | As % of Total Central Government Expenditures | | As % of GNP | |
| | Actual | Difference from International Experience | Actual | Difference from International Experience | Actual | Difference from International Experience | Actual | Difference from International Experience |
| | (1) | (2) | (3) | (4) | (5) | (6) | (7) | (8) |
| Bolivia | -4.4 | -3.6 | -0.3 | -0.4 | 25.6 | 25.5 | 4.0 | 3.8 |
| El Salvador | -3.8 | -2.9 | -0.6 | -0.6 | -3.2 | -3.3 | -0.5 | -0.8 |
| Costa Rica | 15.5 | 16.6 | 4.7 | 4.7 | 0.0 | -2.0 | 2.4 | 2.0 |
| Peru | 0.3 | 1.3 | -0.0 | -0.1 | — | — | — | — |
| Panama | 1.6 | 2.8 | 1.6 | 1.6 | 5.2 | 5.0 | 2.5 | 2.0 |
| Mexico | -3.4 | -2.3 | -0.2 | -0.2 | -16.1 | -16.3 | -0.3 | -0.7 |
| Brazil | 2.8 | 4.0 | 1.2 | -1.2 | -10.8 | -11.0 | -0.0 | -0.6 |
| Chile | -1.9 | -0.8 | -1.4 | -1.4 | -0.6 | -0.8 | -4.1 | -4.5 |
| Uruguay | 3.2 | 4.4 | 0.7 | 0.8 | -2.8 | -3.1 | -1.3 | -2.0 |
| Argentina | — | — | — | — | 12.0 | 11.7 | 3.0 | 2.3 |
| Venezuela | -1.7 | -0.4 | 0.1 | 0.1 | 2.5 | 2.1 | 0.9 | -0.0 |

*Note*: Health-related expenditures include housing, amenities, social security, and welfare.
*Source*: Based on regression estimates by the author.

It might seem that average changes in health expenditures and health-related expenditures by the central government, compared with international experience, would explain the average experience with changes in health and nutrition outcomes, despite the relative deterioration in the indicators of physical health and nutrition inputs. The underlying statistical associations, however, do not support the proposition that countries in which central government expenditures differed substantially from international experience had resulting major differences in health and nutrition outcomes.

### Other Evidence on Health and Nutrition Determinants

Good health is determined by a number of factors, not only preventive and curative health care, but also the environment and the general economy, controllability (i.e., genetics and climate have large effects on health but currently cannot be controlled), and health policies. The existence of so many dimensions of health determination, complicated by limited knowledge about many of these dimensions, makes complete coverage of health determinants and related policies an enormous topic. We will therefore focus only on consumption patterns and direct health-related interventions and institutions.

#### Consumption Patterns: Nutrients, Tobacco and Other Addictive Substances, Sexual Behavior Related to Sexually Transmitted Diseases

**Nutrients.** Inadequate protein-energy nutrition, although much less prevalent than in South Asia and Africa, still afflicts many people in the region. Studies for Barbados, Brazil, and Guatemala suggest that inadequate infant and child protein-energy nutrition can have deleterious effects on intellectual development and school performance, although some of these results must be qualified because of the failure to control for other dimensions of behavior (Gomes-Neto et al., 1992; Klein et al., 1972; Galler et al., 1983 a,b; Johnston et al., 1987).[13] Moreover, inadequate

---

[13] For instance, the first of these studies reports that nutrition indicators are associated with lower school dropout probabilities, higher on-time promotion probabilities, and higher achievement test scores for a sample of 395 students in Ceara, Brazil. The authors conclude that "a student's nutritional and health status affects both expected attainment and performance in school" (p. 21). But this study does not control for the endogenous determination of nutrition and the possibility that parents who are particularly interested in their children invest more in both their children's education and their health and nutrition, so that a positive association between schooling success and nutrition does not necessarily mean that the latter causes the former. For further discussion and illustration that controlling for the en-

protein-energy nutrition is often a contributing factor in infant and child deaths from measles, diarrheal disease, respiratory disease, and malaria —which are in fact the major causes of the region's high infant and child mortality. The totality of these costs in terms of resources, productivity, and life is hard to estimate but is certainly large.

Not long ago, the prevalent view was that inadequate[14] protein-energy nutrition was essentially a reflection of poverty. This view was based in part on the common observation that very poor households spend most of their incremental income on food; with a 10 percent increase in income or total expenditures, food expenditures typically increase by 6 to 8 percent. But recent studies suggest that much of that marginal food expenditure goes to buy more expensive calories or to leakages (for instance, to guests or household employees); as a result, even in low-income households, a 10 percent increase in total expenditure results in only a 1 or 2 percent increase in calories consumed by household members (with a slightly higher value of 2 or 3 percent for very low income households, as estimated for Brazil by Strauss and Thomas, 1992). The difference between increasing caloric consumption by 1 percent versus 8 percent with a 10 percent income increase substantially affects whether income increases can eliminate inadequate protein-energy nutrition. If a household is suffering from a 5 percent shortage of calories relative to accepted standards and if its income grows 2 percent per capita in real terms, the difference in the number of years required to reach those standards is three versus 24. Thus, although income increases are likely to have a role in reducing protein-energy nutritional inadequacies, income increases by themselves are likely to reduce any serious protein-energy inadequacies only slowly. A caveat concerns the possible difference in income under the control of men versus women. A recent study for urban areas in Brazil suggests that the effect of women's income on increasing protein-calorie consumption is much larger than the effect of men's income (Thomas, 1990), so if women's income increases relatively quickly, protein-calorie undernutrition may be reduced more rapidly.

---

dogenous nature of health and nutrition can radically change the inference in another developing country context, see Behrman and Lavy (1994).

[14]Adequate nutrient intake varies with individuals (even after controlling for age and sex), activities, and other considerations. Adequate nutrition for normal growth for a child, for example, depends in part on the experience with diarrhea and infectious diseases. Recent studies in Colombia and Guatemala, to illustrate, suggest that young children who do and do not receive nutritional supplements grow at about the same rates in the absence of diarrhea, but among those who experience diarrhea the children without supplements lag behind (Lutter, Habicht, River, and Martorell, 1992).

For faster eradication of protein-energy inadequacies than will result from income increases, other policies such as targeted food programs (see, for instance, Box 4.2) are likely to be required. Such programs are not easy to target precisely. Efforts to target children by providing food at school, for example, are likely to be offset in substantial part by reduced food intake at home, thus effectively shifting part of the food to other household members. Another important factor in improving protein-energy nutrition is schooling, particularly for females, which seems to have a strong impact on nutrition in Brazil and Nicaragua, even controlling for family background (Chapter 2). However, given the long gestation before schooling investments have their effects, more direct nutritional education would seem to be more effective, but evidence from the region is not readily available.

In addition to protein-energy inadequacies, shortages of some micronutrients may also have important negative health effects, especially iron and iodine deficiencies.[15] Iron deficiency causes anemia, which reduces learning capacity and labor productivity; because of the greater need for iron for menstruation and childbearing, women tend to be more subject to anemia. Iodine deficiency can cause lethargy, mental retardation, and delayed motor development in children, and children born to severely iodine-deficient mothers may suffer cretinism. These micronutrient deficiencies tend to be lessened with increased income and more schooling. Fortifying food (iodized salt) and adding iodine to drinking water are quite cost effective for iodine deficiencies, but a similar approach for treating iron deficiency is much more costly, since it requires that individuals take an iron capsule daily, which creates a compliance problem as well as nausea and other side effects.

Health problems related to nutrition are not, however, only a matter of nutrient deficiencies. Increasingly, health problems in the region are related to dietary excesses. Increases in income, education, and international trade, travel, and communication have led to what Popkin (1992) has called a "nutrition transition," with a shift in energy sources from complex carbohydrates (grains and other starches) to animal fat and sugar consumption, and a shift from vegetable to animal protein sources. These dietary changes are associated with increased incidence of obesity, diabetes, cardiovascular diseases, and cancer, and they abet the epidemiological

---

[15] Vitamin A deficiency is very important in other parts of the developing world, particularly Asia, but not so much in Latin America and the Caribbean. Vitamin A deficiency affects the eyes (with effects ranging from night blindness to blindness) and the functioning of the immune system (so that severe deficiencies that cause blindness are usually followed by death).

## Box 4.2. Targeted Food Subsidies in Mexico

Prior to 1990, food subsidies in Mexico were given through a scheme of generalized price discounts. It is well known, however, that this type of subsidy may not be sufficiently targeted to yield substantial benefits to the poor. Tortillas were the only basic staple subject to a generalized price subsidy. Data from the 1984 National Income-Expenditure Survey show that the Lorenz curve of tortilla consumption in Mexico, by percentile of income, is almost equal to the 45 degree line, indicating that the per capita tortilla consumption is pretty much the same regardless of income level. This finding is confirmed by econometric estimates of the income elasticity of demand for tortillas, which shows values close to zero for all income levels. The implication of these findings is straightforward; if, as some estimates suggest, around 20 percent of the population constitutes the truly poor, then only 20 cents out of every peso of subsidies to tortilla consumption reached the very poor.

Starting in 1990, a new strategy of targeted subsidies has been implemented in Mexico to reach the very poor at lower overall fiscal cost through increasingly targeted interventions. The new strategy eliminates generalized price subsidies and replaces them by directly targeted subsidies, mainly through the *Tortilla-Solidaridad* program. The transition toward directly targeted subsidies has not been complete, however. Most of the changes have been concentrated in urban areas, where it is easier to implement this program.

In rural areas, food support is still offered through generalized price discounts, although these discounts are offered only in selected stores operated through CONASUPO, the government agency in charge of food distribution. In principle, CONASUPO's rural stores are located in remote and poor rural communities, where the spillover of benefits associated with generalized price discounts to the nontargeted population is minimal. Further, if these communities are indeed located in remote areas, transport costs serve as a natural barrier limiting arbitrage opportunities and containing fiscal costs. Thus, the generalized price subsidies offered in rural areas are actually semi-targeted subsidies, with the element of targeting deriving from locational considerations.

In urban areas, families targeted for the Tortilla-Solidaridad program are selected by social workers. The minimum wage is used as a targeting criterion: any family earning less than two minimum wages per month qualifies for the program. (Although not an official poverty line, government agencies sometimes use this criterion to identify the poor.) Selected families receive one free kilogram of tortillas per day. Data from the National Income-Expenditure Survey shows that even the poorest urban families consume an average of two kilograms of tortillas daily. Thus, the amount of tortillas delivered is clearly inframarginal, implying that the consumption decisions of the poor are not distorted by the program: at the margin, the price of tortillas faced by the urban poor is the market price. The subsidy therefore is exactly equivalent to a direct income transfer, equal to the amount of tortillas delivered times its market price. At current prices and income, the transfer given through this program to an urban family in the second decile is approximately equal to 5 percent of its monthly income; for families in the first decile the transfer is somewhat higher. Let us note that means testing for the beneficiaries occurs through an income criterion and not through anthropometric indicators that could serve as direct measurements of malnutrition. Indeed, although superficially *Tortilla-Solidaridad* is seen as a program that provides food for the poor, *de facto* it is an income transfer program and contains no provisions that directly focus on other causes of malnutrition (such as inadequate access to clean water, preventive medicine, and the like).

*The Tortilla-Solidaridad* program covers 2.3 million families, 684 thousand of them located in Mexico City. In 1992, the estimated annual fiscal cost was US$170 million. Interestingly, between 1990 and 1992, the fiscal cost increased less than 30 percent, while the number of families in the program increased by more than 150 percent. This was possible because the strategy of targeted subsidies avoided wasting public funds and made the administrative process more efficient. The delivery mechanisms have by now become somewhat sophisticated: families are given a magnetic card where their daily purchases are recorded; the magnetic card works jointly with a card-reading machine that records the number of tortillas delivered by any *tortillería* or food store. This process allows the owner of the food store to charge the government for the cost of the program. The delivery mechanism is thus based on private operation of the distribution system, minimizing incentives to cheat and to divert resources to other groups; no special stores or distribution networks are required. The key mechanisms of the government intervention are distributing the cards and covering store owners' costs.

If the *Tortilla-Solidaridad* program is evaluated in terms of its ability to transfer income to the urban poor and save fiscal resources, the results are clearly positive. On the other hand, this kind of means tested program has problems from the point of view of incentive structure, since it implies a marginal income tax for the urban poor. Families whose income goes above two minimum wages are disqualified from the program. This effect may or may not have been sufficiently strong to create disincentives for these families to increase their income by their own means. Further research is needed on this point to fully evaluate the merits of switching from generalized price discounts to directly targeted programs.

*Source:* Prepared by Santiago Levy.

transition from largely communicable diseases to chronic, noncommunicable causes of morbidity and mortality. This shift is important because of the low cost effectiveness of medical interventions for many diseases of dietary excess. Behavioral shifts in diets and better exercise regimes both seem to be related to education.

**Nonfood consumption.**   Changes in nonfood consumption, including increased use of tobacco and alcohol, are also having a significant effect on health in the region. Tobacco consumption consistently has been found to be a cause of morbidity and subsequent premature mortality from lung, bladder, and other cancers; from chronic pulmonary disease; and from ischemic heart disease. Chronic alcohol consumption is a known risk factor for cirrhosis and chronic liver disease and for gastrointestinal diseases including ulcers and esophageal cancer. Surveys in several Latin American metropolitan areas have reported that more than a fifth of all hospital admissions were for alcohol-related problems. Alcohol is a major factor in vehicle accidents and in occupational injuries. Consumption of other drugs generally is not so widespread, but some serious health problems have occurred because of drug reactions and from the spread of HIV if delivery is intravenous.

**Sexually transmitted diseases.**   All of these consumption changes, as well as changes in other behaviors such as vehicle use and sexual behavior, imply changing health problems in the region in future decades. There is relatively little evidence from the region on the effectiveness of policies to change these forms of consumption behavior to improve health. But information campaigns in other parts of the world regarding the adverse effects of tobacco and the risks of AIDS are estimated to have the same order of magnitude of cost effectiveness as the most effective direct health interventions, such as immunizations.

### Direct Health-Related Interventions and Institutions

Direct health-related interventions and health institutions in the region resemble schooling in at least four important dimensions.

  • First, as with schooling, there are basic informational problems in measuring the effectiveness of health services. Many assessments of the importance of diseases and the impact of health interventions have focused on deaths from different causes, an advantageous approach in that death is a clear-cut event and such data are widely collected. But the cause of death is often ambiguous even if well-trained medical specialists are present, because the proximate cause (heart failure, pneumonia, dysentery) might mask the cumulative strain of other conditions (immunological deficiencies, malnutrition). And, of course, trained medical personnel often are not present. In addition, many diseases (such as paralysis) make a healthy life impossible even if they do not cause immediate death. For these reasons, the WHO and the World Bank have created a measure in which the present discounted value of each day of life lost from health problems (or saved because of health interventions) is weighted from zero to one depending on the quality of life involved. The measure gives "disability adjusted life years" (DALY) lost from health problems or saved by interventions (see, for instance, World Bank, 1993). Such a measure is not perfect,[16] but it facilitates comparisons in evaluating health conditions and the effectiveness of interventions. Unfortunately, DALY or similar measures were not available for the region at the time this study was written.

 • Second, as with schooling, there is a wide spectrum for cost effectiveness of health services, ranging from some apparently relatively effective interventions (analogous to the provision of textbooks and writing materials) to some that have very low effectiveness (analogous to low teacher-to-pupil ratios). In urban Colombia, for instance, clinics have been found to be much more cost effective than hospitals in lowering child mortality (Rosenzweig and Schultz, 1982). Although the region is well into the epidemiological transition from largely communicable diseases to chronic, noncommunicable causes of morbidity and mortality, communicable diseases remain a major problem. The cost effectiveness of Colombia's expanded program of immunization, therefore, appears to be substantial, especially since the program now offers vaccines for hepatitis B and yellow fever. Family planning services also appear to be highly cost effective (through reducing high-risk pregnancies and related unsafe abortions), as are pregnancy care and childbirth care programs. Cataract extractions and short-course chemotherapy against tuberculosis are also quite cost effective. Cancer surgery, inappropriate drugs, and underutilized hospitals are much less cost effective.

--------

[16] One question is how to weight the quality of life experienced by persons with different disabilities. Among the options are expert judgments, the judgments of a random sample of the population, or productivity weights. Efforts to date have used primarily the first, although the second has been used in some cases. Both are relatively egalitarian in comparison with the third, because they assign the same weight to a condition regardless of who has it (although experts might place a higher value on mental agility while a poor farmer might value physical strength). Such weighing, however, ignores the fact that the social costs of disabilities may differ, and are probably greater for a brilliant young biomedical researcher than for a construction worker of the same age because of the externalities of knowledge that the former is more likely to produce. Also there is some evidence that people with various disabilities judge their quality of life to be better than their lives are judged to be by those who do not have the disabilities. There also are questions about how to weigh different ages and the appropriate discount rate.

• Third, as with schooling, the way health service delivery is organized often does not induce the efficient use of many related inputs. In studies of child anthropometric measures of health and nutritional status (such as height, weight for height) in Chile, Nicaragua, and northeast Brazil, for example, much of the variation appears related to differences across communities in the nature of health services, even though the observed dimensions of the local health services do not have significant effects (Harbert and Scandizzo, 1982; Behrman and Wolfe, 1987a; Thomas, Strauss, and Henriques, 1990). The explanation is that public health interventions (immunizations, enforcement of food and occupational safety standards, epidemiological surveillance, collection and analysis of health data, insect vector control) tend to be underfinanced relative to clinical services. In addition, fee-for-service compensation schemes sometimes encourage the growth of medical care and services that are not very cost effective. Prepayment plans with competitive features, such as HMOs competing on the basis of price and quality, seem to promise better cost containment.

• Fourth, both adult schooling and household income (more women's than men's) play important roles in the demand for health-related services. Household income has a significant effect on health demand for Chile, Nicaragua, and northeast Brazil (Thomas, Strauss, and Henriques, 1990 and 1991; Harbert and Scandizzo, 1982; Behrman and Wolfe, 1987a). Such results confirm the general supposition that health is positively related to family income, which may in part reflect imperfect capital markets to the extent that health is viewed as an investment). For urban Brazil, moreover, unearned income received by women is estimated to have much stronger effects than that received by men on improving child survival and child anthropometric indicators, parallel to the effect of income on nutrition (Thomas, 1990). It is also interesting to note that some estimates for urban Colombia suggest that maternal schooling and public health institutions are substitutes for each other in determining child health (Rosenzweig and Schultz, 1982). For Brazil, as well, there is evidence of intergenerational gender links in the sense that fathers' schooling has greater impact on sons' than on daughters' health and that mothers' schooling has more impact on daughters' than on sons' health (Thomas, 1992). But studies for Nicaragua and Peru suggest that schooling may in part lead to the use of more expensive health care, without any necessary improvement in health itself (Wolfe and Behrman, 1984; Gertler, Locay, and Sanderson, 1987). Finally, in the subset of studies that control for unobserved family background characteristics, the estimated effects of both income and schooling are lessened with such controls. This suggests that increasing income or schooling does not have as large an effect on health as standard estimates imply, because these variables are in part representing other characteristics, such as good health habits learned in childhood.

There also are at least five important dimensions in which health services differ from schooling:

• First, general behavioral patterns and the general environment play a greater role in determining health than they do in determining schooling. The effects of consumption patterns on health were discussed earlier. Occupational hazards can also be considerable, with relatively high health hazards in most countries in agriculture (chemicals and pesticides, vehicle and machinery accidents), construction, transportation, and certain industrial sectors (especially in small-scale industry). Good water supply and sanitation can have important positive effects on health, although investments in these areas in terms of health alone (and not convenience and time saved) have not been cost effective enough to be given priority. Available estimates of other environmental effects on health, such as air pollution, are subject to considerable uncertainty, but suggest that the eradication of these environmental effects is not as cost effective for improving health as are good water supply and sanitation.

• Second, health services focus on a wider range of ages than does schooling. Until recently, much of the policy emphasis on health in the region, as elsewhere in the developing world, has been on infants and preschool children and the communicable diseases that affect them. There also has been increasing recognition of the health issues associated with childbearing, which pertain largely to women 15 to 44 years of age. But DALYs calculations also suggest that the health problems of children 5 to 14 years, who generally are neglected by health services, account for 50 percent as much of the world's health burden as do children under five, and young adults 14 to 44 years old account for about 80 percent as much. Furthermore, older adults account for a substantial share of actual health expenditures, probably larger than their 20 percent share of the health problem burden, which raises questions about the relative efficiency of many health interventions for this group.

• Third, there has been more diversity of experience in financing the health system than the schooling system. Major sources have included social insurance programs related to employment and financed substantially by employees and employers (with large subsidies from general government revenues in many cases), public health services financed by general government revenues, and private funding (Box 4.3).

### Box 4.3. The Diversity of Argentine Health Care Providers: Implications for Equity and Efficiency

Health care in Argentina is provided by three major groups of organizations: private health insurance groups, which cover about 10 percent of the population (biased toward higher-income families); organizations funded by payroll taxes, which cover about 60 percent of the population (with a very slight decline in coverage with higher family incomes); and public hospitals and programs, which cover most of the 30 percent not insured (over a third of whom are in the bottom quintile by family income). Private insurance groups provide health insurance and health care in a single package offering a variety of alternatives. *Obras sociales* (OS) have compulsory membership of all workers, wage earners, and the self-defined employed; are funded primarily by taxes on wages and earnings (formally divided between workers and employers); and are managed under the dominant influence of workers' unions.

Charges in the private sector are not subject to price controls. Public hospital services are free for all who demand them, although sometimes patients are required to pay for part of the medicine they need. In the OS sector, all workers contribute to funding in proportion to their wages or earnings, while the OSs usually recontract their services with the private sector and with medical personnel. Prices and rates in this case are fixed by the central administration after bargaining with both the OS and the medical associations. Rates are set per unit of services performed by doctors, paramedical personnel, and private hospitals and per type of medical examination.

This particular institutional setting and this pricing mechanism allow the coverage of a high proportion of the population. But they have limitations in terms of both efficiency and equity. The inflexibility in the OS sector, for example, has three negative consequences for efficiency: first, it does not allow scale economies to be exploited; second, it rules out any competition; and third, the pricing mechanism leads to overutilization of services. All these factors obviously raise costs above optimal levels. There are also problems in terms of equity. Since there is wide wage dispersion among sectors and the OSs are financed primarily by wages, there are rich and poor OSs, with significant differences in both the quantity and quality of services delivered. Furthermore, there are differences between the OSs and the other two alternatives.

Pressures for reforms are particularly strong in the current era of budgetary stringency. In present circumstances, three lines of action are suggested.

First, progress has to be made in enhancing programs directed to the poorest, particularly programs related to infant and maternal nutrition and health care in public hospitals. Existing programs in these areas can be improved not only by devoting more resources to them but also by more careful targeting and particularly by coordinating education, health, and social worker teams. This policy entails no trade-off between equity and efficiency.

Second, institutional reforms need to be implemented. Resource savings could be achieved by reducing double affiliations and by allowing a larger degree of competition among different organizations delivering health services. In particular, the OSs should be subject to two types of reforms. The first would allow workers to choose the organization with which they want to be affiliated, even if compulsory financing is maintained. The second would be freedom of entry for organizations fulfilling specific quality standards. These two changes would increase efficiency because competition would force resource savings through pressures to lower costs and attain optimal size. Aside from the political implications involved, the major question that this kind of reform raises is how to price services. In the proposed new system, low-wage workers' contributions would probably not be sufficient to pay for full costs. But a compensation scheme could be devised to distribute part of receipts to lower-income members. The greater reliance on markets should be complemented by simpler and more effective information to inform people and public officials, including Congress, of costs and revenues.

Third, the pricing of health services needs to be reformed. If the OS sector is opened to a substantial degree of competition, the present system of centrally fixing input prices should be abandoned. There remains the question of pricing the services of the government sector. Public hospitals and programs currently provide services free for whoever demands them. This policy is quite progressive, on balance. Services of public hospitals are demanded more by the poorest, and hence expenditure there is highly progressive even if complementary private costs are computed. Charging a price to the nonpoor is conceivable for public hospitals, but present use of public hospitals by the nonpoor is so limited that the costs of implementing such a policy likely would be higher than the receipts. Efficiency here could be improved through more effective administrative devices such as budgetary controls and independent *ex post* evaluations.

*Source:* Prepared by Alberto Petrecolla, based in part on Llach, Dieguez, and Petrecolla (1991).

Within the region, social insurance systems have played a major role in financing clinical health activities. Social insurance traditionally has focused on curative medicine for the economically active and on pensions and curative medicine for the retired segment of the population. Social insurance also covers curative medicine for dependents, but with limitations in many cases (for instance, in the Dominican Republic, Ecuador, and Uruguay, spouses are covered for maternity but not sickness, and children are covered only in the first three to 12 months of their lives). Experience with social insurance has varied substantially within the region. Mesa-Lago (1991) identifies three categories of social security systems by how long they have been in existence; i.e., pioneer, intermediate, and latecomer.

Pioneer systems (such as in Argentina, Brazil, Chile, Costa Rica, and Uruguay) were introduced for different occupations over long periods of time. These systems have (or had, if there have been recent unifying reforms, as in Chile) numerous unintegrated subsystems with broad coverage that varies by occupation, and with notably inequitable benefits favoring those in more urban, industrialized areas with higher per capita income. In these systems, expenditures are dominated by pensions rather than health care, and fiscal crises have been common because of generous pension benefits. Because of problems of financing, equity, and efficiency, social insurance reforms have been considered in all of these countries and have actually been undertaken in some. The most radical reform was introduced in Chile in the 1980s with the privatization of social security, but this has affected pensions (covering 85 percent of the active insured as of 1990) more than health care.

For health care, the majority of the population is still covered by the public social insurance system, but a growing percentage (from 9 percent in 1987 to 14 percent in 1990) is affiliated with private prepayment companies, called ISAPRES (*Institutos de Salud Previsional*), which are divided into two types: open ISAPRES accept anyone who pays the commercial rates and therefore cover mostly high-income employee groups; and closed ISAPRES largely cover low-income employee groups, with premiums paid by both insured employees and their employers. A social welfare program provides minimal pensions and health care services for indigents. Costa Rica has undertaken reform that has substantially modified the structure of health care (Box 4.4). For most other countries in this pioneer group, reform efforts to date have not been sufficient to eliminate ongoing fiscal crises stemming from pension obligations.

Intermediate systems (as in Bolivia, Colombia, Ecuador, Mexico, Panama, Peru, and Venezuela) were introduced more recently than systems in the pioneer countries and are more unified and standardized.

Nevertheless, in some cases the systems are quite complicated (Bolivia has 12 major funds, 20 complementary funds, and five health programs; Colombia has 300 institutions with programs for pensions, health care, and family allowances). Furthermore, coverage usually is limited (only as high as 60 percent in Mexico and Panama), and benefits are generous only for limited sectors of society (in Peru in 1985, 30 percent of the productive-age population was covered, but only 1.4 percent of those below 14 years of age; in Colombia, the analogous figures were 15 percent and 3.6 percent). With the exception of Bolivia and Ecuador (which have pioneer-like systems, with pensions dominating), the bulk of expenditures in this intermediate group goes to sickness and maternity programs. Until the 1980s, their social insurance systems appeared to be in better condition than in the pioneer group, but financial problems have increased substantially in the past decade. Reforms are needed to put sickness and maternity programs on a self-sustaining basis, to tighten the entitlements for pension programs, and to expand coverage.

Latecomer systems (such as in the English-speaking Caribbean countries and some Central American countries) have greater unification but much lower coverage (less than a quarter of the population). In the English-speaking Caribbean countries, social insurance includes virtually no health care, but health care is a larger component in the other systems in this group. A serious problem facing these systems (as well as some systems in the intermediate group, as in Bolivia, Colombia, and Ecuador) is that universalization of coverage under present terms would have exorbitant costs. Therefore, reform must involve extension of coverage in a manner that is financially sustainable. With IDB support, Guatemala is extending coverage for sickness and maternity benefits to its less-developed areas, but systematic evaluations by which to judge the replicability of this model in other countries are not yet available.

The social insurance systems in all three groups have tended to have relatively high administrative costs (see Table 4.11, column 1) in comparison with developed country figures of 2 to 4 percent. These high costs stem from low economies of scale, new program development, the complicated administrative structures of multiple funds, and the use of administrative staffing to provide employment (which underlies some of the variance in Table 4.11, column 2). The staff of the social insurance systems in many cases are the best paid in the public sector; strikes by these employees also have been frequent in many countries.

For those in the region who are not covered by social insurance programs, particularly the poorer members of society, public health services provided by ministries of health from general government revenues are a primary source of health care. This sector of society includes almost the

**Box 4.4. Health Dimensions of Social Security Reforms in Costa Rica**

Starting in 1982, changes were introduced in Costa Rica's social security system to attempt to solve the system's serious financial shortfalls. These changes were limited to the administrative and legal sphere because of the perception that the system's worsening financial situation stemmed primarily from administrative problems, exacerbated by the country's severe economic crisis, which began in 1973. These changes included several new models for outpatient care designed to improve the efficiency and quality of services and reduce costs.

**Deterioration of the old CCSS system**. Reduced efficiencies, falling revenues, and rising costs were the three factors responsible for the deterioration of the two health programs managed by the Costa Rican Social Security Fund (*Caja Costarricense del Seguro*, CCSS): Sickness and Maternity (*Enfermedad y Maternidad*, EM) and Disability, Old Age, and Death (*Invalidez, Vejez, y Muerte*, IVM).

CCSS efficiency (or at least productivity per worker) had decreased drastically during the crisis because of the reduction of the system's work week to five days and the introduction of the continuous shift system (which caused a 20 percent loss in the hours of the work shift). To compensate, CCSS had employed special shifts to make up the hours not worked, which worsened its financial situation.

CCSS revenues shrunk in real terms during this time primarily because of payment delays by both the government and employers. The government, since the onset of the crisis, had failed to pay its share of employer and state contributions to CCSS. Similarly, employers, hit by currency devaluation and galloping inflation, had begun to delay or not to pay the contributions for their workers.

At the same time, CCSS expenditures climbed because of excessive personnel costs; moreover, the demand for health services increased as part of the covered population turned to public medical services because of reductions in disposable real income.

In the early 1980s, it was no longer possible within existing budgetary constraints to continue to increase the size and coverage of the EM program. In 1982, health expenditures dropped to a recent low of 5.6 percent of GDP. The IVM program was devalued and lost ten years of capitalization as a result of having to provide financial assistance to the EM program.

**Reforms to stabilize CCSS's financial position and increase its efficiency**. In response to these problems, CCSS in 1982 adopted measures aimed at regulating and stabilizing its financial position. The first measure was the reorganization of its management levels; a financial subdirectorate was added to the two existing subdirectorates, medicine and administration. An effort was also made to eliminate the deficit by implementing measures such as: an increase of 14.75 percent in employer-worker contributions to the EM system (employer contributions rose 9.25 percent and worker contributions 5.5 percent); a government agreement to pay a substantial portion of its accrued debt to CCSS, and the 1983 budget stipulation by Congress that the Office of the Comptroller General would not approve any budget if the government was in arrears to CCSS; extension of the preceding measure to the private sector, so that any private company wishing to participate in a public bidding had to be current in its obligations to CCSS; and reductions in the number and payroll of system employees.

Finally, an effort was made to increase efficiency by introducing four new models for outpatient care to coexist with traditional medical care: Company Medicine, under which companies contract for medical services, with CCSS providing logistical support (medicines and examinations); Mixed Medicine, in which the patient chooses the doctor and pays for the visit, with CCSS providing logistical support; Capitation Model or British Model, in which comprehensive ambulatory care is provided for individuals in their own communities; and Laborer and Worker Clinics, which are fully equipped cooperative clinics providing services to unskilled workers.

As employer-worker contributions increased, the revenues of EM insurance increased from 63 percent of total revenues in 1983 to 83 percent in 1985. In 1982, the government began making its contributions to CCSS on a more timely basis. By 1989, revenues had increased by 34 percent, with growth observed in all categories (contributions, sales of goods and services, and yields on investments) for the first time since 1983. Once the reforms were in place and recovery had started, the programs showed signs of covering their deficits and achieving sustained growth, eventually reaching 1978 CCSS levels.

The new outpatient care models were very successful by several indicators. Between 1982 and 1989, the Company Medicine model tripled its number of consultations, with the average use of medicine at the comparative level of 2.2, a figure below the 2.9 level of the traditional model. Mixed Medicine consultations increased eightfold, and the use of medicines there was slightly higher than in the traditional model. The Capitation Model experienced some initial difficulties because its health care professionals were not sufficiently trained to work with communities; later, however, both patients and staff were satisfied with this program. The Laborer and Worker Clinics performed well, with both the program and the staff of health care professionals producing impressive results.

*Source:* Mesa-Lago (1991), based in part on Miranda (1990).

entire population of the English-speaking Caribbean countries (which have national health systems and very little care provided by social insurance systems) and the majority of the population in most Latin American countries. The per capita financing for public health services is often a fraction of the financing for social insurance programs, although with considerable variance across countries. For instance, on a per capita basis, social insurance funds in the 1980s received 9 times as much as did public health services in the Dominican Republic, 8 times as much in Peru, and 7.5 times as much in Colombia, although such ratios were much lower in Costa Rica and Panama (Mesa-Lago, 1991). In part because of these discrepancies, in Mesa-Lago's words, "The health ministries do not have even the minimum resources needed to provide health care to the majority of the population." He also notes that the gap between the per capita resources of the public health services and those of the social insurance health services has widened over time, which has shifted the allocation from low-cost preventive health services (emphasized much more by the public health services) to high-cost curative health services (emphasized relatively more by the social insurance health services). He also notes that in most countries (with a few exceptions, such as Costa Rica and the English-speaking Caribbean), little progress has been made toward the long-discussed objective of coordinating or integrating public health services with social insurance fund health services. Therefore, duplication, coverage gaps, and resource allocation inefficiencies and inequities continue. Some of these inefficiencies are reflected in the relatively low hospital occupancy rates and the relatively long hospital stays in many of the countries in the region (Table 4.11, columns 3 and 4).

Private financing of sickness care and related health care in the region also appears to be considerable. Of course, part of the private financing is private payment for private curative care by the wealthy or those with high incomes. Private financing also involves private contributions to social insurance funds and general public health expenditures through taxes and other means, which are regressive to the extent that revenues collected from the relatively poor are used to subsidize social insurance curative health care, which benefits primarily middle-class workers or retirees.

Yet another important factor in the costs of poor health is the income lost to illness. Household surveys in Bolivia, Jamaica, Nicaragua, and Peru suggest that the average adult is ill from one to five days a month, which results in 0.5 to 1.5 days of work missed per month—or from 2 to 6 percent of the work time, with commensurately lower productivity and income.

• The fourth difference between health services and schooling is that health service delivery is changing very rapidly, whereas in schooling,

**Table 4.11. Indicators of Social Insurance Administrative and Hospital Efficiency in Latin America and the Caribbean, 1980–87**

| Countries | Percentage of Administrative Expenditures over Total Expenditures (1983–86) | Employees per 1,000 Insured (1980–87) | National Averages (1980–85) Percentage Hospital Occupancy | National Averages (1980–85) Days of Stay |
|---|---|---|---|---|
| | (1) | (2) | (3) | (4) |
| Dominican Republic | 22.0 | 20.5 | 51.7 | 10.4 |
| Honduras | 17.8 | n.a. | n.a. | n.a. |
| Guatemala | 11.8 | 7.4 | n.a. | n.a. |
| Bolivia | 14.5 | 6.7 | n.a. | n.a. |
| El Salvador | 13.7 | 13.5 | n.a. | n.a. |
| Ecuador | 22.5 | 13.2 | 50.0[d] | 8.2[d] |
| Jamaica | 12.8 | 0.6 | n.a. | n.a. |
| Colombia | 11.6 | 7.4 | 56.2[c] | 5.4[c] |
| Costa Rica | 5.0 | 13.0 | 81.0[d] | 6.3[d] |
| Peru | 11.4 | 7.0/10.5[b] | 70.4 | 11.7 |
| Panama | 7.7 | 11.7 | 67.0[d] | 7.0[d] |
| Mexico[a] | 17.1/17.3 | 8.9/10.4 | 67/70 | 4.6/5.7 |
| Brazil | 6.8 | n.a. | n.a. | n.a. |
| Chile | 8.2 | n.a. | 75.3 | 8.5 |
| Uruguay | 5.4 | n.a. | 81.8[c] | 13.3[c] |
| Argentina | 3.4 | n.a. | 61.0 | 7.3 |
| Venezuela | 17.6 | 4.1 | n.a. | n.a. |
| Trinidad and Tobago | 32.4 | n.a. | n.a. | n.a. |
| Bahamas | 21.8 | 3.8 | n.a. | n.a. |
| Barbados | 5.0 | 2.4 | n.a. | n.a. |
| Nicaragua | 28.0 | 4.5 | n.a. | n.a. |

*Notes:*  [a] In the two biggest institutions (IMSS and ISSSTE); hospital efficiency.
[b] The lower is the official figure and the higher is the figure adjusted to correct overestimation of population coverage.
[c] Ministry of Health; in Uruguay, only Montevideo.
[d] Social insurance and Ministry of Health.
n.a.= not available.
*Source:* Mesa-Lago (1991, Table 5).

technological innovations have been relatively slow, despite the use of computers. The epidemiological transition underway in the region, particularly microbial evolution (most importantly, AIDS and drug-resistant tuberculosis) calls for fundamental changes in health services (Box 4.5). Changes in various dimensions of health services and health-related concerns (such as nutrition and pollutants) have also been occurring at a rapid rate, and this is likely to continue in the future. These changes mean that institutional flexibility and timely collection and analysis of data will be increasingly important.

• Fifth, price elasticities for health and nutrition inputs are more related to income than are those for schooling (although evidence for the region is limited). A study for Brazil, for instance, estimates a compensated own-price elasticity of cereal demand of –0.74 for the poor, –0.16 for the middle income, and not significantly different from zero for the rich (Williamson-Gray, 1982). Studies for Peru likewise indicate price elasticities for the lowest quartile of households, by income, that are 2 to 20 times as high as elasticities for the highest quartile, for health care by different providers (private doctors, hospitals, and clinics), with larger responses for care for children than for adults (Gertler, Locay, and Sanderson, 1987; Gertler and van der Gaag, 1988). These results suggest that people, particularly poor people, respond to price incentives by changing their behavior a fair amount. They also suggest that if increased user fees increase prices equally for all, independent of income, the poor are likely to reduce their use of the good or service relatively more than those who are better off. The standard welfare interpretation of this outcome is that the poor suffer smaller welfare losses from such price increases than the rich because they substitute more for the item that has increased in price. But if society wishes to ensure that the poor use these services if prices increase, it may be necessary to target some subsidies to the poor to induce such use.

## Determinants of Training

There are fewer statistical studies that evaluate the region's human resource investment in training than studies that evaluate its human resource investments in schooling and health/nutrition. This section therefore depends more heavily than the previous two sections on a priori analysis and on the judgments of experts such as Amadeo et al. (1993); Mazza (1992); Paredes, Riveros, Balmaceda, Manzur, and Núñez (1993); Riveros (1992a); Zerda Sarmiento (1992); and Middleton, Ziderman, and Van Adams (1991). The section first presents evaluations of some major training programs in the region (also see Box 4.6), then offers some general observations.

SENAI *(Serviço Nacional de Aprendizagem Industrial)*, a major training program in Brazil, is highly regarded on the basis of the occupational and wage experience and subsequent education of its graduates (see Chapter 3). But SENAI does have some definite limitations.

First, for some of the courses with specialized training, a surprisingly small percentage of graduates use that training even in the period immediately afterward, particularly those who were not sent by their employers.

Second, students in the program tend to be workers with relatively high schooling and with employment in good firms—and increasingly so over time as short courses have become more prevalent. Therefore, the SENAI experience does not provide a basis for judging how training might help less prepared or connected workers. Instead, because of the complementarities between schooling and training, the training seems to have served to improve the conditions of the more-schooled workers, and therefore has probably contributed to income inequalities. Some have suggested that SENAI should lower its admission standards in order to train more of the unschooled and poorly schooled members of society and thereby achieve greater equity. But Amadeo et al. (1993) note that since the schooling background of most current trainees is well above the existing minimum requirement, lowering that requirement might not result in the admission of many additional poorly prepared students. They also argue that more equity should be an objective of the general schooling system, not of a relatively small specialized agency such as SENAI. Nevertheless, they argue, SENAI should design programs for small and medium-sized firms.

Third, the SENAI program (or others) has not provided information that enables its effectiveness to be adequately evaluated. Although SENAI graduates have tended to have better subsequent occupation and wage trajectories than their counterparts who have not had training, it is difficult to determine the extent to which these changes stem from the training as opposed to the selection process. Information on the career trajectories of similar individuals who have not had training would be valuable for the purpose of comparison.

Fourth, over time SENAI has shifted increasingly toward providing training tailored specifically to the needs of individual firms; firms have chosen such courses for their exemption from payroll tax. This shift implies, as Amadeo et al. (1993) emphasize, that "a tax meant to finance the provision of a public service, namely, general vocational education, is turned into a tariff to finance the provision of a private service, namely, specific training." Amadeo et al. suggest that in the face of uncertainties from the ongoing adjustment, it is particularly important that the focus be shifted back toward general rather than specific training.

Fifth, SENAI does not have special programs for the unemployed. Clearly, it does not make sense for SENAI to provide specific (as opposed to general) training for the unemployed. But Amadeo et al. argue that it might be desirable to provide general training for the unemployed in order to reduce prospective employers' outlays for specific training.

SENAC is the analog of SENAI for the service and commercial sectors (see Chapter 3). Less information is available for the evaluation of

## Box 4.5. AIDS in Latin America and the Caribbean

Much of the world's attention concerning AIDS has focused on the United States, Sub-Saharan Africa, and Southeast and South Asia, but alarm about AIDS in Latin America and the Caribbean has been increasing because of the rapid growth of estimated cases and HIV infections. Estimates of the number of AIDS cases and HIV carriers in the region vary depending on the sources, with higher values usually given by AIDS workers than by health ministries. Most countries in the region have not conducted detailed surveys to ascertain the incidence of the disease with more precision.

There were fewer than 8,000 full-blown AIDS cases in 1987, but 60,000 or more in 1993. Outside of Africa, Brazil's reported 34,000 cases are second only to the 242,000 cases in the United States; Mexico also is high on the list, with more than 11,000 reported cases in 1992 (compared with 245 in 1986). The highest rates of HIV infection are believed to be in Haiti, where for the largest three cities, 8 to 10 percent of adults are estimated to be infected with the virus. In Brazil, an estimated 1 million people out of a population of 150 million are infected with HIV, about the same number as in the United States population of 255 million. HIV estimates for Mexico range from 225,000 to 500,000 individuals out of a population of 85 million. Estimates for Colombia are 200,000 people infected with HIV out of a population of 33 million, but this number could increase to one million by the year 2000. For Argentina, with a slightly smaller population than Colombia, about 100,000 people are estimated to be infected with HIV. Such estimates indeed are cause for alarm since they imply that in Argentina, Brazil, Colombia, and Mexico alone, the absolute number of individuals currently carrying the HIV virus is from 50 percent to 100 percent greater than in the United States. Since AIDS is newer in Latin America and the Caribbean than in the United States, a surge in the AIDS epidemic is anticipated in the near future.

Apparent HIV transmission patterns in the region vary considerably, with heterosexual sex the major mode in relatively poor Haiti but male homosexual sex and contaminated drug needles the primary mechanisms in Argentina, which has a relatively high per capita income. A major means in many areas

SENAC than for the evaluation of SENAI. Tax exemptions for firm-specific training are not so common for SENAC as for SENAI, so there is less risk that SENAC is providing private training at public expense. Also in contrast with SENAI, during the 1980s SENAC increasingly emphasized longer courses and more hours per student, which means that longer-term, more general (less firm-captured) training is now typical of SENAC. In further contrast to SENAI, most students in SENAC were not working during the course and many had never worked before the course; this program is therefore much more a program for the unemployed and for new appears to be bisexual males with multiple partners, often including wives or cohabiting women. Because of such bisexual activity, the incidence of HIV among women has increased rapidly. Since 1985 the share of Brazilians with AIDS who are women has increased from 3 percent to 20 percent, and the share of Mexicans with AIDS who are women has increased from 1 percent to 16 percent. Surveys in Brazil have found a very high incidence of AIDS among pregnant women, from 1 to 2.6 percent (25 to 70 times as high as had been anticipated prior to the surveys).

Policies to deal with AIDS in the region have varied substantially in nature and effectiveness. At one extreme, Cuba has limited the number of reported cases of HIV infection to less than 1,000 in a population of 10 million through mandatory testing for the HIV virus and quarantining those who test positive. Other countries in the region have not implemented such policies, in part because of the costs in terms of individual freedom. On the technical side, almost universal testing of hospital blood supplies in the region has sharply reduced new infections coming from blood transfusions. But public health programs apparently have been limited by pressures from the Catholic Church in Colombia, Mexico, and elsewhere. Radio and television information campaigns about AIDS and the effectiveness of condoms have been withdrawn because of such pressures. Condom prices are relatively high (the equivalent of one kilogram of rice or two kilograms of beans for a package of three condoms in Brazil), and quality control is poor. Misinformation about transmission also appears widespread; for example, a recent survey of female prostitutes in São Paulo found that 90 percent of those who use condoms also use lubricant creams that make latex porous for HIV. But the limited nature of policy actions to stem the AIDS epidemic in the region appears to be due in large part to resistance to recognizing the severity of the epidemic and the role of sexual behavior that is not accepted by many in the region. The cost of limiting interventions to stem the spread of HIV is likely to be enormous in terms of future AIDS cases, associated health system use, and lost productivity.

*Source:* Based in substantial part on Brooke (1993).

entrants into the job market. The wages of employed graduates from SENAC have been relatively low in comparison with those of SENAI graduates, with only 23 percent receiving more than three minimum wages. Therefore, it is not clear that SENAC has a large impact on wages, although it may have an important impact on trainees' probability of actually attaining employment. Finally, SENAC students, like SENAI students, have high levels of schooling (in 1989, 88 percent had completed primary school and 54 percent had completed secondary school), so experience with this program does not indicate possible outcomes for those with lim-

Box 4.6. Responding to Unemployment Costs of Structural Reform: Training in Mexico

In the mid 1980s, Mexico introduced comprehensive trade reforms aimed at opening the trade account by eliminating all price and nonprice barriers. These reforms were accompanied by other policy measures aimed at reducing the size and role of the state in the economy and at deregulating the country's product and factor markets. Given the high expected short-term social costs of adjustment, entrepreneurs, government, and labor unions signed a formal agreement (Social Pact) designed to facilitate these policy reforms and associated macroeconomic policies needed to achieve price stabilization and structural economic reform.

A long-term feature of the Mexican labor market has been relatively low open unemployment, although some commentators claim that there has been high underemployment. The reforms of the 1980s were expected to exert significant pressures on the labor market, in direct association with the need for substantial labor mobility from the contracting sectors and industries toward those in expansion. Even if there were enough wage flexibility to allow for this labor reallocation, there was a significant likelihood of high mismatch unemployment. That is, some of those who departed from the contracting firms would not have the skills needed by the expanding firms and would have been openly unemployed because of the skills mismatch. This would have weakened the political support for the program, and in the absence of an adequate social safety net, would have produced higher structural poverty. Within the framework of the Social Pact, an innovative training program *(Programa de Becas de Capacitación para Trabajadores)* was designed to achieve the objectives of reducing the social cost of adjustment and facilitating the redeployment of labor.

The *Programa de Becas* was instituted in 1987. Since then it has provided more then 9,000 training courses to more than 250,000 unemployed. It is administered through state employment offices, thereby facilitating the identification of potential beneficiaries and the diagnosis of regional economic scenarios.

ited prior schooling. Although information simply is not available for estimating the rate of return to this program, controlling for who enrolls in it, there would seem to be a substantial payoff to more careful monitoring and evaluation.

The present Chilean training system under SENCE *(Servicio de Capacitación y Empleo)*, also described in Chapter 3, has three components. The largest, covering almost 2,000 workers in 1990, are the company-level training programs, financed through a tax deduction to Chilean businesses that fund training for their employees. Paredes et al. note four problems with this component. First, the cost limitation for subsidies en

Through formal liaison with private enterprises, these offices also help trainees to find jobs. Participants are selected on the basis of factors such as previous formal education and work experience, length of unemployment, and number of economic dependents. During the training period, participants receive a grant equivalent to one month's minimum wage. A low grant level was set so that the program would not attract trainees from higher-income families, thus focusing the program's benefits on lower-income households through self-targeting. Finally, the specific activities and areas of vocational courses are programmed on the basis of periodic diagnoses of local labor market conditions.

Questions regarding the success of the *Programa de Becas* have been raised with regard to two issues: its effectiveness in promoting the reemployment of trainees and its ability to raise their productivity and earnings. Analysis for a cohort of trainees has indicated that their job prospects are generally better than for those unemployed who did not undergo training activities. But it has also been found that the program does not shorten the duration of unemployment for participants without work experience. In other words, it seems that the training is not a substitute for work experience. With regard to the second issue, it has been found that program participation does not have any effect on hourly wages. But on average, the monetary benefit of workers finding jobs more quickly outweighs the cost of the program.

Three policy implications derive from these findings. First, in order to increase the program's effectiveness, it is necessary to better target individuals likely to remain in the labor market. Second, a specific program for youth, directed toward increasing their first-time employment probabilities, seems advisable. Third, to foster greater links between the program and market needs and to improve the impact on earnings, it is important that the private sector become more directly involved in the programming and execution of training activities. Reliance on labor market diagnoses is insufficient to establish an efficient link between training and jobs.

*Source:* Prepared by Luis Riveros.

courages training that is not intensive in terms of equipment; as a result, 60 percent of the trainees in 1990 were concentrated in administration, computers, and languages. Second, there is a lag of 16 months between the time when enterprises incur training expenses and the effective remuneration for those expenses, which biases the programs toward larger firms not constrained by liquidity. In part for this reason, only 5.4 percent of the potential funding is actually used, and primarily by large firms. Third, the program's coverage is procyclical rather than anticyclical; therefore, it tends to reinforce rather than mitigate business cycle movements. Fourth, the coverage has been regressive, higher for highly paid than for less well-paid workers, even though the tax subsidy is greater for the latter. In addition to these four problems, the company-level training scheme seems to encourage the use of public funds for firm-specific training. Information to evaluate the selectivity of the program and its impact on subsequent productivity and wages has not yet been collected.

The other two Chilean training programs, the training scholarship program and the apprenticeship program, are much smaller. The training scholarship program for unemployed first-time job seekers and independent workers, which covered fewer than 15,000 individuals in recent years, has four major problems (Paredes et al., 1992). First, the scholarship courses are not well matched with future labor market needs. Second, many potential beneficiaries have limited resources and credit access and so cannot benefit from the program. Third, overlapping responsibilities of SENCE and the municipal employment offices cause confusion and disorganization. Fourth, there are information problems regarding what the program has to offer and what it should offer. The apprentice program covered only 2,324 apprentices in the 1988–1990 period and appears to have been used less for training than for obtaining cheap unskilled labor (Paredes et al., 1993). As with company-level training, information on these programs is very limited, so it is difficult to know who is selected and to evaluate the precise impact of the programs as a function of the selection criteria.

Preparing youth for work—through vocational and technical education, and employee and pre-employment training—has an extensive history in Latin America. Corvalan (1988) distinguishes five types of programs: prevocational training (usually within schools); vocation preparation (usually outside of schools); vocational training (with well-defined courses in a training center); work programs (combining training and paid employment); and technical-vocational and agricultural education (in specialized schools with fixed, relatively long-term curricula). Many of these programs have been limited, however, by high cost and low quality, limited links to employers, and limited access to the poor, particularly from rural areas. An enduring concern is whether the recipients of the training have sufficient basic skills to benefit from these programs, or whether training resources should be used to strengthen their basic skills.

Development of entrepreneurs also has been spreading in the region as a result of efforts by the Carvahal Foundation (Colombia) and other organizations (Chapter 3). To date, the experience with entrepreneurship training has been mixed. Classroom courses often are not tailored to either the educational level of the trainees or the specific business of the microentrepreneurs. Training should be made more innovative and appropriate, perhaps through workshops led by successful small-scale entrepreneurs.

There are six general considerations that come out of the Latin American and Caribbean experience with public training policies. First, the purpose of publicly subsidized training is to provide more skilled and productive workers, not to serve as social assistance programs. In the increasingly dynamic markets of the region, the general skills required for a worker to be more productive over time include greater flexibility. Therefore, training programs should have a broad range, giving workers the skills to adapt to rapidly changing markets.

Second, to become effective workers, trainees need a sufficient basic general education, which can probably be more effectively provided through formal schooling than by teaching basic skills in training programs. Dougherty and Tan (1991) note that "there appears to be a systematic tendency for policymakers to overlook the complementarity between basic education and later skills development, and the consequence is that resources may be spent on expensive, low-volume training programs when they might more cost effectively and more equitably be used to upgrade the quality of basic education."

Third, to be effective, training programs need to be closely integrated with the needs of a country's expanding employers (most of whom are now more likely to be found in the private sector than in the public sector, for which much training was undertaken in the past). Employers' needs are likely to change more and more rapidly in the region because of greater integration into fast-changing international markets; therefore, employers need to be involved in designing and implementing training programs.

Fourth, the most rapidly expanding employers in many instances may be small and medium-sized firms. Therefore, training arrangements should not discriminate against such firms. In fact, there may be a case for targeting interventions to stimulate training in such firms, given that they are more likely than larger firms to be constrained by other related market imperfections (such as those in capital markets).

Fifth, although close links to a country's expanding employers are desirable, care needs to be taken that training remains general (which merits subsidies on efficiency grounds) and does not become firm specific (for which public subsidies are not warranted).

Sixth, more resources should be devoted to collecting, evaluating, and disseminating information about the effectiveness of training programs. Since some information is inherently difficult to obtain in a timely fashion, efforts should be made to develop institutional arrangements, such as the Chilean open-bidding processes, that encourage the efficient provision of training.

## Conclusions

Some general themes come out of the experience with human resource investments in Latin America and the Caribbean. For one thing, price responses in such investments appear to be fairly substantial and probably larger for poorer than for richer households—a finding that has implications regarding the impact of increased user charges. Within the standard model of consumer behavior, this result means that the poor are able to adjust to such price changes better than those who are more well-off. But if certain human resource investments have a social value beyond their private value to the individuals making those investments, then the relatively great price responsiveness of the poor means that if user charges are increased, the poor may reduce such investments below the levels that society deems important.

Human resource investments also seem responsive to the quality of available social services. The current quality of public supplies of related services varies substantially, but it often is low. Furthermore, the specific dimensions of inputs that determine such quality are only poorly identified, although there do appear to be some large gains from improving a few specific dimensions of that quality, such as the availability of textbooks and writing materials in lower-level school systems and the availability of appropriate basic drugs in health clinics. The importance of quality also means that there may be important quality/quantity trade-offs that imply equity/productivity trade-offs.

Human resource investments also seem responsive to expectations regarding rates of return. Thus, investment choices are likely to be sensitive to the nature of labor markets (including any discriminatory factors therein) and to perceptions regarding the general development of the economy.

Furthermore, there are important interactions and complementarities among human resource investments. Options in a country's health sector depend on the composition of investments in its educational sector, for instance, and the extent of schooling investments in turn depends on a country's child health. (Interestingly, for the more cost-effective health policies, the personnel needs are not so much for highly specialized physicians as for lower-level technicians, health service managers, and public health specialists.)

Incentives for creating value added in the provision of such related social services seem quite limited. Monitoring value added is infrequent, and tying staff compensation to performance is so rare as to be almost nonexistent. Pricing usually seems to be at best weakly related to marginal social costs and benefits. In many cases, regulations and control are fairly centralized, and responsiveness to local conditions is rather limited. Some technical education, for instance, does not appear to have very high returns (except when there are close ties to potential employers, perhaps because of greater awareness of the nature of user demand). Because of the weak links to the marginal benefits of the services being produced and to the opportunity costs of the resources used in producing services, provision seems, on the whole, to be quite inefficient.

The region's highly subsidized education and health services related to human resource investments, as they now stand, tend to encourage overuse and therefore low quality in order to keep benefits widespread. But they frequently have limited benefits for the poor, in part because they also tend to increase pressures on government deficits.

Efforts to establish increasingly incentive-compatible systems—by privatizing services and linking them more closely to private demand and to the decentralization process—hold great promise in many cases.

Targeting is most effective when carried out through self-targeting mechanisms (such as low wages for trainees in subsidized training programs), in part because of problems in accurately identifying the desired recipients by income.

Information problems commonly hamper evaluation of the quality of services related to human resource investments, and private entities do not have incentives to provide the socially optimal degree of information (because of the public good characteristics of information). Therefore, especially in view of privatization and decentralization, it is essential that the region's governments encourage the collection, analysis, and dissemination of relevant information.

The region's human resource investments are being made in a dynamic environment of increasingly rapid changes in technology and in the international economy. Therefore, such investments must seek to increase the flexibility of human capital and must not be overly tied to specific activities of production.

# CHAPTER

**5**

# HUMAN RESOURCE POLICIES FOR THE 1990s

## Which Human Resource Investments Should the State Subsidize?

A number of human resource investments in the region have strong productivity effects (Chapter 2). This justifies public subsidies for such investments on distributional grounds alone. Nevertheless, strong productivity (or efficiency) effects do not justify public subsidies for all human resource investments, or for investments in a particular type of human resource in which a country might be limited relative to other countries at a similar level of development.[1] To justify subsidies on any of these grounds, social returns to the investments must exceed private returns.

Major sources of distortions between private and social incentives were discussed in Chapter 4. Let us review all four. (1) Technological externalities: these are effects of one entity on another that are not transferred through markets; competitive markets generally do not create the right incentives for the production and use of goods and services that have benefits expressed largely as externalities. (2) Increasing returns to scale over the relevant range: under this condition, producers can gain from restricting supplies so that marginal benefits to users are greater than marginal costs. An extreme example of increasing returns to scale is a public good—a good or service for which one individual's having more does not mean that others have less. (3) Missing or imperfect markets: under this condition, individuals may not be able to produce, consume, or invest efficiently (in the sense of equating marginal benefits with marginal costs). (4) Policy distortions: most policies, no matter how well they attain their objectives, introduce distortions between social and private marginal costs and benefits.

---

[1] However, if a country has a relatively scarce stock of certain human resources in comparison with other countries at a similar level of development, the rate of return to further investments in human resources of that type may be high because of their relative scarcity.

The art of good policy for increasing productivity and efficiency is to identify the distortions between private and social incentives and to select policies high in the policy hierarchy to address such distortions. Policies high in the policy hierarchy tend to focus directly on the distortion and to work through prices, whereas quantitative regulations often have unintended effects. Such policies should be as transparent as possible so that their effects can be monitored and assessed despite endemic information problems. Also because of inadequate information, policies that create incentives for efficient behavior are likely to be higher in the policy hierarchy than those that require substantial information to monitor, evaluate, and change behavior. Because almost all policies have distortionary and direct resource costs, there may be distortions between social and private marginal costs and benefits for which no available policy can promise gains greater than the costs.

Evidence from the region, and informed judgments, support the proposition that social rates of return to some human resource investments are indeed higher than private rates of return. The social costs of adjustment, for example, probably exceed the private costs because of problems of macro-unemployment, and because more schooling (at least above the primary level) seems to facilitate adjustment. Also, epidemiological evidence strongly suggests externalities for control of contagious diseases. There are, in such cases, positive externalities to innovations (whether in product or input markets or technologies) in that others learn whether or not to imitate them; and improving human resources seems to increase such innovation. More schooling almost always facilitates the dissemination of information of all sorts, because the more-schooled can understand more media at lower cost, and this increases efficiency because of the public good characteristic of information. These and similar cases are good reasons to consider whether policies high in the policy hierarchy should be used to promote public subsidization of selected human resource investments, particularly since capital markets and insurance markets are imperfect for financing human resource investments, in that expected returns from such investments cannot be insured or used as collateral.

There is only limited systematic quantitative evidence on whether social returns to selected human resource investments are higher than private returns, and that evidence is sometimes interpreted incorrectly. As a result, policies are often advocated on efficiency and productivity grounds without a good rationale in terms of distortions between social and private costs, or without their being high in the policy hierarchy. Advocacy of such policies may make it more difficult to select policies that are relatively effective. A few examples are useful.

First, the rates of return to some human resource investments appear high but are subject to considerable risk. Earnings for individuals with additional schooling, for instance, may increase enough to imply a high average return, but there may be considerable variance in earnings across individuals. There are no private insurance markets to pool such risks, which might seem to be an argument for public subsidies for human resource investments. The same argument, however, could be applied to all risky investments, whether in schooling, starting a shoe repair stand on the streets of Santiago, or buying land in Porto Alegre.

Second, the fact that fertility falls with increases in female schooling is often cited as an externality that justifies subsidies for female schooling. But whether or not the phenomenon is truly an externality depends on the underlying mechanism. If more schooling for women enables them to absorb information about contraception at lower cost, then increased dissemination may have social benefits because of the public good characteristics of information; but there is nothing special about contraception as opposed to other goods and services in this respect. If more schooling for women changes their preferences toward more material goods and away from child care, that may reduce the number of children they have; but the effects on their welfare are ambiguous. If more schooling reduces the preferred number of children by changing the effective price of women's time for child rearing through increasing their productivity in other activities, then the reduction in children reflects the private adjustment to changed prices. But where is the difference between the private and social benefits? One possibility is that the difference between the private and social benefits derives from having schooling and health services provided by society, so that the private costs are less than the social costs. In this case, however, increasing subsidies for the schooling of little girls, so that they might have fewer children in the future, would not seem to be high in the policy hierarchy. A preferable policy would remove the distortion between the private and social costs of schooling and health services in the present by increasing prices, so that private prices are less than social marginal costs only by an amount that offsets the greater-social-than-private rate of return, but not by more.

Third, estimates that labor market rates of return to primary schooling are higher than to secondary and tertiary schooling are often used to support the argument that primary schooling should be subsidized on grounds of efficiency as well as equity. But the standard estimates (Table 2.4) do not provide any evidence that the social benefits of primary schooling exceed private benefits. If such comparisons were made for all levels of schooling, they would perhaps show that social benefits exceed private benefits to a greater extent for higher levels of schooling, because of the closer relation to producing knowledge with public good character-istics. This would imply an efficiency reason for subsidizing higher rather than lower schooling levels; it would also imply an efficiency/equity trade-off.

Fourth, the fact that more parental, particularly maternal, schooling seems to produce more human resource investments in the schooling, health, and nutrition of children and other household members is often cited as an externality to women's schooling. If the improved health of children reduces contagious diseases, there is a clear externality; but this is equally true for the woman's own health. There is nothing special about the effects through children's health. Moreover, for many contagious dis-eases, investing more in the schooling of little girls to improve the health of their family members decades in the future is not likely to be high in the policy hierarchy, in light of the highly cost-effective immunizations that are now available.

If more schooling for women improves family members' health and thereby reduces the demand on health systems that are socially under-priced, there is divergence between the social and private benefits, but again—as for fertility—the first-best remedy would seem to be to increase the price of health services. If increasing women's schooling changes women's tastes so that they prefer to have more-schooled or healthier chil-dren, there may be social benefits beyond the private ones if these human resources have externalities, but the welfare effects are ambiguous because of the induced changes in preferences. If more-schooled women are more likely to produce healthier and more-educated children and if they value such children, then clearly there is private gain to having more-schooled women. But this is not an externality (and therefore the basis for arguing for subsidies on efficiency grounds) in itself, any more than it would be if more schooling for one factory worker increased the productivity of train-ing for coworkers.

The point of these examples is not to suggest that the social rates of return to investments in some human resources probably do not exceed the private rates of return and that some selected state subsidies are war-ranted. To the contrary, we have already discussed why selected state sub-sidies are indeed warranted. The point is that a lot of the discussion in this area is murky, and the rationale for policy interventions is ambiguous, of-ten because of limitations of information and analysis. This lack of preci-sion may lead to mistaken policy choices and a waste of public resources. At any point, policy should be based on the best available information; from a policy perspective, therefore, it would be useful to invest resources in obtaining better information and analysis, in order to improve the knowledge basis for future policy.

## Specific Examples for Relevant Policy Areas

Successful human resource policies for Latin America and the Caribbean should address a wide range of macro and micro policy areas. Of course, not every policy is desirable in the context of every country. To the contrary, as already noted, policies must be tailored to the ever-evolving conditions of specific countries and to the inevitably imperfect information available to policymakers. Bearing this in mind, let us now consider some general insights about policies specifically directed toward human resources (schooling, health/nutrition, and training), as well as certain basic macro and labor market policies that are related directly to human resources.

### Schooling Policies

High returns can accrue to such relatively simple changes in schooling systems as the wider provision of textbooks and writing materials, which can reduce the enormous quantity of resources devoted to grade repetition. Most schooling systems, however, appear inefficient (and inequitable) enough to warrant major reforms to become more responsive to the needs of users (students, their families, and potential employers) and more efficient in the use of resources. Governments should therefore encourage the development of various institutions to provide schooling services, without undue restrictions on innovations, while at the same time providing information with which interested parties (including students and parents) can make schooling decisions.

Primary and some secondary schooling is often considered a basic right; it probably has equalizing distributive effects, as well as social benefits that exceed private benefits. Higher levels of secondary and tertiary schooling are less frequently considered basic rights; and while possibly having an unequalizing effect on distribution, may still have important social benefits that exceed private benefits by increasing contributions to knowledge and expanding workers' adjustment capacity. Increasingly throughout the region, schooling-related constraints to faster economic development are likely to be found at the secondary and tertiary levels.

For such reasons, countries in the region (and elsewhere) have provided large subsidies for schooling, primarily in the form of public schools at all levels. But the creation of a wider scope of institutions should be encouraged, given the limited success of much existing schooling in the region. Mechanisms to make schools more responsive to users, such as voucher systems, should be explored. Laws, procedures, subsidies, and regulations that discriminate against alternative schooling institutions, including private schools (which, limited evidence suggests, are relatively cost effective), should be reexamined and probably eliminated in most cases. In public educational institutions, pay systems that tie teachers' salaries to merit should be explored. Laws or traditions that serve more to guarantee employment of teachers than to encourage efficient schooling need to be changed—for instance, in Guatemala the state is obliged by law to hire all graduates of teaching institutions (Infante, Matter, and Sancho, 1992).

Most of these changes are not likely to be easy, in part because of vested interests in present systems. But many individuals engaged in the present systems could become interested in the rewards of using their talents more efficiently. The most successful basic educational reforms exploit this potential. Encouraging such innovations in schooling will result in some failures; problems of asymmetric information about the value added of schooling are going to continue and probably increase; and geographical monopolies in remote areas may become more troublesome as decentralization increases. Therefore, it is critical that the region promote the publicly subsidized (private incentives are inadequate) collection, analysis, and timely dissemination of information on the value added of different schools at all levels (not just information on, say, the cognitive achievement of graduates). Such information constitutes an appropriate public concern from an efficiency and productivity point of view. The better the region's school system performs this educational-information function, the more effective these systems are likely to be. There are also other means through which public policy can encourage a more effective schooling environment. For instance, some of the problems of monopolies in remote areas could be alleviated by radio classes, which have been very cost effective in some cases.

There are additional policy concerns at the tertiary and advanced schooling levels. In much of the region, for instance, the per capita subsidies to tertiary schooling have been very large relative to subsidies to lower schooling levels, and have mainly benefitted the upper and middle classes (Table 5.1); the nature and the rationale of these subsidies need to be addressed. To be sure, as Brunner (1989) and others have emphasized, it is crucial that countries in the region have engineering, scientific, and technological capacities to be competitive in international markets. Such capacities, moreover, are likely to have considerable knowledge externalities and therefore warrant public support. Some important developments have occurred in the region in the past two decades that have strengthened the countries' endogenous capacities for such education, but there remain many needs, such as: more training of engineers and scientists; doctoral and other advanced programs in institutions that provide con-

**Table 5.1. Who Gets Schooling Subsidies?**

| Country and Sector | Year of Survey | Percentage of Government Subsidy Received, by Income Group | | |
| --- | --- | --- | --- | --- |
| | | Lower 40 Percent | Middle 40 Percent | Upper 20 Percent |
| **All education** | | | | |
| Dominican Republic | 1976–77 | 24 | 43 | 14 |
| Colombia | 1974 | 40 | 39 | 21 |
| Costa Rica | 1983 | 42 | 38 | 20 |
| Chile | 1983 | 48 | 34 | 17 |
| Uruguay | 1983 | 52 | 34 | 14 |
| Argentina | 1983 | 48 | 35 | 17 |
| **Higher education** | | | | |
| Dominican Republic | 1976–77 | 2 | 22 | 76 |
| Colombia | 1974 | 6 | 35 | 60 |
| Costa Rica | 1983 | 17 | 41 | 42 |
| Chile | 1983 | 12 | 34 | 54 |
| Uruguay | 1980 | 14 | 52 | 34 |
| Argentina | 1983 | 17 | 45 | 38 |

*Source:* Jiménez (1990).

tinuous research engagement with full-time students; development of complementary subregional, regional, and interregional programs and networks; closer academic-producer links; lifelong education of researchers, with the development of better information bases for education and research; and better-trained higher education and research administrators.

This is a long list, and its components need to be evaluated with care for each context. The overarching point, however, is that there are likely to be important policy reasons for supporting some dimensions of tertiary and advanced education (although with reforms to make this enterprise more efficient from a social perspective), but there are other dimensions of tertiary and advanced education for which public subsidies do not seem warranted. An important example is the training of physicians, who are relatively abundant in most countries in the region and whose presence probably skews health services inefficiently and inequitably toward expensive curative health treatment.

In the process of evaluating the amount and composition of public subsidies for tertiary and advanced education, some hard questions need to be asked to establish the appropriate balance between tertiary/advanced and lower levels of schooling (subsidies appear to be too skewed toward tertiary/advanced schooling in many cases), between liberal arts and science/engineering (subsidies often appear to favor liberal arts too much), between local and foreign education, between basic and applied research, and among different types of health service training.

## Health and Nutrition Policies

Most countries in the region have the possibility of some health or health-related interventions that are attractive from a cost effectiveness point of view. These include: extending the basic immunization package to all children, with more control over vaccine quality and extension (perhaps to cover hepatitis B and yellow fever) when necessary; iodine supplements; information campaigns on tobacco and alcohol (and perhaps other addictive drugs), on sexually transmitted diseases (STDs), and on AIDS; subsidizing condoms and other means of restricting the spread of STDs;[2] safe motherhood and infant monitoring and care; short-course chemotherapy against tuberculosis; provision of medical or drug manuals (that include descriptions of use, dose, and adverse reactions) to drug providers; provision of adequate basic drug supplies to clinics; use of generic drugs; rationalizing the selection and procurement of drugs; and development of chronic care facilities so that resource-intensive acute care facilities are not used for chronic care. Such opportunities clearly should be grasped where they exist.

In most countries in the region, however, the mechanisms for providing health and nutrition services have major interrelated problems of inefficiencies, inequities (particularly when there are multiple systems, with large numbers of poor being the residual responsibility of resource-poor public health systems), and financial insolvency. Let us examine four major dimensions of needed reform.

First, clarification is needed regarding the efficiency and equity reasons for policy support, and public subsidies should be shifted toward those ends. From the point of view of either efficiency or equity, the present distribution of subsidies goes far too much toward tertiary curative care rather than for public health measures and preventive care, and far too much toward training physicians rather than nurses, technicians, and public health specialists.

Second, institutions and mechanisms need to be developed that are more responsive to the needs of users, and more efficient in terms of the

---

[2] In 1990 retail prices were more than US$0.50 per condom in Brazil and Venezuela, for example, as compared with prices as low as US$2.00 per hundred condoms in China and Egypt.

use of inputs and incentives for personnel. This shift may require substantial innovations such as decentralization, the introduction of user charges (to encourage the more efficient use of resources and to eliminate subsidies not justified on efficiency or equity grounds), the contracting out of certain functions to private groups and NGOs, and the privatization of some functions. For equity reasons, it may be important to maintain or institute some self-targeted subsidies such as subsidized clinics in very poor areas or the provision of food consumed primarily by the poor.

Third, there are also major financial problems that have to be addressed, although many of the reforms described above would substantially alleviate them. International experience with limiting the growth of health costs in ways that are transferable to Latin America and the Caribbean is not conclusive, but does seem to suggest that: copayment provisions have advantages in inducing more efficient resource use; client prepayment plans are more effective in restraining clinic cost increases and ensuring adequate concern for preventive care than fee-for-service plans, which pass on all costs to the client; and state-financed or compulsory insurance has been more successful in containing costs and avoiding perverse equity effects (such as not covering the sick or the elderly because they are "bad risks") than private voluntary insurance.

Fourth, informational problems are endemic in this sector, and the social returns to lessening some of these problems are likely to be large. Improvements in the collection of basic epidemiological and nutritional data may have high payoffs in terms of timely response to health and nutrition problems. Publicly subsidized collection, analysis, and timely dissemination of information about the value added or effectiveness of different health service providers would probably increase efficiency, and this function is likely to become more important as institutions become more innovative. The development of mechanisms such as managed health plans, whereby large groups of individuals (defined, say, by geographical area) are represented by informed bargainers vis-à-vis potential health service providers, may lessen the problems of informational asymmetry between individual users and the providers of health services.

Many groups working in health and nutrition-related services may be resistant to change (Infante, Matte, and Sancho, 1992), but will perhaps be supportive if they can see their skills being used more efficiently in a reformed system. Furthermore, the problems in the sector are constantly changing, in part because of the demographic, epidemiological, and nutrition transitions taking place in the region and in part because of the rapid spread of new challenges such as AIDS and drug-resistant tuberculosis. In any case, effective policies for health and nutrition should be designed taking these concerns into account.

## Training Policies

The region has a long and sometimes innovative history in public policy support for training. Although training policy alone cannot offset deficiencies in the region's schooling systems, labor markets, or income distribution, it can probably effectively address differences between social and private incentives and increase efficiency, if directed toward providing general training to individuals with sufficient basic schooling to benefit from that training at relatively low cost. Let us examine seven general considerations that emerge from the Latin American and Caribbean experience with respect to public training policies.

First, the purpose of publicly subsidized training is to provide more-skilled and more-productive workers, not to serve as social assistance programs. In the increasingly dynamic markets of the region, the general skills required for workers to be more productive over time include the capacity to be more flexible than may have been necessary in the past.

Second, trainees need a sufficient basic general education, which is provided more effectively through formal schooling than by teaching basic skills in training programs.

Third, training programs should be closely integrated with the needs of employers who have expanding labor demands (now more likely to be found in the private sector rather than in the public sector, for which much training was undertaken in the past). These labor needs are likely to change with increasing speed in the region because of greater integration into rapidly changing international markets. Therefore, training programs should be driven by the demands of labor markets, with private sector participation encouraged at all levels, including initial curriculum and program design, selection and placement of trainees, staff development, and administration and management of the program.

Fourth, some of the most rapidly expanding employers may be small and medium-sized firms. Therefore, training arrangements should not discriminate against such firms, as they might if the smaller firms are very sensitive to liquidity constraints because of delays in public compensation. If small and medium-sized firms face particular problems that cause inefficiencies, such as relatively limited access to capital markets, and if such problems cannot be rectified through other policies, it may be desirable to take such problems into account when designing the programs.

Fifth, although close links to expanding employers are desirable, care needs to be taken that the training is not thereby changed from general training (which merits subsidies on efficiency grounds) to firm-specific training (for which public subsidies are not warranted). This could possibly happen in a situation in which employers have more information about what is needed than do the overseers of the public training subsidies.

Sixth, youth training for new labor market entrants has different objectives than training for experienced workers, and it should probably be treated as a separate program. Youth training makes sense only if the trainees have basic skills and if the training is of high quality, focuses on productivity, and is linked to available jobs.

Seventh, given past difficulties with many training programs, pilot programs may be desirable, and strict evaluation systems should be built into such programs to measure their effectiveness. A new Multilateral Investment Fund (MIF) has been established to provide support for pilot programs and new training programs (Box 5.1).

### Policies Related to Macro Balance

The major thrust of policy packages in most of the countries in the region in the past decade has been to reestablish and maintain both internal and external macro balance. Many countries have substantially improved their macro balance, with reductions in internal governmental deficits, inflation, external account deficits, and debt, although some countries (such as Brazil and Peru) still have a long way to go in regard to macro balance. Maintaining such balance is critical for human resource investments because some investments, such as in the health and education of children, often have long gestation periods. If there is not macro balance, uncertainty about the longer-run relative prices and thus about the returns to human resource investments will discourage such investments. Moreover, if macro imbalances cause human resource returns to deteriorate or their future levels to be uncertain in a particular country, individuals with relatively high human resources will have greater incentives to migrate to other economies or not to return from training and education abroad. The establishment of macro balances is not likely to be sufficient in itself to induce adequate human resource investments (because of various micro market failures), and in any case, the specific policy options best suited for attaining and sustaining such balances are beyond the scope of this book. Nevertheless, it is important to recognize that reasonable macro balances are necessary to induce adequate levels of longer-run human resource investments.

Sustainable levels of fiscal balance for many countries in the region will require reductions in government employment and possibly in public human resource expenditures; such labor market adjustments are a critical part of the overall adjustment process. With the probable changes in incentives and in the composition of production that follow from key components of the macro reforms (reduction of the government deficit,

**Box 5.1. New Multilateral Facility for Human Resources
in Latin America and the Caribbean**

A new fund for investing in human resources in Latin America has been created
under the Multilateral Investment Fund (MIF) in 1992. The MIF was established by donors from the United States, Japan, Canada, Europe, and Latin
America as part of the Enterprise for the Americas Initiative. The purpose of the
MIF is to promote increased private investment in Latin America and support
the economic reform process underway in the region. The MIF represents the
most significant new international infusion of capital for human resources in the
region in many years.

The donors have created three separate windows, or facilities, under the
MIF: window one, the **Technical Cooperation Facility**, will provide technical
assistance for investment and financial reforms; window two, the **Human Resources Facility**, will help train and develop the labor resources needed by the
private sector; and window three, the **Small-Enterprise Development Facility**, will provide technical assistance and make equity and quasi-equity investments in small and medium-sized enterprises. The creation of a separate facility
for human resources demonstrates the importance donor nations have placed
on human resources for increasing investment and growth in the region.

More than $1.3 billion has been pledged by the donors for the MIF for a
five-year period. Funding for the three windows is expected to be roughly
equivalent; no one facility may receive more than 40 percent of the funds. The
new MIF thus holds the promise of bringing around $433 million to the region
in Human Resources Facility projects. This level of funding is even more significant because the funds will nearly all be grant resources.

The Human Resources Facility will meet the objectives of the MIF
through two principal functions. First, funds will be available to provide a quick
response to labor market needs during critical periods of adjustment by helping
countries get over the initial hurdles in reallocating displaced labor and providing trained labor for new investment. These short-term interventions, however,
will not be sufficient to expand the private sector and stimulate private investment over the long run. Thus, a second function will be to help build permanent capabilities within countries to develop human capital. More specifically,
funds will be available to carry out human resource programs such as training

privatization, integration into the international economy), there are likely
to be considerable mismatches in labor market skills, creating unemployment and underemployment. How quickly and successfully the labor market can accommodate and resolve these problems critically affects both the
shorter-run prospects of maintaining the reforms and the longer-run prospects of attaining sustainable and equitable growth. Thereafter, both reac-
tive policies that deal with short-term problems and proactive policies that

and retraining and labor market services (such as information and employment services). Funds will also be used for institution strengthening and reform projects such as improving management and operations, developing curricula and new services, and encouraging private sector participation in human resource development.

The Human Resources Facility is intended to be a relatively flexible instrument that can be adapted to country circumstances. Funds can go not only to national governments but also to the private sector, educational institutions, private training institutes, and nongovernmental organizations. Thus, funding can be directed to the institutions and program ideas that are most promising in a given country.

Not all Latin American and Caribbean countries will be eligible for the new human resource funds. The donors have specified that MIF funds will be available only to countries that are making significant investment and private sector reforms. The satisfaction of this requirement can be demonstrated most easily if the country has an investment sector loan (ISL) with the Inter-American Development Bank (IDB), since such reforms are required under an ISL. Latin American and Caribbean countries are automatically eligible for the MIF if they have an ISL. Currently, Bolivia, Chile, Colombia, and Jamaica have ISLs with the IDB, and many more are being processed. Countries could also be determined eligible, on a case-by-case basis, if they have made substantial investment sector reforms without the assistance of an ISL.

Once a country is determined by the donor committee to be eligible for the MIF, the national government, nongovernmental organizations, and private sector firms in the country will be eligible to apply for MIF funds to carry out projects. The Inter-American Development Bank has been designated the administrator of the new fund. Projects can be initiated by national governments, local organizations, or the IDB.

By aiding countries in investment and financial reforms and in building up human resources and small-business capabilities, the MIF is intended to stimulate new private sector investment and growth in Latin America. Development of human resources has been clearly recognized as an integral part of this strategy.

*Source:* Prepared by Jacqueline Mazza.

facilitate the development of human resources for longer-run growth may be critical for attaining macro balance (Riveros, 1992a).

## Labor Market Policies

Labor market policies impinge very directly on human resource investments and on the returns to those investments (and, thus, on incentives for further investments) because the economic productivity and earnings returns to human resources are determined primarily in labor markets. A flexible and transparent labor market is central for attracting foreign and domestic investment, which feeds on the demand for human resources (positively if such investment is complementary with more-skilled labor, as generally appears to be the case). Therefore, policies that improve the functioning of labor markets tend to be conducive to human resource investments.

The structural reform agenda in the region, of course, also implies an important role for the labor market. Economic transformation frees labor from the shrinking industries, thereby changing relative wages across industries and reducing real consumption wages to achieve stabilization. In the medium term, labor will be absorbed by new expanding industries, causing a recovery in real wages. Frictional unemployment and declining real wages in the short run, however, imply a social cost that may lessen the political sustainability of the reforms.

Riveros (1992a) characterizes the recent adjustment experience in the region as displaying two stylized facts about labor markets. First, aggregate adjustment policies have been impeded by important rigidities in these labor markets (including job security regulations, wage indexation laws, and labor market segmentation), which have increased open unemployment and lessened employment creation in expanding sectors, and ultimately have made the continuation of the reform less sustainable politically. Second, there is considerable mismatch unemployment, which, in combination with poor information, has made the recovery yet more difficult.

Various remedies have been suggested to improve the functioning of labor markets in the region (see, for instance, Infante et al., 1992; Mazza, 1992; and Riveros, 1992a). It is beyond the scope of this book to fully evaluate these remedies, but it is useful to briefly mention six of them, with the caveat that specific conditions vary across countries.

First, job search and outplacement assistance may improve information flows and thereby accelerate adjustment. The possibilities range from low-cost information centers that compile lists of job openings to more extensive services with counselors who assess workers' skills, assist them in writing resumes and identifying firms for job searches, and test and place them in private firms. Such assistance may complement training and retraining programs. Employment service institutions in the region need strengthening. A few countries (such as Bolivia, Chile, Mexico, and Panama) have labor exchange programs, but such programs are generally limited, in part because of the dominant traditional role of government in employment. Rural areas and the informal sector are not as well served as they should be. Private employment services exist but are not likely to take into account the social gains beyond the private gains of having well-functioning labor markets unless there is cost sharing with the public sector. Decentralization may be important, particularly if target areas are large.

Second, unemployment compensation programs can cushion some of the private and social costs of adjustment, but few countries in the region (for instance, Argentina, Brazil, Chile, Ecuador, and Uruguay) have such programs. Unemployment compensation programs also encourage mobility by lessening severance pay arrangements, which have been fairly common in the region and tend to have the opposite effect.[3] For instance, in Colombia, the labor code requires employers to provide one month's severance pay per year of service and additional severance pay for dismissal without just cause. In Mexico, employers are required to pay dismissed employees a lump sum equal to three months' pay plus 20 days' pay for each year of service. Unemployment compensation systems could be designed or reformed to stress better human resource development and to create better linkages with retraining and unemployment services, but their budgetary costs are usually not small.

Third, the ranks of displaced workers may increase in a number of countries in the region because of efforts to achieve fiscal balance, privatization, and trade liberalization. Displaced workers may represent a constraint on growth, private investment, and general transformation. Special programs may be helpful in assisting these workers if their numbers are large relative to the total labor market and if they have special problems

---

[3] Amadeo et al. (1993) note, however, that the Brazilian labor code may encourage workers to change jobs too often, so that employers are not willing to invest much in the workers' human capital. In Brazil, there is a complex set of institutional rules: (1) the labor code (the *Consolidação das Leis do Trabalho,* CLT), which is a comprehensive set of laws dealing with individual and collective rights and duties of workers and employers; (2) the compensation fund for dismissed workers; (3) unemployment insurance law; (4) wage adjustment clauses, linked to inflation. The cost of dismissing workers has two components: (1) the *aviso previo* (one month prior notification), during which a worker is allowed at least two hours per day to look for other employment, which implies at least 25 percent of the monthly salary, although firms often fire workers immediately with a month's salary; and (2) a fine on the dismissal compensation fund, *Fundo de Garantia por Tempo de Serviço,* FGTS (in which firms deposit 8 percent of a worker's wage into a bank account every month, with a 3 percent real return to the worker) of an additional 40 percent of what is due to the worker from FGTS. This is equal to 3.2 percent of the average wage times the months the worker has been with the firm. After 2 years these costs total 2.15 wages; after 10 years, 4.84 wages. In addition, the worker also has access to the FGTS, which he/she would otherwise have only upon retirement or for purchasing a house. The total (including the FGTS) can be large, 1.67 wages after six months and 2.34 wages after 12 months. This creates incentives for workers to obtain other jobs and force dismissals, thus discouraging firms from investing in the workers.

relating to reemployment.[4] If special programs are implemented, eligibility requirements need to be established and interpreted. The general considerations for retraining programs are similar to those for training programs, with the caveat that displaced workers tend to be older, and if they have been unemployed for some time, to have suffered some depreciation of basic skills that may need to be remedied. Based on industrial country experience, job search assistance in the period immediately following dismissal may be critical.

Rapid response teams or industrial adjustment services, as in Canada, may facilitate such adjustments. The premise is that timely action in cooperation with labor and management can facilitate job and training transitions. Legislation requiring early notification of plant closings usually is necessary for the system to be effective. The service acts as an advisor when a plant closing is imminent. It assists the company, workers, and unions to devise plans to move workers into new jobs or training before plants actually close, with interim benefits such as health insurance. Key components such as labor exchanges, retraining, and unemployment compensation must be in place before the plant closes for such a service to be effective. The Canadian experience suggests that working cooperatively and flexibly at the local level can have high payoffs. Similar systems are being developed in Colombia.

Fourth, improved public information collection would permit not only better functioning of labor markets but also better assessment of the social situation and of the effectiveness of programs.

Fifth, reform of wage policy is needed. In most countries, minimum wage policies and wage indexation are not fundamental issues, because of the drop in inflation (Brazil is an important exception). Instead, emphasis on wage reform should be on making the wage-bargaining process more responsive to the market through the introduction of policy guidelines and institutional changes. The government could play a coordinating and informational role in this process. Also, reform is needed in nonwage payments, to promote productivity-related payments and flexible wages.

Sixth, workfare programs can help to cushion adjustment problems. Success at incorporating training components into such programs, however, has been limited. Self-targeting through low wages can be used to focus on the poor, because those who are better off are not likely to choose to participate in low-wage programs.

---

[4] It is not clear that many former government employees, for example, have special problems relating to reemployment since they tend to be relatively well educated and well connected and in major labor markets—although it may be necessary to have programs for them on political, if not economic, grounds.

## Other Policies

Human resources may also be affected, within the market and nonmarket interactions of economies, by all other policies. A few examples are described below.

First, competition policies and market policies may be important in providing an incentive regime through trade and domestic competition that puts pressure on enterprises to improve quality and productivity and to keep up with new products and services; in fostering cooperation in such areas as joint research consortia; and in encouraging socially optimal explorations of new markets (given that the private incentives for exploring markets are less than the social ones, because innovators provide information to other possible entrants).

Second, financial and capital market policies may be important in fostering flexible financial markets that can redeploy resources out of declining areas of economic activity to new areas; in fostering the development of an efficient and modern financial sector that can tap into international financial systems; in avoiding subsidized credit that might induce capital-intensive investments; and in providing appropriate financial instruments to finance new knowledge-based ventures and human resource investments, which typically have few physical assets to offer as collateral.

Third, policies regarding the acquisition of foreign technology may be important in exploiting positive externalities and linkages to the world economy by actively attracting the kind of foreign investment that can most contribute to the country's development; in promoting better information on foreign technology and helping to negotiate better terms for technology licensing; in facilitating imports of knowledge goods and stimulating such foreign linkages as exports and international subcontracting, which can provide a window on the world and technological externalities through knowledge transfer from foreign buyers; and in supporting the acquisition of human resources abroad that have social returns higher than private returns.

Fourth, policies for local research and development may be important in restructuring the incentives of public research and development institutes to make them responsive to the needs of the production sector; in stimulating local enterprises to carry out research and development; in protecting the property rights of local firms investing in research and development; and in identifying, in consultation with the production sector, specific priority research and development areas that warrant local research and development because of particular local circumstances.

Fifth, policies affecting dissemination and effective use of knowledge may be important in ensuring the compatibility of national systems with international norms and standards; in ensuring the use of standards, testing, and quality control to stimulate the diffusion and appropriate use of technology; and in promoting public and private providers of technological information and extension services, including engineering and other consulting firms and other knowledge agents.

Sixth, infrastructure policy may be important in developing the telecommunications, ports, and transportation infrastructure necessary for plugging the country efficiently into the growing global network of trade and knowledge; and in developing the legal infrastructure necessary for making and enforcing contracts, given that development is largely a process of increasing specialization and requires an increasing number and variety of contracts that must be enforceable.

# REFERENCES

Aedo, Mario Cristián, and Osvaldo Larrañaga. 1993. *Sistemas de entrega de los servicios sociales: La experiencia chilena.* Working Paper Series No. 152. Washington, D.C.: Inter-American Development Bank.

Ahmad, Sultan. 1993. Improving Inter-Spatial and Inter-Temporal Comparability of National Accounts. Paper presented at the Conference on Data Base of Development Analysis, 15–16 May. New Haven: Yale University.

Albuquerque, R.C. de. 1991. A Situação Social: O que Diz o Passado e o que Promete o Futuro. In *Perspectivas da Economia Brasileira –1992.* Brasília: Instituto de Pesquisa Econômica Aplicada (IPEA).

Albuquerque, R.C. de, and R. Villela. 1991. A Situação Social no Brasil: um Balanço de Duas Décadas. In *A Questão Social no Brasil.* Nobel.

Altimir, Oscar. 1991. *Magnitud de la Pobreza en América Latina en los Años Ochenta.* ECLAC Studies and Reports, No. 81. Santiago: ECLAC.

Altimir, Oscar, and Sebastián Pinera. 1979. Análisis de Descomposiciones de las Desigualdades del Ingreso en América Latina. In *La Distribución del Ingreso en América Latina,* O. Muñoz. Buenos Aires: El Cid Editores.

Amadeo, Edward J., Ricardo Paes de Barros, José Marcio Camargo, Rosane S.P. de Mendonça, Valeria Lucía Pero, and André Urani. 1993. *Human Resources in the Adjustment Process.* Working Paper Series No. 137. Washington, D.C.: Inter-American Development Bank.

Amadeo, Edward J., José Marcio Camargo, Antonio Emilio S. Marques, and Cândido Gomes. 1992. Fiscal Crisis and Asymmetries in the Educational System in Brazil. Rio de Janeiro: Pontifícia Universidade Católica do Rio de Janeiro. Mimeo.

Armitage, J., B. João, Ralph W. Harbison, D. Holsinger, and Raimundo Helio Leite. 1986. *School Quality and Achievement in Rural Brazil.* EDT Discussion Paper No. 25. Washington, D.C.: World Bank.

Azariadis, Costas, and Allan Drazen. 1990. Threshold Externalities in Economic Development. *Quarterly Journal of Economics* 105 (No. 2, May): 501–526.

Balmaceda M., Felipe. 1992. Antigüedad en el Empleo y los Salarios en Chile. *Estudios de Economía* 19 (No. 1): 1–20.

Barros, Ricardo Paes de, and Rosane S.P. de Mendonça. 1992. The Quality of Education in Brazil. Mimeo.

Barros, Ricardo Paes de, and Lauro Ramos. 1992. A Note on the Temporal Evolution of the Relationship between Wages and Education among Brazilian Prime-Age Males. Brasília: IPEA. Mimeo.

Barros, Ricardo Paes de, Rosane S.P. de Mendonça, Lauro Ramos, and Sonia Rocha. 1992. Welfare, Inequality, Poverty and Social Conditions in Brazil in the Last Three Decades: An Overview. Brasília: IPEA. Mimeo.

Bautista, Arturo, Patrick A. Barker, John T. Dunn, Max Sánchez, and Donald L. Kaiser. 1982. The Effects of Oral Iodized Oil on Intelligence, Thyroid Status, and Somatic Growth in School-Age Children from an Area of Endemic Goiter. *The American Journal of Clinical Nutrition* 35:127–134.

Beccaria, Luis, and Ricardo Carciofi. 1992. Social Policy and Adjustment During the Eighties: An Overview of the Argentine Case. Buenos Aires: CEPAL. Mimeo.

Becker, Gary S. 1967. Human Capital and the Personal Distribution of Income: An Analytical Approach. Ann Arbor: University of Michigan, Woytinsky Lecture. Reprinted in *Human Capital,* Gary S. Becker, 2nd edition, pp. 94–117. New York: NBER. 1975.

Behrman, Jere R. 1990a. *Human Resource-Led Development?* New Delhi: ARTEP/ILO.

_____. 1990b. *The Action of Human Resources and Poverty on One Another: What We Have Yet to Learn.* Washington, D.C.: Population and Human Resources Department, World Bank.

_____. 1990c. Women's Schooling and Non-market Productivity: A Survey and a Reappraisal. Paper prepared for the Women in Development Division of the Population and Human Resources Department of the World Bank.

_____. 1993a. Human Resources in Latin America and the Caribbean. Background study prepared for this IDB Report. Philadelphia: University of Pennsylvania.

_____. 1993b. Health and Economic Growth: Theory, Evidence, and Policy. *Proceedings of International Conference on Macroeconomics and Health in Countries in Greatest Need, 24–26 June 1992, World Health Organization.* Vol. 1: 7–42. Geneva: World Health Organization.

Behrman, Jere R., and Nancy Birdsall. 1983. The Quality of Schooling: Quantity Alone is Misleading. *American Economic Review* 73: 928–946.

_____. 1988. Implicit Equity-Productivity Tradeoffs in the Distribution of Public School Resources in Brazil. *European Economic Review* 32.

Behrman, Jere R., Nancy Birdsall, and Robert Kaplan. 1993. The Quality of Schooling and Labor Market Outcomes in Brazil: Some Further Explorations. Williamstown, MA: Williams College, and Washington, D.C.: World Bank. Mimeo.

Behrman, Jere R., and Anil B. Deolalikar. 1988. Health and Nutrition. In *Handbook on Economic Development*, Hollis B. Chenery and T.N. Srinivasan, eds. Vol. 1, pp. 631–711. Amsterdam: North-Holland Publishing Co.

_____. 1991. The Poor and the Social Sectors During a Period of Macroeconomic Adjustment: Empirical Evidence for Jamaica. *World Bank Economic Review* 3 (No. 2, May): 291–313.

Behrman, Jere R., Masako Ii, and David Murillo. 1992. Household Demands for Schooling Investments in Urban Bolivia: Multivariate Analysis with Control for Unobserved Community Factors. La Paz: UDAPE/Grupo Social. Mimeo.

Behrman, Jere R., and Victor Lavy. 1993. Child Health and Schooling Achievement: Association or Causality? Washington, D.C.: Population and Human Resources Department, World Bank. Mimeo.

Behrman, Jere R., and Mark R. Rosenzweig. 1993. The Quality of Aggregate Inter-Country, Time-Series Data on Educational Investments and Stocks, Economically Active Populations, and Employment. Paper presented at the Conference on Data Base of Development Analysis, 15–16 May 1992. New Haven: Yale University.

Behrman, Jere R., and Barbara L. Wolfe. 1987a. How Does Mother's Schooling Affect the Family's Health, Nutrition, Medical Care Usage, and Household Sanitation? *Journal of Econometrics* 36: 185–204.

_____. 1987b. Investments in Schooling in Two Generations in Pre-Revolutionary Nicaragua: The Roles of Family Background and School Supply. *Journal of Development Economics* 27 (No. 1–2, October): 395–420. Reprinted in *International Trade, Investment, Macro Policies and History: Essays in Memory of Carlos F. Díaz-Alejandro*, Pranab Bardhan, Jere R. Behrman, and Albert Fishlow, eds., 395–420. Amsterdam: North-Holland Publishing Co. 1987.

_____. 1989. Does More Schooling Make Women Better Nourished and Healthier? Adult Sibling Random and Fixed Effects Estimates for Nicaragua. *Journal of Human Resources* 24 (No. 4, Fall): 644–663.

Birdsall, Nancy. 1985. Public Inputs and Child Schooling in Brazil. *Journal of Development Economics* 18 (No. 1, May–June): 67–86.

_____. 1988. Public Spending on Higher Education in Developing Countries: Too Much or Too Little? Washington, D.C.: World Bank. Mimeo.

Bonilla, Elssy. 1990. Working Women in Latin America. *Economic and Social Progress in Latin America: 1990 Report*. Washington, D.C.: Inter-American Development Bank, pp. 208–260.

Booth, Jerome. 1991a. Welfare Consequences of Social Security Schemes. Washington, D.C.: U.S. Government Strategic Planning Office. Mimeo.

_____. 1991b. Government Use and Misuse of Social Security Reserves. Washington, D.C.: U.S. Government Strategic Planning Office. Mimeo.

Bour, Juan Luis. 1993. *Sistemas de seguridad social en la región: Problemas y alternativas de solución.* Working Paper Series No. 148. Washington, D.C.: Inter-American Development Bank.

Briscoe, John. 1990. *Brazil: The New Challenge of Adult Health.* Washington, D.C.: World Bank.

Brooke, James. In Deception and Denial, an Epidemic Looms: AIDS in Latin America. *The New York Times.* 24 January 1993.

Brunner, José Joaquín. 1989. *Recursos Humanos para la Investigación Científica en América Latina.* Santiago: ODRC.

Bucheli, Marisa. 1992a. Los Logros Educativos y los Niveles de Ingreso. Montevideo: Universidad de la República.

Bucheli, Marisa, Adriana Cassoni, Rafael Diez de Medina and Máximo Rossi. *Recursos humanos en el proceso de ajuste: El caso uruguayo.* Working Paper Series No. 140. Washington, D.C.: Inter-American Development Bank.

Cademartori, Ligia, ed. 1991. *O desafio da escola básica: qualidade e eqüidade.* Série IPEA No. 132. Brasília: IPEA.

Castañeda, Tarsicio. 1990. *Para combatir la pobreza: Política social y descentralización en Chile durante los '80.* Santiago: Centro de Estudios Públicos.

Chamie, Joseph. 1993. Population Databases in Development Analysis. Paper presented at the Conference on Data Base of Development Analysis, 15–16 May 1992. New Haven: Yale University.

Cline, William. 1991. *Facilitating Labor Adjustment in Latin America.* Working Paper Series No. 129. Washington, D.C.: Inter-American Development Bank.

Colclough, C. 1982. The Impact of Primary Schooling on Economic Development: A Review of the Evidence. *World Development* 10: 167–185.

Corbo, Vittorio. 1992. *Development Strategies and Policies in Latin America: A Historical Perspective.* Occasional Paper Series No. 22. San Francisco: International Center for Economic Growth.

Corden, Max. 1974. *Trade Policy and Economic Welfare.* Oxford: Clarendon Press.

Cornia, Giovanni Andrea, and F. Stewart. Country Experience with Adjustment. In *Adjustment with a Human Face: Protecting the Vulnerable and Promoting Growth*, G.A. Cornia, Richard Jolly, and F. Stewart, eds., pp. 105–131. UNICEF.

Cornia, A.P., Richard Jolly, and F. Stewart, eds. 1987. *Adjustment with a Human Face: Volume 1.* Oxford: Clarendon Press for UNICEF.

_____. 1988. *Adjustment with a Human Face: Volume 2.* Oxford: Clarendon Press for UNICEF.

Corvalan Vásquez, Oscar. 1988. Youth Employment Problems and Training Programmes in Latin America. In *Paving Pathways to Work: Comparative Perspectives on the Transition from School to Work*, D.D. Fortuijn, W. Hoppers and M. Morgan, eds. The Hague: Centre for the Study of Education in Developing Countries.

Coupal, Françoise Praline. 1992. Human Resources in Costa Rica: the Raison d'Être of Development. Washington, D.C.: Inter-American Development Bank. Mimeo.

de Mello, Guiomar Mamo, and Rose Neubauer da Silva. 1992. Política Educacional no Governo Collor: Antecedentes e Contradições. Mimeo.

de Mello e Souza, Alberto. 1979. Financiamento da Educação e Acesso à Escola no Brasil. Rio de Janeiro.

de Oliveira, Francisco Eduardo Barreto. 1992. A Liberalização da Economia e a Saúde. Mimeo.

de Oliveira, Francisco Eduardo Barreto, Kaizô Iwakami Beltrão and André Cezar. 1993. *Brazilian Social Security System: Problems and Alternatives.* Working Paper Series No. 163. Washington, D.C.: Inter-American Development Bank.

Díaz Santana, Míriam, et al. 1992. Programa de Cooperación Técnica para el Fortalecimiento del Sistema de Enseñanza Técnico-Vocacional en la República Dominicana. BID-FUNDAPEC. Mimeo.

Dougherty, Christopher, and Jee-Peng Tan. 1991. Financing Training: Issues and Options. Washington, D.C.: World Bank. Mimeo.

Dubey, Ashutosh, Eric Swanson, and Vikram Nehru. 1992. IEC's Education Stock Data—A Brief Commentary on the Methodology, Sources, and Results. Washington, D.C.: World Bank. Mimeo.

ECLA. 1992. *Education and Knowledge: Basic Pillars of Changing Production Patterns with Social Equity.* Santiago: Economic Commission for Latin America and the Caribbean, United Nations.

Farrell, J., and Ernesto Schiefelbein. 1985. Education and Status Attainment in Chile: A Comparative Challenge to The Wisconsin Model of Status Attainment. *Comparative Education Review* 29 (No. 4): 490–506.

Figueroa, Adolfo. 1992. Social Policy and Economic Adjustment in Peru. Lima: Catholic University of Peru. Mimeo.

Fletcher, P.R., and S. Costa Ribeiro. 1987. O Fluxo de Alunos no Ensino Formal de Primeiro Grau no Brasil. Brasília. Mimeo.

Fundação Instituto Brasileiro de Geografia e Estatística. 1990. *Educação, Indicadores Sociais.* Vol. 1. Rio de Janeiro.

Galler, Janina R., Frank Ramsey, Giorgio Solimano, and Walter E. Lowell. 1983a. The Influence of Early Malnutrition on Subsequent Behavioral Development: II. Classroom Behavior. *American Academy of Child Psychiatry* 22: 16–22.

Galler, Janina R., Frank Ramsey, Giorgio Solimano, Walter E. Lowell, and Elaine Mason. 1983b. The Influence of Early Malnutrition on Subsequent Behavioral Development: I. Degree of Impairment in Intellectual Performance. *American Academy of Child Psychiatry* 22: 8–15.

Gershberg, Alec Ian, and Til Schuermann. 1993. Welfare Considerations in the Provision of Public Services: Educational Expenditures and Outcomes in Mexico in 1980 and 1990. Philadelphia: University of Pennsylvania. Mimeo.

Gertler, Paul, and Paul Glewwe. 1990. The Willingness to Pay for Education in Developing Countries: Evidence from Rural Peru. *Journal of Public Economics*: 251–275.

Gertler, Paul, Luis Locay, and Warren Sanderson. 1987. Are User Fees Regressive? The Welfare Implications of Health Care Financing Proposals in Peru. *Journal of Econometrics* 36: 67–88.

Gertler, Paul, and Jacques van der Gaag. 1988a. *Measuring the Willingness to Pay for Social Services in Developing Countries*. Washington, D.C.: World Bank.

Gomes-Neto, João Batista, Eric A. Hanushek, Raimundo Helio Leite, and Roberto Claudio Frota-Bezzera. 1992. *Health and Schooling: Evidence and Policy Implications for Developing Countries*. Working Paper No. 306. Rochester University Center for Economic Research.

Greene, Lawrence S. 1977. Hyperendemic Goiter, Cretinism, and Social Organization in Highland Ecuador. In *Malnutrition, Behavior, and Social Organization*, Lawrence S. Greene, ed. New York: Academic Press.

Hanushek, Eric A., João Batista Gomes-Neto, and Ralph W. Harbison. 1992. Self-financing Educational Investments: The Quality Imperative in Developing Countries. University of Rochester. Mimeo.

Harbert, Lloyd, and Pasquale L. Scandizzo. 1982. *Food Distribution and Nutrition Intervention: The Case of Chile*. Staff Working Papers No. 512. Washington, D.C.: World Bank.

Harbison, Ralph W., and Eric A. Hanushek. 1992. *Educational Performance of the Poor: Lessons from Rural Northeast Brazil*. New York: Oxford University Press.

Heckman, James J., and V. Joseph Hotz. 1986. The Sources of Inequality for Males in Panama's Labor Market. *Journal of Human Resources* 21 (No. 4, Fall): 507–542.

Heston, Alan. 1993. A Brief Review of Some Problems in Using National Accounts Data in Level Comparisons and Growth Studies. Paper presented at the Conference on Data Base of Development Analysis, 15–16 May 1992. New Haven: Yale University.

Iglesias, Enrique V. 1992. *Reflections on Economic Development: Toward a New Latin American Consensus*. Washington, D.C.: Inter-American Development Bank.

Ii, Masako. 1992. The Willingness to Pay for Medical Care: Evidence from Urban Areas in Bolivia. Madison: University of Wisconsin. Mimeo.

Immink, M., and V. Viteri. 1981. Energy Intake and Productivity of Guatemalan Sugarcane Cutters: An Empirical Test of the Efficiency Wages Hypothesis, Parts I and II. *Journal of Development Economics* 92: 251–287.

Infante, Teresa B., Patricia Matte L., and Antonio Sancho M. 1992. *Reform of Social Service Delivery Systems in Latin America*. Working Paper Series No. 130. Washington, D.C.: Inter-American Development Bank.

Inter-American Development Bank. 1989. Peru: Socioeconomic Report. Washington, D.C.: Inter-American Development Bank. Mimeo.

_____. 1991. Chile: Socioeconomic Report. Washington, D.C.: Inter-American Development Bank. Mimeo.

_____. 1992a. *Economic and Social Progress in Latin America: 1992 Report*. Washington, D.C.: Inter-American Development Bank, pp. 175–216.

_____. 1992b. Dominican Republic Socioeconomic Report. Washington, D.C.: Inter-American Development Bank. Mimeo.

_____. 1992c. Brazil: Socioeconomic Report. Washington, D.C.: Inter-American Development Bank. Mimeo.

_____. 1992d. Reforma Social y Pobreza. Washington, D.C.: Inter-American Development Bank.

Instituto de Pesquisa Econômica Aplicada (IPEA). 1990a. *Tecnologia, produtividade e participação*. 2d ed. Série IPEA No. 130. Brasília: IPEA.

_____. 1990b. *Educação e Cultura - 1987: Situação e Políticas Governamentais.* Série IPEA No. 128. Divonzir Arthur Gusso, ed. Brasília: IPEA.

_____. 1992. *Sistemas de Seguridade Social na Região: Problemas e Alternativas de Solução. Estudo Nacional.*

Instituto de Planejamento Econômico e Social. 1989. *Para a Década de Prioridades e Perspectivas de Políticas Públicas, Políticas Sociais e Organização do Trabalho.* Brasília: IPEA-IPLAN.

_____. 1990. *Para a Década de Prioridades e Perspectivas de Políticas Públicas, População, Emprego, Desenvolvimento Urbano e Regional.* Brasília: IPEA-IPLAN.

Jamison, Dean T., and W. Henry Mosley. 1990. Selecting Disease Control Priorities in Developing Countries. Washington, D.C.: World Bank. Mimeo.

Jamison, Dean T., B. Searle, K. Galda, and S. Heyneman. 1981. Improving Elementary Mathematics Education in Nicaragua: An Experimental Study of the Impact of Textbooks and Radio on Achievement. *Journal of Educational Psychology* 74 (No. 4): 556–557.

Jiménez, Emmanuel. 1990. Social Sector Pricing Policy Revisited: A Survey of Some Recent Controversies. In *Proceedings of the World Bank Annual Conference on Development Economics 1989.* (Supplement to *World Bank Economic Review* and *World Bank Research Observer*), pp. 109–138.

Jiménez, Emmanuel, B. Kugler, and R. Horn. 1989. National In-Service Training Systems in Latin America: An Economic Evaluation of Colombia's SENA. *Economic Development and Cultural Change* 37 (No. 3): 595–610.

Jiménez, Emmanuel, Marlaine E. Lockheed, and Vicente Paqueo. 1991. The Relative Efficiency of Private and Public Schools in Developing Countries. *The World Bank Research Observer* 6 (No. 2, July): 205–218.

Johnston, Francis E., Setha M. Low, Yetilu de Baessa, and Robert B. MacVean. 1987. Interaction of Nutritional and Socioeconomic Status as Determinants of Cognitive Development in Disadvantaged Urban Guatemalan Children. *American Journal of Physical Anthropology* 73: 501–506.

King, Elizabeth M. 1990. *Educating Girls and Women: Investing in Development*. Washington, D.C.: World Bank.

_____. 1991. Economics of Gender and Educational Choices. Washington, D.C.: World Bank. Mimeo.

King, Elizabeth M., and R. Bellew. 1988. Education Policy and Schooling Levels in Peru. Washington, D.C.: World Bank. Mimeo.

Klein, Robert E., Howard E. Freeman, Jerome Kagan, Charles Yarbrough, and Jean-Pierre Habicht. 1972. Is Big Smart? The Relation of Growth to Cognition. *Journal of Health and Social Behavior* 13 (No. 3): 219–225.

Levin, Henry M., Ernesto Pollitt, Rae Galloway, and Judith McGuire. 1991. Micronutrient Deficiency Disorders. Forthcoming in *Disease Control Priorities in Developing Countries*, Dean T. Jamison and W. Henry Mosley, eds. New York: Oxford University Press for the World Bank.

Levy, Santiago. 1991. Poverty Alleviation in Mexico. Washington, D.C.: World Bank. Mimeo.

Llach, H., H. Dieguez, and A. Petrecolla. 1991. El Gasto Público Social. *Desarrollo Económico* 31. Buenos Aires.

Lockheed, Marlaine E., and Eric A. Hanushek. 1988. Improving Educational Efficiency in Developing Countries: What Do We Know? *Compare* 18 (No. 1): 21–38.

López, R., and L. Riveros. 1990. *Do Labor Market Distortions Cause Overvaluation and Rigidity of the Real Exchange Rate?* PRE Working Paper No. 416. Washington, D.C.: World Bank.

Lucas, Robert E. 1988. On the Mechanics of Economic Development. *Journal of Monetary Economics* 21: 3–42.

Marcel, Mario, and Alberto Arenas. 1992. *Social Security Reform in Chile*. Washington, D.C.: Inter-American Development Bank.

Mardones, Francisco. 1991. An Update on Cholera in the Americas. Washington, D.C.: World Bank. Mimeo.

Márquez, Gustavo, and Clementina Acedo. 1993. *El sistema de seguros sociales en Venezuela: Problemas y alternativas de solución.* Working Paper Series No. 151. Washington, D.C.: Inter-American Development Bank.

Mazza, Jacqueline. 1993. *Human Resource Adjustment in Latin America: A Preliminary Program for the Human Resources Facility of the Multilateral Investment Fund.* Working Paper Series No. 132. Washington, D.C.: Inter-American Development Bank.

McGinn, Noel, Fernando Reimers, Armando Loera, María del Carmen Soto, and Sagrario López. 1992. Why Do Children Repeat Grades? A Study of Rural Primary Schools in Honduras. Cambridge: Harvard Institute for International Development. Mimeo.

Medici, André Cezar, Francisco Eduardo Barreto de Oliveira, and Kaizô Iwakami Beltrão. 1991. A Política de Medicamentos no Brasil. ENCE. Mimeo.

_____. 1992. Seguridade Social. Análise e Proposições. Sumário Executivo. Rio de Janeiro: IPEA. Mimeo.

_____. 1992. O Sistema de Saúde Chileno: Mitos e Realidades. Rio de Janeiro: IPEA. Mimeo.

Medici, André Cezar, and Francisco Eduardo Barreto de Oliveira. 1991. A Saúde dos Anos Noventa: os Recursos Federais e a Descentralização. Mimeo.

_____. 1991. A Política de Saúde no Brasil: Subsídios para uma Reforma. Rio de Janeiro: IPEA. Mimeo.

Mesa-Lago, Carmelo. 1991. Social Security in Latin America. *Economic and Social Progress in Latin America: 1991 Report.* Washington, D.C.: Inter-American Development Bank, pp. 175–216.

Middleton, John, Adrian Ziderman, and Arvil Van Adams. 1991. *Vocational and Technical Education and Training.* World Bank Policy Paper. Washington, D.C.: World Bank.

Ministério da Educação. 1990. *A Educação no Brasil na Década de 80.* Brasília: Secretaria de Administração Geral, Coordenação Geral de Planejamento Setorial. Coordenação de Informações para o Planejamento.

Miranda, Guido. 1990. *Repercusión de la crisis económica en la caja costarricense del seguro social.* IDB Work Report 1990. Washington, D.C.: Inter-American Development Bank.

Mujica, Patricio R. 1993. *Sistemas de seguridad social: La experiencia chilena.* Working Paper Series No. 149. Washington, D.C.: Inter-American Development Bank.

Nash, Nathaniel C. Latin American Indians: Old Ills, New Politics. *New York Times.* 24 August 1992.

Palloni, Alberto, and Marta Tienda. 1992. Demographic Responses to Economic Recessions in Latin America Since 1990. *Sociological Inquiry* 62 (No. 2): 244–270.

Palma, Oscar Arcos. 1992. Capacitación e intermediación de recursos humanos en el proceso de ajuste económico en Colombia. Bogotá: Universidad Nacional de Colombia. Mimeo.

Paredes, Ricardo, and Luis Riveros. 1993. Recursos humanos en el proceso de ajuste: El caso de Chile. Working Paper Series No. 138. Washington, D.C.: Inter-American Development Bank.

Popkin, Barry M. 1992. Development and the Nutrition Transition. Mimeo.

PREALC. 1991. *Labour Market Adjustment in Latin America: An Appraisal of the Social Effects in the 1980's.* PREALC Working Paper No. 357. Santiago.

Preston, Samuel H. 1986. Review of *The Impact of World Recession on Children,* by Richard Jolly and Giovanni Andrea Cornia, eds. *Journal of Development Economics* 21 (No. 2, May): 374–376.

Psacharopoulos, George. 1985. Returns to Education: A Further International Update and Implications. *Journal of Human Resources* 20: 583–597.

_____. 1993. Ethnicity, Education and Earnings: A Comparative Analysis of Bolivia and Guatemala. *Comparative Education Review* 37 (No. 1, February).

Psacharopoulos, George, Samuel Morley, Ariel Fiszbein, Haeduck Lee, and Bill Wood. 1992. *Poverty and Income Distribution in Latin America: The Story of the 1980s.* Washington, D.C.: World Bank.

_____. 1993. *Human Resources in Latin America and the Caribbean: Priorities and Action.* Washington, D.C.: World Bank.

Psacharopoulos, George, and Eduardo Vélez. 1992. Does Training Pay, Independent of Education? Some Evidence from Colombia. *International Journal of Educational Research* 17 (No. 6): 581–591.

Puryear, J. 1979. Vocational Training and Earnings in Colombia: Does a SENA Effect Exist? *Comparative Education Review* 23: 283–292.

Raut, L.K., and T.N. Srinivasan. 1992. Theories of Long-run Growth: Old and New. New Haven: Yale University. Mimeo.

Reimers, Fernando. 1990a. Education for All in Latin America in the XXI Century and the Challenges of External Indebtedness. *New Education* 12 (No. 2): 16–30.

_____. 1990b. The Impact of the Debt Crisis on Education in Latin America: Implications for Educational Planning. *Prospects* 20 (No. 4): 539–554.

_____. 1991a. Adjustment and Education in Latin America. *Journal of Educational Planning and Administration* 5 (No. 3): 249–258.

_____. 1991b. The Role of Organization and Politics in Government Financing of Education: The Effects of Structural Adjustment in Latin America. *Comparative Education* 27 (No. 1): 35–51.

_____. 1991c. The Impact of Economic Stabilization and Adjustment on Education in Latin America. *Comparative Education Review* 35 (No. 2): 319–353.

_____. 1992. Necesidades de una política de educación inicial en América Latina y el Caribe. *Boletín* 28: 65–84.

Riveros, Luis. 1990a. Recession Adjustment and the Role of Urban Labor Markets in Latin America. *Canadian Journal of Development Studies* 11 (No. 1): 33–59.

_____. 1990b. The Economic Return to Schooling in Chile: An Analysis of its Long-term Fluctuations. *Economics of Education Review* 9 (No. 2): 111–121.

_____. 1992. Labor Markets, Economic Restructuring and Human Resource Development in Latin America. Santiago: University of Chile. Mimeo.

Romer, Paul M. 1986. Increasing Returns and Long-run Growth. *Journal of Political Economy* 94 (No. 5): 1002–1036.

Rosenzweig, Mark R., and T. Paul Schultz. 1982. Child Mortality and Fertility in Colombia: Individual and Community Effects. *Health Policy and Education* 2. Amsterdam: Elsevier Scientific Publishing Co., pp. 305–348.

Sancho M., Antonio. 1991. Participación del sector privado en la prestación de servicios sociales. Universidad Católica de Chile. Mimeo.

Santana López, Isidoro, and Magdalena Rathe. 1993. *Sistema de servicios sociales en la República Dominicana: Una agenda para la reforma*. Working Paper Series No. 150. Washington, D.C.: Inter-American Development Bank.

Schiefelbein, Ernesto, and Laurence Wolff. 1992. Repetition and Inadequate Achievement in Latin America's Primary Schools: A Review of Magnitudes, Causes, Relationships and Strategies. Washington, D.C.: World Bank. Mimeo.

Srinivasan, T.N. 1993. Data Base for Development Analysis: An Overview. Paper presented at the Conference on Data Base of Development Analysis, 15–16 May 1992. New Haven: Yale University.

Strauss, John, and Duncan Thomas. 1992. The Shape of the Calorie Expenditure Curve. New Haven: Yale University. Mimeo.

Summers, Robert, and Alan Heston. 1991. The Penn World Table (Mark 5): An Expanded Set of International Comparisons, 1950–1988. *Quarterly Journal of Economics* 106 (No. 2, May): 327–368.

Sussangkarn, Chalongphob. 1988. *Production Structures, Labor Markets and Human Capital Investments: Issues of Balance for Thailand*. Nihon University Population Research Institute Research Paper Series No. 46. Tokyo.

Thomas, Duncan. 1990. Intra-household Resource Allocation: An Inferential Approach. *Journal of Human Resources* 25 (No. 4, Fall): 635–664.

Thomas, Duncan, and John Strauss. 1992. Prices, Infrastructure, Household Characteristics and Child Height. *Journal of Development Economics* 39: 301–331.

Thomas, Duncan, John Strauss, and Maria Helena Fernandes Henriques da T. 1990. Child Survival, Height for Age and Household Characteristics in Brazil. *Journal of Development Economics* 33 (No. 2, October): 197–234.

_____. 1991. How Does Mother's Education Affect Child Height? *Journal of Human Resources* 26 (No. 2, Spring): 183–211.

Trejos, Juan Diego. 1993. *Sistemas de entrega de los servicios sociales: Una agenda para la reforma en Costa Rica*. Working Paper Series No. 153. Washington, D.C.: Inter-American Development Bank.

UNESCO. 1991. *Statistical Yearbook, 1991*. Paris: UNESCO.

UNICEF. 1984. The Impact of World Recession on Children: A UNICEF Special Study. In *The State of the World's Children 1984*. Oxford: Oxford University Press.

Urrutia, Miguel, ed. 1991. *Long-Term Trends in Latin American Economic Development*. Washington, D.C.: Inter-American Development Bank.

Williamson-Gray, C. 1982. *Food Consumption Parameters for Brazil and Their Application to Food Policy*. Research Report 32. Washington, D.C.: International Food Policy Research Institute.

Wolfe, Barbara L., and Jere R. Behrman. 1984. Determinants of Women's Health Status and Health-Care Utilization in a Developing Country: A Latent Variable Approach. *Review of Economics and Statistics* 56 (No. 4, November): 696–703.

_____. 1986. Child Quantity and Quality in a Developing Country: The Importance of Family Background, Endogenous Tastes and Biological Supply Factors. *Economic Development Cultural Change* 34: 703–720.

_____. 1987. Women's Schooling and Children's Health: Are the Effects Robust with Adult Sibling Control for the Women's Childhood Background? *Journal of Health Economics* 6 (No. 3): 239–254.

World Bank. 1990. *World Development Report*. Oxford: Oxford University Press.

_____. 1992. *World Development Report*. Oxford: Oxford University Press.

_____. 1993. *World Development Report*. Oxford: Oxford University Press.

Zerda Sarmiento, Alvaro, Oscar Arcos Palma, et al. 1993. *Capacitación e intermediación de recursos humanos en el proceso de ajuste económico en Colombia*. Working Paper Series No. 139. Washington, D.C.: Inter-American Development Bank.

Zuckerman, Elaine. 1989. Adjustment Programs and Social Welfare. Washington, D.C.: World Bank. Mimeo.

# INDEX